THE COMPLETE STEP-BY-STEP ITALIAN COOKBOOK

Notes on the recipes:
Please note that the measurements provided in this book are presented as 'metric/imperial/US cups', with practical
equivalents; certain foods and cooking items that are termed differently in the UK and in North America are presented as
'UK term/US term'; and eggs are medium (UK)/large (US) and large (UK)/extra-large (US).

Each recipe has been given a **handy Health Rating**, from 1 to 5 points; the higher the score, the 'healthier' the recipe.
This is a basic at-a-glance way to check whether a recipe may be particularly healthy or unhealthy in terms of its overall
fat, sugar or salt content versus its vegetable or nutrition content. It is important to remember that balance and variety are
key to a healthy diet, so mix up your choice of recipes, saving those with few points for occasional treats. This rating is in
no way intended to constitute a comprehensive guide to a healthy diet.

Publisher and Creative Director: Nick Wells
Project Editor: Catherine Taylor
Art Director: Mike Spender
Layout Design: Jane Ashley
Digital Design and Production: Chris Herbert
Proofreader: Dawn Laker

Special thanks to Caitlin O'Connell and Laura Bulbeck

12 14 16 15 13

1 3 5 7 9 10 8 6 4 2

This edition first published 2012 by
FLAME TREE PUBLISHING
Crabtree Hall, Crabtree Lane
Fulham, London SW6 6TY
United Kingdom

www.flametreepublishing.com

Flame Tree Publishing is part of Flame Tree Publishing Ltd

© Flame Tree Publishing Ltd

All pictures courtesy of Foundry Arts, except the following:which are courtesy of Shutterstock.com
and © the following contributors:
3, 23 Svetlana Lukienko; 8 Olga Miltsova; 9t wavebreakmedia ltd; 9b michaeljung; 11l Joe Gough; 11r, 18 Robyn Mackenzie;
12t brieldesign; 12c marco mayer; 12b Crisferra; 13l matka_Wariatka;13r inacio pires; 14t, 20t Monkey Business Images;
14c Pieralfonso; 15t elena moiseeva; 15c Robert Anthony; 15b, 16l KAppleyard; 16r Subbotina Anna; 17l Mirabelle Pictures;
17r Luiz Rocha; 19c, 20b Jiri Hera; 19t Fotografiche; 19b LUCARELLI TEMISTOCLE; 21l Tyler Olson; 22 martiapunts

ISBN 978-0-85775-520-9

A CIP Record for this book is available from the British Library upon request

Printed in China

THE COMPLETE STEP-BY-STEP ITALIAN COOKBOOK

General Editor: Gina Steer

FLAME TREE
PUBLISHING

Contents

This chapter provides the necessary guidelines for making Italian cooking easy and fun. From tips on hygiene in the kitchen to essential ingredients and information on the different varieties of pasta, this section is full of invaluable information you will refer to again and again. There are even instructions on how to make your own pasta from scratch, making this chapter an excellent base for mastering all aspects of Italian cookery.

This section provides you with an excellent selection of hearty soups and delicious starters. Whether you are in the mood for a Classic Minestrone or a White Bean Soup with Parmesan Croutons, you'll find the recipe you are looking for. The starter recipes, such as Antipasti with Focaccia or Pasta with Walnut Sauce, make for excellent snacks, light lunches, or appetizers, so you will not be lacking in options for your guests or for you.

Seafood is a healthy option for a main course, and one that features prominently in Italian cooking, especially in dishes that originated in coastal cities. Featuring many different types of fish and shellfish and a plethora of preparation methods, this chapter has recipes that will delight the seafood enthusiast and tempt even the most reluctant fish eater. Why not try Fish Lasagne or Pan-fried Salmon with Herb Risotto for a delicious new dinner alternative?

Meat..................126

No Italian cookbook would be complete without favourite recipes such as Spaghetti & Meatballs. This section features many well-loved classic Italian recipes, such as Traditional Lasagne and Spaghetti Bolognese, hearty and familiar dishes that you, your family and your guests will love. It also includes a number of equally delicious but less familiar recipes, such as Prosciutto & Gruyère Carbonara and Roasted Lamb with Rosemary & Garlic that will soon become new favourites.

Poultry & Game..................178

Who says that poultry has to be boring? In this section, there are many excellent recipes that will prove how delicious and exciting poultry can be. From Chicken Cacciatore to Turkey Escalopes Marsala with Wilted Watercress, you are sure to find something to suit your tastes. You also need not be afraid to try the easy-to-follow game recipes, such as the Pheasant with Sage & Blueberries or the Braised Rabbit with Red Peppers.

Vegetables, Cheese & Salads..................222

Vegetables add vital nutrients to your diet, but that does not mean that eating your daily dose needs to be a chore. This section is filled with recipes such as Spaghetti with Pesto, Melanzane Parmigiana and Spring Vegetable & Herb Risotto that can be served as a whole meal or as an accompaniment, and that will all provide a delicious and healthy addition to your daily meals.

Entertaining & Desserts..................286

This section is filled with excellent recipes that will delight your family and friends. The first half is devoted to savoury dishes for dinner parties, such as Pasta Triangles with Pesto & Walnut Dressing and Tagliatelle with Stuffed Pork Escalopes. The second half is filled with recipes for baking and desserts, beginning with Italian bread such as Rosemary & Olive Focaccia before moving on to sweet treats. The Tiramisu will provide an excellent pick-me-up, while other desserts such as the Bomba Siciliana and the Almond Angel Cake with Amaretto Cream are sure to make you a success at any dinner party.

Index 350

Italian Cooking

This chapter provides the necessary guidelines for making Italian cooking easy and fun. From tips on hygiene in the kitchen to essential ingredients and information on the different varieties of pasta, this section is full of invaluable information you will refer to again and again. There are even instructions on how to make your own pasta from scratch, making this chapter an excellent base for mastering all aspects of Italian cookery.

Good Cooking Rules

When handling and cooking food, there are a few rules and guidelines that should be observed so that food remains fit to eat and uncontaminated with the bacteria and bugs that can result in food poisoning.

Good Hygiene Rules

- Personal hygiene is imperative when handling food. Before commencing any preparation, wash hands thoroughly with soap, taking particular care with nails. Always wash hands after going to the bathroom. Wash again after handling raw foods, cooked meats or vegetables. Do not touch any part of the body or handle pets, rubbish or dirty laundry during food preparation.
- Cuts should be covered with a waterproof plaster/bandage, preferably blue so it can be easily seen if lost.
- Do not smoke in the kitchen.
- Keep pets off all work surfaces and out of the kitchen, if possible. Clean surfaces with an antibacterial solution. Wash pet eating bowls separately.
- Ensure that hair is off the face and does not trail into food or machinery.
- Use a dishwasher wherever possible and wash utensils and equipment in very hot, soapy water.

- Use clean cloths and dish towels, replacing regularly. Boil to kill any bacteria, and use absorbent paper towels where possible to wipe hands and equipment.
- Chopping boards and cooking implements must be clean. Boards should either be washed in a dishwasher or scrubbed after each use. Keep separate boards for meat, fish and vegetables and wash knives before using on different types of food. Do not use the same board for raw and cooked food: wash in between or, better still, use a different board.
- Use dustbin liners/garbage bags for rubbish and empty regularly, cleaning your bin with disinfectant. Dustbins should be outside.

Guidelines for Using a Refrigerator

- Ensure that the refrigerator is situated away from any equipment that gives off heat, such as the cooker, washing machine or tumble drier, to ensure the greatest efficiency. Ensure that the vents are not obstructed.
- If not frost-free, defrost regularly, wiping down with a mild solution of bicarbonate of soda/baking soda dissolved in warm water and a clean cloth.
- Close the door as quickly as possible so that the motor does not have to work overtime to keep it at the correct temperature.
- Ensure that the temperature is 5°C/40°F. A thermometer is a good investment.
- Avoid overloading – this just makes the motor work harder.
- Cool food before placing in the refrigerator, and always cover to avoid any smells or transference of taste to other foods.

Stacking Your Refrigerator

- Remove supermarket packaging from raw meat, poultry and fish, place on a plate or dish, cover loosely and store at the base of the refrigerator to ensure that the juices do not drip on other foods.
- Store cheese in a box or container, wrapped to prevent the cheese drying out.
- Remove food to be eaten raw 30 minutes before use so it can return to room temperature.
- Cooked meats, bacon and all cooked dishes should be stored at the top – this is the coldest part.
- Store eggs in the egg compartment and remove 30 minutes before cooking in order to return them to room temperature.
- Butter and all fats can be stored in the door, as can milk, cold drinks, sauces, mayonnaise and preserves with low sugar content.
- Cream and other dairy products, as well as pastries such as chocolate éclairs, should be stored on the middle shelf.

- Vegetables, salad and fruit should be stored in the salad boxes at the bottom of the refrigerator.
- Soft fruits should be kept in the salad boxes, along with mushrooms, which are best kept in paper bags.
- To avoid cross-contamination, raw and cooked foods must be stored separately.
- Use all foods by the sell-by date – once opened, treat as cooked foods and use within two days.

General Rules

- Use all foods by the use-by date and store correctly. This applies to all foods: fresh, frozen, canned and dried. Potatoes are best if removed from polythene/plastic, stored in brown paper and kept in the cool and dark.
- Ensure that all food is thoroughly thawed before use, unless meant to be cooked from frozen.
- Cook all poultry thoroughly at the correct temperature (190°C/375°F/Gas Mark 5), ensuring that the juices run clear
- Leave hot foods to cool thoroughly before placing in the refrigerator; cover while cooling.
- Do not re-freeze any thawed frozen foods unless cooked first.
- Date and label frozen food and use in rotation.
- Reheat foods thoroughly until piping hot. Remember to allow foods to stand when using the microwave and stir to distribute the heat.

- Microwaves vary according to make and wattage – always refer to manufacturers' instructions.
- Only reheat dishes once and always heat until piping hot.
- Ensure that eggs are fresh. If using for mayonnaise, soufflés or other dishes that use raw or semi-cooked egg, do not give to the vulnerable – the elderly, pregnant women, those with a recurring illness, toddlers and babies.
- When buying frozen foods, transport in freezer-insulated bags, placing in the freezer as soon as possible after purchase.
- Chilled foods, such as cold meats, cheese, fresh meat, fish and dairy products, should be bought, taken home and placed in the refrigerator immediately. Do not keep in a warm car or room.
- Avoid buying damaged or unlabelled canned goods. Keep store cupboards clean, wiping down regularly and rotating the food.
- Flour, nuts, rice, pulses/legumes (peas, beans, etc), grains and pasta should be checked regularly and, once opened, placed in airtight containers.
- Do not buy eggs or frozen or chilled foods that are damaged in any way.
- Keep dried herbs and ready-ground spices in a cool, dark place, not in a spice rack on the work surface. They quickly lose their pungency and flavour when exposed to light.

Useful Conversions

Liquid Measures
Metric, Imperial and US Cups/Quarts

2.5 ml	½ tsp	–	
5 ml	1 tsp	–	
15 ml	1 tbsp	–	
25 ml	1 fl oz	⅛ cup	2 tbsp
50 ml	2 fl oz	¼ cup	3–4 tbsp
65 ml	2½ fl oz	⅓ cup	5 tbsp
75–85 ml	3 fl oz	⅓ cup	6 tbsp
100 ml	3½ fl oz	⅓ cup	7 tbsp
125 ml	4 fl oz	½ cup	8 tbsp
135 ml	4½ fl oz	½ cup	9 tbsp
150 ml	5 fl oz	¼ pint	⅔ cup
175 ml	6 fl oz	⅓ pint	scant ¾ cup
200 ml	7 fl oz	⅓ pint	¾ cup
225–50 ml	8 fl oz	⅜ pint	1 cup
275 ml	9 fl oz	½ pint	1⅛ cups
300 ml	10 fl oz	½ pint	1¼ cups
350 ml	12 fl oz	⅔ pint	1½ cups
400 ml	14 fl oz	⅝ pint	1⅔ cups
450 ml	15 fl oz	¾ pint	1¾ cups
475 ml	16 fl oz	⅞ pint	scant 2 cups
500 ml	18 fl oz	⅞ pint	2 cups
600 ml	20 fl oz	1 pint	2½ cups
750 ml	26 fl oz	1¼ pints	3¼ cups
900 ml		1½ pints	scant 1 quart
1 litre		1¾ pints	1 quart
1.1 litres		2 pints	1¼ quarts
1.2 litres		2 pints	1¼ quarts
1.25 litres		2¼ pints	1⅓ quarts
1.3 litres		2⅓ pints	1⅓ quarts
1.4 litres		2½ pints	1½ quarts
1.5 litres		2½ pints	1⅔ quarts
1.6 litres		2¾ pints	1¾ quarts
1.7 litres		3 pints	1¾ quarts
1.8 litres		3⅛ pints	1⅞ quarts
1.9 litres		3⅓ pints	2 quarts
2 litres		3½ pints	2 quarts
2.25 litres		4 pints (½ gal)	2⅜ quarts
2.5 litres		4½ pints	2⅔ quarts
2.75 litres		5 pints	3 quarts
3 litres		5¼ pints	3 quarts
4.5 litres		8 pints (1 gal)	scant 5 quarts

Temperature Conversion

–4°F	–20°C
5°F	–15°C
14°F	–10°C
23°F	–5°C
32°F	0°C
41°F	5°C
50°F	10°C
59°F	15°C
68°F	20°C
77°F	25°C
86°F	30°C
95°F	35°C
104°F	40°C
113°F	45°C
122°F	50°C
212°F	100°C

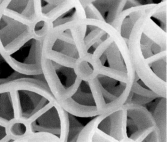

Dry Weights
Metric/Imperial

10 g	¼ oz
15 g	½ oz
20 g	¾ oz
25 g	1 oz
40 g	1½ oz
50 g	2 oz
65 g	2½ oz
75 g	3 oz
100 g	3½ oz
125 g	4 oz
150 g	5 oz
165 g	5½ oz
175 g	6 oz
185 g	6½ oz
200 g	7 oz
225 g	8 oz
250 g	9 oz
275 g	10 oz
300 g	11 oz
325 g	11½ oz
350 g	12 oz
375 g	13 oz
400 g	14 oz
425 g	15 oz
450 g	1 lb

Oven Temperatures
Bear in mind that if using a fan oven you should reduce the stated temperature by around 20°C – check the manufacturer's instructions.

110°C	225°F	Gas Mark ¼	Very slow (low) oven
120/130°C	250°F	Gas Mark ½	Very slow oven
140°C	275°F	Gas Mark 1	Slow oven
150°C	300°F	Gas Mark 2	Slow oven
160/170°C	325°F	Gas Mark 3	Moderate oven
180°C	350°F	Gas Mark 4	Moderate oven
190°C	375°F	Gas Mark 5	Moderately hot oven
200°C	400°F	Gas Mark 6	Moderately hot oven
220°C	425°F	Gas Mark 7	Hot oven
230°C	450°F	Gas Mark 8	Hot oven
240°C	475°F	Gas Mark 9	Very hot oven

Essential Ingredients

Italian cuisine is popular all over the world and basic Italian store-cupboard ingredients are commonplace items on supermarket shelves. Even fresh ingredients that used to be difficult to find are available all year round, often in parts of the world where previously they were unheard of. For those who enjoy Italian food and cooking, this is good news – delicious, authentic Italian cuisine can now be enjoyed anywhere and at any time.

Cheeses

Dolcelatte This cheese, which translates as 'sweet milk', comes from the Lombardy region. Dolcelatte is a creamy, blue cheese and has a luscious, sweet taste. It is very soft and melts in the mouth, often appealing to those who find more traditional blue cheeses, such as Roquefort and Gorgonzola, too strongly flavoured.

Fontina This is a dense, smooth and slightly elastic cheese with a straw-coloured interior. Fontina is made in the Valle d'Aosta region and has a delicate nutty flavour with a hint of mild honey. It is often served melted, in which case the flavour becomes very earthy.

Gorgonzola This is a traditional blue cheese from the Lombardy region. Made from cows' milk, the cheese has a sharp, spicy flavour as well as being rich and creamy.

Mascarpone Technically, mascarpone is not a cheese but a by-product obtained from making Parmesan. A culture is added to the cream that has been skimmed off the milk that was used to make the cheese. This is then gently heated and allowed to mature and thicken. Mascarpone is most famous as the main ingredient in Tiramisu, but it is a very versatile ingredient and is used in all sorts of sweet and savoury recipes.

Mozzarella di Bufala Mozzarella is a fresh cheese, prized more for its texture than its flavour, which is really quite bland. Mozzarella cheese melts beautifully, however, on pizzas and in pasta dishes, and is also good served cold in salads. It is usually sold in tubs along with its whey and should have a floppy rather than a rubbery texture. The fresher it is when eaten, the better.

Parmigiano-Reggiano (Parmesan) One of the world's finest cheeses, Parmigiano-Reggiano is also one of the most versatile cooking cheeses. Its production is very carefully regulated to guarantee a consistent high-quality result. The trademark is branded all over the rind, so that even a small piece is easily identified. Buy it in pieces, rather than ready-grated.

Pecorino This is the generic term for cheeses made purely from sheep's milk. All pecorino cheeses are excellent for grating or shaving onto both hot and cold dishes. Each type of pecorino is characteristic of a particular region and a particular breed of sheep. Pecorino Romano is made in the countryside around Rome between November and late June. Pecorino Sardo is made in Sardinia and Pecorino Toscano comes from Tuscany and tends to mature younger than other pecorino cheeses.

Ricotta When cheese is made, the solids in the milk are separated from the liquid by coagulation; however, some solids are always lost to the whey. To retrieve these solids, the milk is heated until they come to the surface. They are then skimmed off and drained in woven baskets until the curd is solid enough to stick together. The resulting cheese is ricotta (literally meaning 'recooked'). Good-quality ricotta should be firm but not solid and consist of fine, delicate grains. Ricotta is used in both savoury and sweet dishes.

Cured Meats

Coppa This boned shoulder of pork is rolled and cured with salt, pepper and nutmeg and then aged for about three months. It has a flavour not unlike prosciutto but contains equal amounts of fat and lean. It is excellent for larding the breasts of game birds, adding both fat and flavour, or for wrapping leaner types of meats.

Pancetta Essentially, pancetta is Italian streaky/fatty bacon, but its depth of flavour is unrivalled by ordinary bacon. It is often

flavoured with herbs, cloves, nutmeg, garlic, salt and pepper and sometimes fennel seeds – it is then often air-dried. It is also available smoked. Use it in slices or cut into lardons.

Prosciutto There are many types of cured ham available, but the two best types are Prosciutto di San Daniele and Prosciutto di Parma. The first comes from the Friuli region, where the pigs feed in the fields and oak woods, accounting for the leanness of the meat. The second type, also known as Parma ham or prosciutto crudo, is made from pigs that have been fed on local grain as well as the whey left over from the making of Parmigiano-Reggiano. This meat is usually fattier.

Salami Italy produces a huge range of salamis, each with its own local character. You may be most familiar with Milano salami, which comes sliced in packets or in one piece from major supermarkets.

Vegetables and Herbs

Artichokes Very popular in Italian cooking, artichokes are available in many different varieties and forms: from tiny, young artichokes cooked and eaten whole to enormous globe artichokes, prized for their meaty hearts which can be sliced, stuffed or grilled. Artichokes are often cooked and preserved and served as an antipasto, on pizzas or in pasta dishes.

Aubergines These vegetables are popular all over the Mediterranean, probably because of their affinity with olive oil and garlic. Where you live, aubergines may tend to be fatter and somewhat juicier than the Mediterranean varieties, which are often elongated and marked with bright purple streaks.

Broad/Fava beans Fresh broad beans are a prized early-summer speciality and in Italy are eaten raw with pecorino cheese. As the season progresses, they are best cooked and peeled, as they tend to become coarse and grainy.

Cavallo Nero A member of the cabbage family, cavallo nero has long, slender, very ridged leaves which are dark green in colour. It has a strong but rather sweet cabbage flavour. Large supermarkets stock it in season, but if it is unavailable, use Savoy cabbage instead.

Garlic Garlic is one of the most important flavours in Italian cooking. When buying garlic, check it carefully – the heads should be firm without soft spots. Look for fresh, green garlic in spring.

Herbs A number of fresh herbs are used in Italian cooking, but the most important ones are basil, parsley, rosemary, sage, marjoram and oregano. These are all widely used herbs and are available from most supermarkets, but are also very easy to grow, even on a windowsill.

Lemons Lemons are an essential flavour in many Italian dishes, especially seafood and sweet dishes.

Pumpkins and Squashes Pumpkins and the many varieties of squash are widely used in Italian cooking. They are excellent for enriching stews – some varieties have flesh which breaks down during cooking. They are also used for risottos and pasta fillings. Pumpkins and squashes have an affinity with prosciutto, sage, pine nuts, Parmesan cheese and mostardo di cremona (see the Dry Ingredients section on page 15).

Rocket/Arugula This peppery salad leaf has become popular in recent years and is now very easy to find. It is known by many other names, including rucola, rughetta and roquette. It does not keep well.

Tomatoes Tomatoes are another essential flavour in Italian recipes. It is best to use tomatoes only in season and, at other times, to use good-quality, canned Italian tomatoes.

Wild Mushrooms Mushroom hunting is a very popular and lucrative business in Italy, so much so that there are strict regulations regarding the minimum size for picking mushrooms. Many excellent edible varieties of wild mushrooms grow in Britain and North America, but it is vital to seek expert advice before picking them on your own, as some varieties are poisonous. Many large supermarkets now sell varieties of wild mushrooms in season.

Bread

Italian breads tend to be fairly coarse and open-textured. They are made with unbleached flours and are left to prove for quite some time so that the flavour develops fully. Italian breads also tend to have a fairly crusty exterior. Look out for Pugliese and ciabatta breads. Focaccia, a soft-crusted bread, is also popular and can be flavoured with herbs, sun-dried tomatoes or garlic.

Seafood

Italy has a large coastline relative to its size and, as a result, seafood is a very popular choice. A huge variety of fish and shellfish are available, and large meals such as those served at weddings or other special celebrations will always include a fish course.

Meat, Poultry and Game

Italians are amongst the world's greatest meat eaters. Most meals will be based on meat of some kind. Popular choices include beef, chicken, pork and lamb, but duck, guinea fowl, pheasant, pigeon, rabbit, veal and many kinds of offal are also used.

Dry & Preserved Ingredients

As with fresh ingredients, many items previously unavailable have, in recent years, appeared on supermarket and delicatessen shelves. Many dry ingredients keep well and are worth stocking up on.

Savoury

Anchovies These come in several forms and are an essential Italian ingredient. Anchovies can be treated almost as a seasoning in many recipes. Salted anchovies are sold in bottles and must be

rinsed thoroughly to remove the excess salt. If the anchovies are whole, remove the heads and bones before using. If they are preserved in oil, remove them from the oil and drain them on absorbent kitchen paper. Some recipes require that anchovies are soaked in milk for 10–15 minutes (this makes the fillets less salty and less oily). By doing so, the anchovies will simply melt on cooking. Do not soak the anchovies in milk if the fillets are to be used uncooked, as in salads, for example.

Bottarga This is the salted and sun dried roe of either grey mullet or tuna. It is available from Italian delicatessens or speciality shops (tuna bottarga is less delicately flavoured). Spaghetti with mullet bottarga, olive oil and chilli flakes is listed on every restaurant menu in Sardinia. Bottarga can also be finely shaved into a salad of raw fennel, lemon juice and olive oil.

Canned tomatoes Good–quality, canned Italian plum tomatoes are the next best thing to outdoor grown, sun ripened tomatoes for making sauces. The fruit should be deep red and the liquid should be thick and not watery. Buy them whole or chopped.

Sun-dried tomatoes Although they seem ubiquitous now, sun-dried tomatoes were unavailable outside Italy until the end of the 1980s. Sun-dried tomatoes are ripe plum tomatoes which have been dried in the sun. Often they have been rehydrated by being soaked in water and then preserved in oil. To use them, simply drain them on absorbent kitchen paper and chop as necessary. Also available now are semi-dried tomatoes, which have a sweeter, fresher flavour and a softer, less leathery texture. If you find sun-dried tomatoes which are not in oil, put them into a bowl and cover with boiling water. Leave for about 30 minutes, or until softened, before using.

Sun-dried-tomato purée/paste As the name suggests, this is a paste made from sun–dried tomatoes. Use it in the same way as you would tomato purée/paste. Sometimes it has other flavours added, such as garlic or herbs, in which case it can be used in salad dressings or mixed with pesto to dress pasta.

Capers The flower buds of a bush native to the Mediterranean, capers are available both salted and preserved in vinegar. Small capers generally have a better flavour than larger ones. When using

salted capers, it is important to soak and rinse them to remove the excess salt. Those preserved in vinegar should be drained and rinsed before use.

Coffee Italians prefer dark, roasted coffee and they pioneered the drinking of cappuccino and espresso. It is best to buy whole beans, as freshly roasted as possible, and grind them yourself as needed.

Dried herbs These days, most recipes call for fresh herbs, but dried herbs still have their place. Oregano dries particularly well and has a much less astringent flavour when dried; it is essential in tomato sauces. Other herbs that dry well are rosemary, sage and thyme. Dried basil, however, is no substitute for fresh.

Dried mushrooms The most commonly available – and most affordable – type of dried mushroom is porcini. They should be soaked in almost-boiling water or stock for 20–30 minutes, until tender. Carefully squeeze out any excess liquid – it will still be hot – and then chop as needed. Reserve the liquor, as it contains a great deal of flavour. It is wise, however, to strain it before use, as it can contain grit.

Flour In most Italian recipes where flour is required, plain/all-purpose flour can easily be substituted. However, when making pizza or pasta dough, look for Tipo '00' flour, which is very fine and very strong, making it ideal for these two dishes. If you cannot find it, use strong bread flour instead.

.**Semolina** Not to be confused with the semolina used in puddings, 'semola di grano duro' is flour from Italian durum wheat. This produces a granular-textured flour as opposed to finer-textured flour used in bread-making. Large supermarkets and Italian delicatessens sell semola di grano duro, but if it is unavailable, use strong bread flour instead.

Nuts Almonds, hazelnuts, walnuts and pistachios are all popular in Italian cooking, particularly in dessert recipes. Buy from a supplier with a quick turnover to guarantee that the nuts are fresh.

Pine nuts An essential ingredient in pesto sauce, pine nuts are found in all sorts of Italian recipes, both savoury and sweet. They are widely available and are delicious toasted and tossed in with pasta. They burn very easily, however, and are relatively expensive, so take care when toasting.

Olives Olives grow all over Italy and are synonymous with Italian cooking. Olives are available in most supermarkets, although it is worth looking for them in specialist shops that might preserve them with more interesting flavours. If you are lucky enough to find fresh olives, soak them in a very strong brine for a couple of weeks, then rinse them and preserve in oil and flavourings of your choice.

Dried Pulses

Pulses are an excellent source of carbohydrate and also contain protein, making them particularly useful to vegetarians. Dried pulses should all be treated in the same way – soak them overnight in plenty of water (two to three times their volume), then drain and cover with fresh water. Bring to the boil and boil hard for 10 minutes, reduce the temperature and simmer gently until tender (check packet instructions for full cooking times). Do not add salt to dried pulses until they are cooked, as salt will make the skins tough. Italians make use of a large number of different types of pulses and lentils.

Cannellini beans These beans are long and slender with a creamy texture. Cannellini beans take up other flavours very well, especially garlic, herbs and olive oil.

Borlotti beans These are large, rounded beans which cook to a uniform brown colour. They also have a creamy texture and are very good in soups and stews.

Broad/Fava beans These are available dried; either whole with skins or split. The whole ones are excellent in soups. The split beans are popular in Eastern European countries, as well as Greece and Turkey, where they are used in dishes such as falafel.

Chickpeas *Ceci* in Italian, chickpeas were introduced from the Middle East. Look out for big ones when buying them dry. They are excellent in soups and also in vegetable dishes. Chickpeas need a long cooking time.

Lentils Look for Lentilles de Puy. Although not Italian, these lentils are possibly the best flavoured of the lentil family. They are small and beautifully coloured from green–brown to blue. They also hold their shape well when cooked, making them easy to serve as a side dish – simply dress with olive oil. Similar lentils named Castelluccio are grown in Umbria. They are also small, but paler green in colour.

Lentils are traditionally served with Bollito Misto, a famous New Year's Eve dish consisting of various meats, lentils and mostarda di cremona.

Sweet

Amaretti biscuits/cookies These delicious little crisp biscuits are made from almonds and most closely resemble macaroons. They come individually wrapped in beautiful paper and are good to eat on their own or with a sweet dessert wine. They are also useful as ingredients in desserts, as they add crunch and flavour.

Candied peel Citrus fruit plays an important part in Italian cooking. Candied peel is found in all sorts of desserts. Buy it whole and chop it finely for the best flavour.

Mostarda di cremona Also known as 'mostarda di frutta', it is made of candied fruits such as peaches, apricots, pears, figs and cherries, which are preserved in a honey, white wine and mustard syrup. It is available from large supermarkets and specialist shops.

Raisins Italy is a large grape–producing nation, so, not surprisingly, raisins feature alongside citrus fruits in many recipes. Look for plump, juicy–looking fruit and try to buy only what you need, as raisins can become sugary if kept for too long.

Panettone Generally available around Christmas, panettone is a sweet bread enriched with egg and butter, similar to French brioche. It is usually flavoured with candied citrus fruits, although it can be plain. It keeps very well and is delicious toasted and spread with butter or used in bread and butter pudding.

How to Make Pasta

Home-made pasta has a light, almost silky texture and is different from the fresh pasta that you can buy vacuum-packed in supermarkets. It is also easy to make and little equipment is needed, just a rolling pin and a sharp knife. If you make pasta regularly, it is perhaps worth investing in a pasta machine.

Basic Egg Pasta Dough

225 g/8 oz/2 cups type '00' pasta flour, plus extra for dusting
1 tsp salt, 2 eggs, plus 1 egg yolk
1 tbsp olive oil, 1–3 tsp cold water

1 Sift the flour and salt into a mound on a work surface and make a well in the centre, keeping the sides high so that the egg mixture will not trickle out when added.

2 Beat the eggs, yolk, oil and 1 teaspoon water together. Add to the well, then gradually work in the flour, adding extra water if needed, to make a soft but not sticky dough.

3 Knead on a lightly floured surface for 5 minutes, or until the dough is smooth and elastic. Wrap in plastic wrap and leave for 20 minutes at room temperature.

Using a Food Processor

Sift the flour and salt into a food processor fitted with a metal blade. Add the eggs, yolk, oil and water and pulse-blend until mixed and the dough begins to come together, adding extra water if needed. Knead for 1–2 minutes, then wrap and rest as before.

Rolling Pasta

By Hand

1 Unwrap the pasta dough and cut in half. Work with just half at a time and keep the other half wrapped in plastic wrap.

2 Place the dough on a lightly floured work surface, then flatten and roll out. Always roll away from you. Start from the centre, giving the dough a quarter turn after each rolling. Sprinkle a little more flour over the dough if it starts to get sticky.

3 Continue rolling and turning until the dough is as thin as possible, ideally 3 mm/¹/₈ inch thick.

Drying

Fresh pasta should be dried before cutting. Drape over a wooden pole for 5 minutes, or place on a dish towel sprinkled with a little flour for 10 minutes.

Shaping Up

For shaping freshly made pasta, have several lightly floured dish towels ready. Arrange the pasta in a single layer, spaced slightly apart, or you may find that they stick together. When they are dry, you can freeze them successfully for up to 6 weeks, by layering in suitable freezer containers between sheets of baking parchment. Spread them out on baking parchment for about 20 minutes, or slightly longer if stuffed, before cooking. When making pasta, do not throw away the trimmings. They can be cut into tiny shapes or thin slivers and used in soups.

Farfalle Use a fluted pasta wheel to cut the pasta sheets into rectangles 2.5 x 5 cm/1 x 2 inches. Pinch the long sides of each rectangle in the centre to make a bow. Spread on a floured dish towel. Leave for 15 minutes.

Lasagne Trim the pasta sheets until neat and cut into lengths. Spread the sheets on a dish towel sprinkled with flour.

By Machine

A machine makes smoother, thinner, more even pasta than that made by hand-rolling. Most pasta machines work in the same way, but you should refer to the manufacturers' instructions before using.

1   Clamp the machine securely and attach the handle. Set the rollers at their widest setting and sprinkle with flour.

2   Cut the pasta dough into four pieces. Wrap three of them in plastic wrap and reserve. Flatten the unwrapped dough slightly, then feed it through the rollers.

3   Fold the strip of dough in three, rotate and feed through the rollers a second time. Continue to roll the dough, narrowing the roller setting by one notch every second time and flouring the rollers if the dough starts to get sticky. Only fold the dough the first time it goes through each roller width. If it is hard to handle, cut the strip in half and work with one piece at a time.

Macaroni This is the generic name for hollow pasta. Cut the rolled-out pasta dough into squares, then wrap each around a chopstick, thick skewer or similar, starting from one of the corners. Slip the pasta off, curve slightly if liked and leave to dry for at least 15 minutes.

Noodles If using a pasta machine, use the cutter attachment to produce tagliatelle or fettucine, or use a narrower one for tagliarini or spaghetti. To make by hand, sprinkle the rolled-out pasta with flour, then roll up like a Swiss/jelly roll and cut into thin slices. The thickness of these depends on the noodles required. For linguine, cut into 5 mm/¼ inch slices and for tagliatelle cut into 8 mm/⅓ inch slices. Unravel immediately after cutting. To make thicker ribbon pasta such as pappardelle, use a serrated pastry wheel to cut into wide strips. Leave over a wooden pole for 5 minutes to dry.

Ravioli Cut the rolled-out sheet of dough in half widthways. Cover one half with plastic wrap to stop it drying out too quickly. Brush the other sheet of dough with beaten egg. Pipe or spoon small mounds – using about 1 teaspoon filling in even rows, spacing them at 4 cm/1½ inch intervals. Remove the plastic wrap from the reserved pasta sheet and, using a rolling pin, carefully lift over the dough with the filling. Press down firmly between the pockets of filling to push out any air. Finally, cut into squares with a pastry cutter or sharp knife. Leave on a floured dish towel for 45 minutes before cooking.

You can also use a ravioli tray *(raviolatore)* to produce perfect even-sized ravioli. A sheet of rolled-out dough is laid over the tray, then pressed into the individual compartments. The filling can then be spooned or piped into the indentations and the second sheet of dough placed on top. To create the individual ravioli squares, a rolling pin is gently rolled over the serrated top. These tins are excellent for making small ravioli containing a little filling.

Three or four simple ingredients combined together make the best fillings. Always season generously with salt and freshly ground black pepper and, where the filling is soft, stir in a little beaten egg. Why not try chopped cooked spinach, ricotta and freshly grated nutmeg; finely ground turkey, curd cheese, tarragon and Parmesan cheese; white crab meat with mascarpone, finely grated lemon zest and dill; or ricotta, roasted garlic and fresh herbs.

Silhouette Pasta If rolled out very thinly, fresh herb leaves can be sandwiched between two layers of pasta for a stunning silhouette effect. Put the pasta through a machine set on the very last setting, so that it is paper-thin. Cut in half and lightly brush one piece with water. Arrange individual fresh herb leaves at regular intervals over the moistened pasta (you will need soft herbs for this – flat-leaf parsley, basil and sage are all ideal). Place the second sheet of dry pasta on top and gently press with a rolling pin to seal them together. Sprinkle the pasta with a little flour, then put it through the machine on the second-to-finest setting. Use a pastry wheel, dipped in flour, to cut around the herb leaves to make squares, or use a round or oval cutter to stamp out the pasta if preferred. Leave to dry on a floured dish towel for 20 minutes before cooking.

Tortellini Use a plain cookie cutter to stamp out rounds of pasta about 5 cm/2 inches in diameter. Lightly brush each with beaten egg, then spoon or pipe about 1 teaspoon of filling into the centre of each round. Fold in half to make a half-moon shape, gently pressing the edges together to seal. Bend the two corners round and press together to seal. Allow to dry on a floured dish towel for 30 minutes before cooking. To make tortelloni, use a slightly larger cutter; about 6.5 cm/2½ inches.

Automated

You can also buy electric pasta machines that carry out the whole pasta-making process, from dough mixing and kneading, to extruding it through cutters into the required shapes – all you have to do is weigh out and add the individual ingredients. They can make over 900 g/2 lb of pasta at a time, but are expensive to buy and take up a lot of space.

Variations

Flavoured pastas are simple, and there are dozens of delicious ways that you can change the flavour and colour of pasta. You will find that you get a more even colour when using a machine, but the speckled appearance of flavoured hand-rolled pasta can be equally attractive.

Chilli Add 2 teaspoons crushed, dried red chillies to the egg mixture before you mix with the flour.

Herb Stir 3 tablespoons chopped fresh herbs such as basil, parsley, marjoram or sage or 2 tablespoons finely chopped, strongly flavoured herbs such as thyme or rosemary into the flour.

Olive Blend 2 tablespoons of black olive paste with the egg mixture, leaving out the water.

Porcini Soak 15 g/½ oz dried porcini mushrooms in boiling water for 20 minutes. Drain and squeeze out as much water as possible, then chop very finely. Add to the egg mixture. (Reserve the soaking liquor, strain and use to flavour the pasta sauce.)

Saffron Sift 1 teaspoon powdered saffron with the flour.

Spinach Cook 75 g/3 oz prepared spinach in a covered pan with just the water clinging to the leaves, until wilted. Drain and squeeze dry, then chop finely. Add to the egg mixture.

Sun-dried tomato Blend 2 tablespoons sun-dried tomato paste into the egg mixture, leaving out the water.

Wholemeal pasta Substitute half the wholemeal flour for half of the white flour and add an extra 1–2 teaspoons water to the mixture.

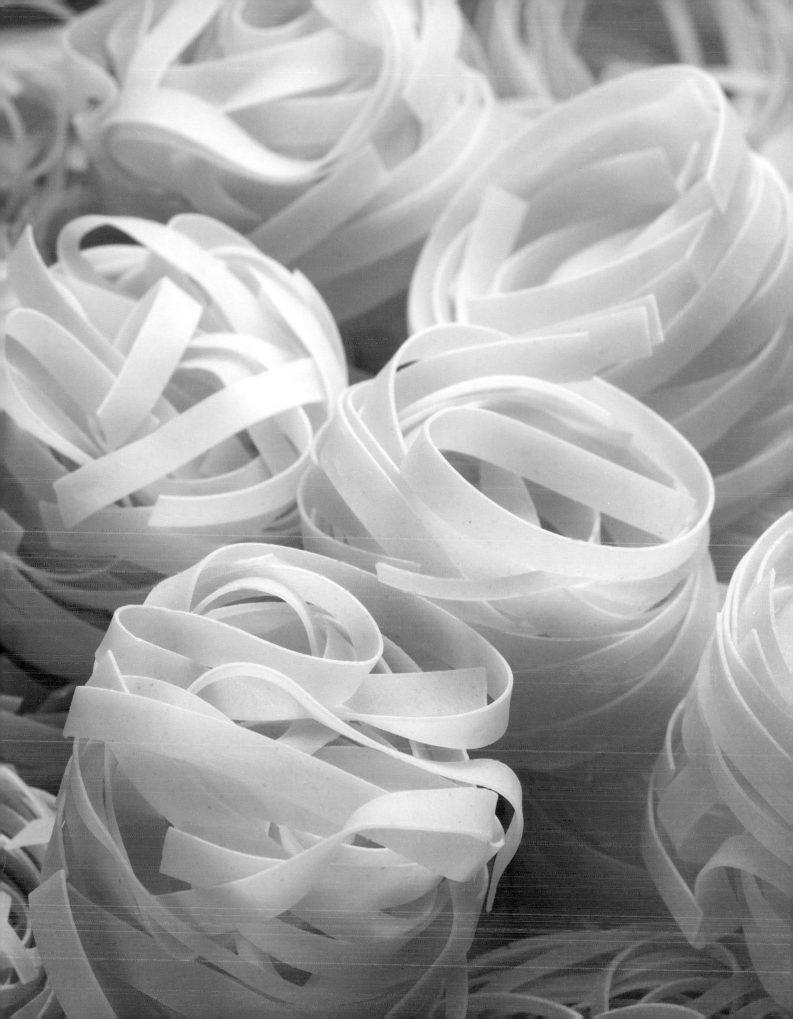

Soups & Starters

This section provides you with an excellent selection of hearty soups and delicious starters. Whether you are in the mood for a Classic Minestrone or a White Bean Soup with Parmesan Croutons, you'll find the recipe you are looking for. The starter recipes, such as Antipasti with Focaccia or Pasta with Walnut Sauce, make for excellent snacks, light lunches, or appetizers, so you will not be lacking in options for your guests or for you.

White Bean Soup with Parmesan Croutons

Serves 4

Ingredients

3 thick slices white bread, cut into 1 cm/½ inch cubes

3 tbsp groundnut/peanut oil

2 tbsp finely grated Parmesan cheese

1 tbsp light olive oil

1 large onion, peeled and finely chopped

50 g/2 oz/¼ cup unsmoked bacon lardons (or diced thick slices)

1 tbsp fresh thyme leaves

800 g/28 oz canned cannellini beans, drained

900 ml/1½ pints/3¾ cups chicken stock

salt and freshly ground black pepper

1 tbsp prepared pesto sauce

50 g/2 oz piece pepperoni sausage, diced

1 tbsp fresh lemon juice

1 tbsp roughly shredded fresh basil

Preheat the oven to 200°C/400°F/Gas Mark 6. Place the bread cubes in a bowl and pour over the groundnut/peanut oil. Stir to coat the bread, then sprinkle the Parmesan cheese over. Place on a lightly oiled baking sheet and bake in the preheated oven for 10 minutes, or until crisp and golden. Reserve.

Heat the olive oil in a large saucepan and cook the onion for 4–5 minutes until softened. Add the bacon and thyme and cook for a further 3 minutes. Stir in the beans, stock and black pepper and simmer gently for 5 minutes.

Place half the bean mixture and liquid into a food processor and blend until smooth. Return the purée to the saucepan. Stir in the pesto sauce, pepperoni sausage and lemon juice and season to taste with salt and pepper.

Return the soup to the heat and cook for a further 2–3 minutes until piping hot. Ladle the soup into each serving bowl, garnish with shredded basil and serve immediately with the croutons scattered over the top.

Health Rating: 3 points

Rice Soup with Potato Sticks

Serves 4

Ingredients

175 g/6 oz/³/₄ cup (1½ sticks) butter

1 tsp olive oil

1 large onion, peeled and finely chopped

4 slices Parma ham/prosciutto, chopped

100 g/3½ oz/½ cup Arborio/risotto rice

1.1 litres/2 pints chicken stock

350 g/12 oz frozen peas

salt and freshly ground black pepper

1 medium/large egg

125 g/4 oz self-raising flour

175 g/6 oz mashed potato

1 tbsp milk

1 tbsp poppy seeds

1 tbsp finely grated Parmesan cheese

1 tbsp freshly chopped parsley

Preheat the oven to 190°C/375°F/Gas Mark 5. Heat 25 g/1 oz/2 tbsp of the butter and the olive oil in a saucepan and cook the onion for 4–5 minutes until softened, then add the Parma ham/ prosciutto and cook for about 1 minute. Stir in the rice, the stock and the peas. Season to taste with salt and pepper and simmer for 10–15 minutes until the rice is tender.

Beat the egg and 125 g/4 oz/½ cup (1 stick) of the butter until smooth, then beat in the flour, a pinch salt and the potato. Work the ingredients together to form a soft, pliable dough, adding a little more flour if necessary. Roll the dough out on a lightly floured surface into a rectangle 1 cm/½ inch thick and cut into 12 thin, long sticks. Brush with milk and sprinkle on the poppy seeds. Place the sticks on a lightly oiled baking tray and bake in the oven for 15 minutes, or until golden.

When the rice is cooked, stir the remaining butter and the Parmesan into the soup and sprinkle the chopped parsley over the top. Serve immediately with the warm potato sticks.

Health Rating: 3 points

Wild Mushroom Soup

Serves 4

Ingredients

15 g/¹⁄₂ oz dried porcini mushrooms

125 g/4 oz chestnut/cremini mushrooms

175 g/6 oz assorted wild mushrooms

3–4 tbsp olive oil

1 medium onion, peeled and chopped

2–3 garlic cloves, peeled and chopped

1 small red chilli, deseeded and chopped

125 g/4 oz potatoes, peeled and chopped

900 ml/1¹⁄₂ pints/3³⁄₄ cups vegetable or chicken stock

salt and freshly ground black pepper

3–4 tbsp single/light cream

2 medium/large egg yolks

warm Italian bread, to serve

Soak the dried mushrooms, in enough warm water to cover, for 20 minutes. Drain and reserve the soaking liquor. Chop the drained soaked mushrooms. Wipe the chestnut/cremini mushrooms and trim the tops of the stalks. Chop the stalks and both the wild and chestnut mushrooms and reserve.

Heat 3 tablespoons of the oil in a large saucepan, add the onion, garlic, chilli and potatoes and fry for 5 minutes, stirring, or until well covered in the oil. Add the remaining oil if all the oil in the pan has been used, then add all the mushrooms and stalks and fry for a further 2 minutes.

Pour in the stock together with the soaking liquor and bring to the boil. Cover with a lid, reduce the heat to a simmer and cook for 15 minutes, or until the mushrooms are tender. Cool slightly, then place in a blender or food processor until smooth. Return to the cleaned saucepan and add the remaining stock and the seasoning to taste.

Beat the cream and egg yolks together and stir slowly into the soup. Place over a gentle heat and cook, stirring. Bring to the boil, then reduce the heat and simmer for 5 minutes. When slightly thickened, serve with warm Italian bread.

Health Rating: 4 points

Rich Tomato Soup with Roasted Red Peppers

Serves 4

Ingredients

2 tsp light olive oil

700 g/1¹⁄₂ lb red peppers, halved

3 plum tomatoes, halved

2 onions, unpeeled and quartered

4 garlic cloves, unpeeled

600 ml/1 pint/2¹⁄₂ cups chicken stock

salt and freshly ground black pepper

4 tbsp sour cream

1 tbsp freshly shredded basil

Preheat the oven to 200°C/400°F/Gas Mark 6. Lightly oil a roasting tin/pan with 1 teaspoon of the olive oil. Place the peppers and tomatoes cut-side down in the roasting tin with the onion quarters and the garlic cloves. Spoon over the remaining oil.

Bake in the preheated oven for 30 minutes, or until the skins on the peppers have started to blacken and blister. Allow the vegetables to cool for about 10 minutes, then remove the skins, stalks and seeds from the peppers. Peel away the skins from the tomatoes and onions and squeeze out the garlic.

Place the cooked vegetables in a blender or food processor and blend until smooth.

Add the stock and blend again to form a smooth purée. Pour the puréed soup through a sieve, if a smooth soup is preferred, then pour into a saucepan. Bring to the boil, simmer gently for 2–3 minutes, and season to taste with salt and pepper. Serve hot with a swirl of sour cream and a sprinkling of shredded basil on the top.

Health Rating: 4 points

Bread & Tomato Soup

Serves 4

Ingredients

6 very ripe tomatoes

4 tbsp/¼ cup olive oil

1 onion, peeled and finely chopped

1 tbsp freshly chopped basil

3 garlic cloves, peeled and crushed

¼ tsp hot chilli powder

salt and freshly ground black pepper

600 ml/1 pint/2½ cups chicken stock

175 g/6 oz/6 slices stale white bread

50 g/2 oz/¼ small cucumber, cut into small dice

4 whole basil leaves

Health Rating: 4 points

Make a small cross in the base of each tomato, then place in a bowl and cover with boiling water. Allow to stand for 2 minutes, or until the skins have started to peel away, then drain, remove the skins and seeds and chop into large pieces.

Heat 3 tablespoons of the olive oil in a saucepan and gently cook the onion until softened. Add the skinned tomatoes, chopped basil, garlic and chilli powder and season to taste with salt and pepper. Pour in the stock, cover the saucepan, bring to the boil and simmer gently for 15–20 minutes.

Remove the crusts from the bread and break into small pieces. Remove the tomato mixture from the heat and stir in the bread. Cover and leave to stand for 10 minutes, or until the bread has blended with the tomatoes. Season to taste.

Serve warm or cold with a swirl of olive oil on the top, garnished with a spoonful of chopped cucumber and basil leaves.

Rocket & Potato Soup with Garlic Croutons

Serves 4

Ingredients

14–18 baby new potatoes

1.25 litres/2¼ pints/5¼ cups chicken or vegetable stock

50 g/2 oz/2 cups rocket/arugula leaves

4 thick slices sliced white bread

50 g/2 oz/4 tbsp unsalted butter

1 tsp groundnut/peanut oil

2–4 garlic cloves, peeled and chopped

1 stale ciabatta loaf, crusts removed

4 tbsp olive oil

salt and freshly ground black pepper

2 tbsp finely grated Parmesan cheese

Place the potatoes in a large saucepan, cover with the stock and simmer gently for 10 minutes. Add the rocket/arugula leaves and simmer for a further 5–10 minutes until the potatoes are soft and the rocket has wilted.

Meanwhile, make the croutons. Cut the thick, white sliced bread into small cubes and reserve. Heat the butter and groundnut/peanut oil in a small frying pan and cook the garlic for 1 minute, stirring well. Remove the garlic. Add the bread cubes to the butter and oil mixture in the frying pan and sauté, stirring constantly, until they are golden brown. Drain the croutons on absorbent paper towels and reserve.

Cut the ciabatta bread into small cubes and stir into the soup. Cover the saucepan and leave to stand for 10 minutes, or until the bread has absorbed a lot of the liquid.

Stir in the olive oil, season to taste with salt and pepper and ladle into individual bowls with a few of the garlic croutons scattered over the top and a little grated Parmesan cheese.

Health Rating: 3 points

Classic Minestrone

Serves 6–8

Ingredients

25 g/1 oz/2 tbsp butter

3 tbsp olive oil

3 slices streaky/fatty bacon

1 large onion, peeled

1 garlic clove, peeled

1 celery stalk, trimmed

2 carrots, peeled

400 g/14 oz/2 cups canned chopped tomatoes

1.25 litres/2¼ pints/5¼ cups chicken stock

175 g/6 oz/2½ cups finely shredded green cabbage

50 g/2 oz/½ cup trimmed and halved French/green beans

3 tbsp frozen petits pois

50 g/2 oz spaghetti

salt and freshly ground black pepper

Parmesan cheese shavings, to garnish

crusty bread, to serve

Heat the butter and olive oil together in a large saucepan. Chop the bacon and add to the saucepan. Cook for 3–4 minutes, then remove with a slotted spoon and reserve.

Finely chop the onion, garlic, celery and carrots and add to the saucepan, one ingredient at a time, stirring well after each addition. Cover and cook gently for 8–10 minutes until the vegetables are softened.

Add the chopped tomatoes, with their juice and the stock, bring to the boil, then cover the saucepan with a lid, reduce the heat and simmer gently for about 20 minutes.

Stir in the cabbage, beans, petits pois and spaghetti, broken into short pieces. Cover and simmer for a further 20 minutes, until all the ingredients are tender. Season to taste with salt and pepper.

Return the cooked bacon to the saucepan and bring the soup to the boil. Serve the soup immediately, with Parmesan shavings sprinkled on top and plenty of crusty bread.

Health Rating: 3 points

Cream of Pumpkin Soup

Serves 4

Ingredients

4 tbsp olive oil
900 g/2 lb/6 cups peeled, deseeded and cubed pumpkin
1 large onion, peeled and finely chopped
1 leek, trimmed and finely chopped
1 carrot, peeled and diced
2 celery stalks, diced
4 garlic cloves, peeled and crushed
salt and freshly ground black pepper
¼ tsp freshly grated nutmeg
150 ml/¼ pint/⅔ cup single/light cream
¼ tsp cayenne pepper
warm herby bread, to serve

Heat the olive oil in a large saucepan and cook the pumpkin for 2–3 minutes, coating it completely with oil.

Add the onion, leek, carrot and celery to the saucepan with the garlic and cook, stirring for 5 minutes, or until they have begun to soften. Cover the vegetables with 1.7 litres/3 pints/1¾ quarts water and bring to the boil. Season with plenty of salt and pepper and the nutmeg, cover and simmer for 15–20 minutes until all of the vegetables are tender.

When the vegetables are tender, remove from the heat, cool slightly, then pour into a food processor or blender. Liquidize to form a smooth purée, then pass through a sieve into a clean saucepan.

Adjust the seasoning to taste and add all but 2 tablespoons of the cream and enough water to obtain the desired consistency. Bring the soup to boiling point, add the cayenne pepper and serve immediately, swirled with cream and accompanied by warm herby bread.

Health Rating: 3 points

Fresh Herb & Egg Soup

Serves 4

Ingredients

900 ml/1½ pints/3¾ cups stock, such as chicken, beef
   or vegetable
1 tsp unsalted butter
2 tbsp freshly chopped parsley
1 tbsp freshly chopped coriander/cilantro
2 tbsp freshly chopped basil
1 tbsp freshly chopped dill
1 medium/large egg
1 medium/large egg yolk
salt and freshly ground black pepper

To serve:
freshly grated Parmesan cheese
warm bread

Pour the stock into a large saucepan, add the butter together
with the herbs, bring to the boil, then reduce the heat to a
gentle boil.

Beat the egg and egg yolk with seasoning to taste, then pour
slowly into the gently simmering soup. Use a whisk to do this
and make sure that you whisk constantly so that the beaten egg
does not curdle.

Ladle into warm soup bowls and sprinkle with plenty of grated
Parmesan cheese. Serve with more grated Parmesan cheese, if
liked, and chunks of warm bread.

Health Rating: 2 points

Lettuce Soup

Serves 4

Ingredients

2 iceberg lettuces, quartered and with hard core removed
1 tbsp olive oil
50 g/2 oz/4 tbsp butter
125 g/½ cup trimmed and chopped spring onions/scallions
1 tbsp freshly chopped parsley
1 tbsp plain/all-purpose flour
600 ml/1 pint/2½ cups chicken stock
salt and freshly ground black pepper
150 ml/¼ pint/⅔ cup single/light cream
¼ tsp cayenne pepper, or to taste
thick slices stale ciabatta bread
parsley sprigs, to garnish

Bring a large saucepan of water to the boil and blanch the
lettuce leaves for 3 minutes. Drain and dry thoroughly on
absorbent paper towels, then shred with a sharp knife.

Heat the oil and butter in a clean saucepan and add the lettuce,
spring onions/scallions and parsley and cook together for 3–4
minutes until very soft.

Stir in the flour and cook for 1 minute, then gradually pour in
the stock, stirring throughout. Bring to the boil and season to
taste with salt and pepper. Reduce the heat, cover and simmer
gently for 10–15 minutes until soft.

Allow the soup to cool slightly, then either sieve or purée in
a blender. Alternatively, leave the soup chunky. Stir in the
cream, add more seasoning to taste, if liked, then add the
cayenne pepper.

Arrange the slices of ciabatta bread in a large soup dish or in
individual bowls and pour the soup over the bread. Garnish with
parsley sprigs and serve immediately.

Health Rating: 3 points

Italian Bean Soup

Serves 4

Ingredients

2 tsp olive oil
1 leek, washed and chopped
1 garlic clove, peeled and crushed
2 tsp dried oregano
75 g/3 oz/³⁄₄ cup trimmed and chopped green beans
410 g/14 oz canned cannellini beans, drained and rinsed
75 g/3 oz/³⁄₄ cup small pasta shapes
1 litre/1³⁄₄ pints/4 cups vegetable stock
8 cherry tomatoes
salt and freshly ground black pepper
3 tbsp freshly shredded basil

Heat the oil in a large saucepan. Add the leek, garlic and oregano and cook gently for 5 minutes, stirring occasionally.

Stir in the green beans and the cannellini beans. Sprinkle in the pasta and pour in the stock. Bring the stock mixture to the boil, then reduce the heat to a simmer.

Cook for 12–15 minutes until the vegetables are tender and the pasta is cooked to *al dente*. Stir occasionally.

In a heavy-based frying pan, dry-fry the tomatoes over a high heat until they soften and the skins begin to blacken.

Gently crush the tomatoes in the pan with the back of a spoon and add to the soup.

Season to taste with salt and pepper. Stir in the shredded basil and serve immediately.

Health Rating: 4 points

Tomato & Basil Soup

Serves 4

Ingredients

7 ripe tomatoes, cut in half
2 garlic cloves, unpeeled
1 tsp olive oil
1 tbsp balsamic vinegar
1 tbsp dark brown sugar
1 tbsp tomato purée/paste
300 ml/½ pint/1¼ cups vegetable stock
6 tbsp natural/plain yogurt
2 tbsp freshly chopped basil
salt and freshly ground black pepper
small basil leaves, to garnish

Health Rating: 4 points

Preheat the oven to 200°C/400°F/Gas Mark 6. Evenly spread the tomatoes and garlic in a single layer in a large roasting tin/pan.

Mix the oil and vinegar together. Drizzle over the tomatoes and sprinkle with the dark brown sugar.

Roast the tomatoes in the preheated oven for 20 minutes until tender and lightly charred in places.

Remove from the oven and allow to cool slightly. When cool enough to handle, squeeze the softened flesh of the garlic from the papery skins. Place with the charred tomatoes in a nylon sieve over a saucepan.

Press the garlic and tomato through the sieve with the back of a wooden spoon. When all the flesh has been sieved, add the tomato purée/paste and vegetable stock to the pan. Heat gently, stirring occasionally.

In a small bowl, beat the yogurt and basil together and season to taste with salt and pepper. Stir the basil yogurt into the soup. Garnish with basil leaves and serve immediately.

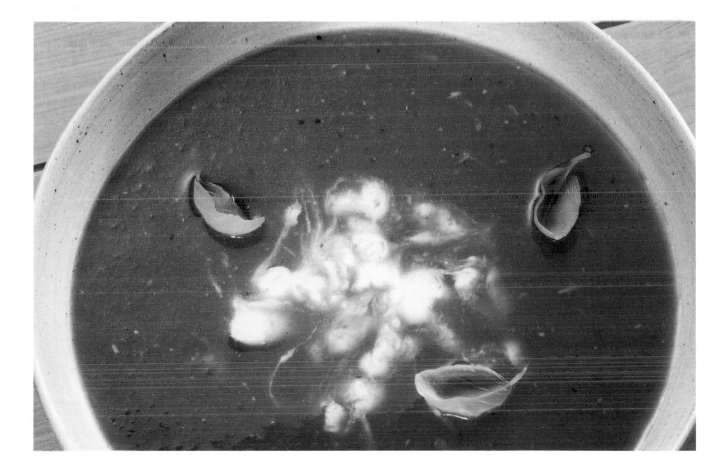

Wild Mushroom Crostini

Serves 4

Ingredients

15 g/¹/₂ oz dried porcini mushrooms
125 g/4 oz/1¹/₄ cups assorted wild mushrooms
125 g/4 oz/¹/₄ cups button/white mushrooms
3 tbsp olive oil
2 shallots, peeled and thinly sliced
2–3 garlic cloves, peeled and sliced
1 small yellow pepper, deseeded and thinly sliced
125 g/4 oz baby plum tomatoes, halved
salt and freshly ground black pepper
1 ciabatta loaf, cut into 8 slices
25 g/1 oz rocket/arugula or watercress
basil-flavoured oil, for drizzling

Soak the dried mushrooms, in enough warm water to cover, for 20 minutes, then drain. Chop the rehydrated mushrooms. Wipe the button/white mushrooms and slice.

Preheat the grill/broiler or griddle pan. Heat the olive oil in a large frying pan, add the shallots and garlic and fry for 2 minutes. Add all the mushrooms together with the pepper, tomatoes and seasoning to taste. Continue to cook over a gentle heat for 5–8 minutes until tender.

Meanwhile, toast the bread under the grill, or cook in a heated griddle pan which has been lightly brushed with oil.

Place the rocket/arugula or watercress on the toasted bread, then spoon the mushrooms on top, drizzle with a little basil-flavoured oil and serve.

Health Rating: 4 points

Fried Whitebait with Rocket Salad

Serves 4

Ingredients

450 g/1 lb whitebait/smelt, fresh or frozen
vegetable oil, for deep-frying
100 g/3¹/₂ oz/³/₄ cup plain/all-purpose flour
¹/₂ tsp cayenne pepper
salt and freshly ground black pepper

For the salad:
125 g/4¹/₂ oz/4 cups rocket/arugula leaves
8 cherry tomatoes, halved
¹/₂ cucumber, cut into cubes
3 tbsp olive oil
1 tbsp fresh lemon juice
¹/₂ tsp Dijon mustard
¹/₂ tsp caster/superfine sugar

If the fish are frozen, thaw completely, then wipe dry with absorbent paper towels.

Start to heat the oil in a deep-fat fryer. Arrange the fish in a large, shallow dish and toss well in the flour, cayenne pepper and salt and pepper.

Deep-fry the fish in batches for 2–3 minutes until crisp and golden. Keep the cooked fish warm while deep-frying the remaining fish.

For the salad, arrange the leaves, tomatoes and cucumber on individual serving dishes. Whisk the olive oil and the remaining ingredients together and season lightly. Drizzle the dressing over the salad. Serve with the fish.

Health Rating: 2 points

Mozzarella Frittata with Tomato & Basil Salad

Serves 6

Ingredients

For the salad:
6 ripe but firm tomatoes, thinly sliced
2 tbsp fresh basil leaves
2 tbsp olive oil
1 tbsp fresh lemon juice
1 tsp caster/superfine sugar
freshly ground black pepper

For the frittata:
7 medium/large eggs, beaten
salt
300 g/10 oz/2 cups grated mozzarella cheese
2 spring onions/scallions, trimmed and finely chopped
2 tbsp olive oil
warm crusty bread, to serve

To make the tomato and basil salad, place the tomatoes in a dish, tear up the basil leaves and sprinkle over. Make the dressing by whisking the olive oil, lemon juice and sugar together well. Season with black pepper before drizzling the dressing over the salad.

To make the frittata, preheat the grill/broiler to a high heat just before starting to cook. Place the eggs in a large bowl with plenty of salt and whisk. Stir the mozzarella into the egg with the finely chopped spring onions/scallions.

Heat the oil in a large, nonstick frying pan. Pour in the egg mixture, stirring with a wooden spoon to spread the ingredients evenly over the pan. Cook for 5–8 minutes until the frittata is golden brown and firm on the underside. Place the whole pan under the preheated grill and cook for about 4–5 minutes until the top is golden brown.

Slide the frittata onto a serving plate, cut into six large wedges and serve immediately with the tomato and basil salad and plenty of warm crusty bread.

Health Rating: 4 points

Antipasti with Focaccia

Serves 4

Ingredients

3 fresh figs, quartered

125 g/4 oz/²⁄₃ cup cooked and halved green beans

1 small head radicchio, rinsed and shredded

125 g/4 oz/8–12 large prawns/shrimp, peeled and cooked

25 g/1 oz/2 tbsp pitted black/ripe olives

125 g/4 oz canned sardines, drained

25 g/1 oz/2 tbsp stuffed green olives

125 g/4 oz/1 cup sliced mozzarella cheese

50 g/2 oz/½ cup Italian thinly sliced salami sausage

3 tbsp olive oil

275 g/10 oz/2½ cups strong white/bread flour

pinch sugar

175 g/6 oz fine semolina

1 tsp salt

3 tsp easy-blend quick-acting yeast or 15 g/½ oz/1¼ tsp fresh yeast

a little extra olive oil for brushing

1 tbsp coarse salt crystals

Preheat oven to 220°C/425°F/Gas Mark 7, 15 minutes before baking. Arrange the fresh fruit, vegetables, prawns/shrimp, olives, sardines, cheese and meat on a large serving platter. Drizzle over 1 tbsp of the olive oil, then cover and chill while making the bread.

Sift the flour, sugar, semolina and salt into a mixing bowl, then sprinkle in the dried yeast. Make a well in the centre and add the remaining 2 tablespoons of the olive oil. Add 300 ml/½ pint/1¼ cups warm water, a little at a time, and mix together until a smooth, pliable dough is formed. If using fresh yeast, cream the yeast with the sugar, then gradually beat in half the warm water. Leave in a warm place until frothy, then proceed as for dried yeast.

Place onto a lightly floured board and knead until smooth and elastic. Place the dough in a lightly greased bowl, cover and leave in a warm place for 45 minutes.

Knead again and flatten the dough into a large, flat oval shape about 1 cm/½ inch thick. Place on a lightly oiled baking tray.

Prick the surface with the end of a wooden spoon and brush with olive oil. Sprinkle on the coarse salt and bake in the oven for 25 minutes, or until golden. Serve the bread with the prepared platter.

Health Rating: 3 points

Bruschetta with Pecorino, Garlic & Tomatoes

Serves 4

Ingredients

6 ripe but firm tomatoes
125 g/4 oz/1¼ cups finely grated pecorino cheese
1 tbsp chopped oregano leaves
salt and freshly ground black pepper
3 tbsp olive oil
3 garlic cloves, peeled
8 slices Italian flat bread, such as focaccia
8 thin slices mozzarella cheese
marinated black/ripe olives, to serve

Preheat the grill/broiler and line the rack with foil just before cooking. Make a small cross in the tops of the tomatoes, then place in a small bowl and cover with boiling water. Leave to stand for 2 minutes, then drain and remove the skins. Cut into quarters, remove the seeds. Chop the flesh into small cubes.

Mix the tomato flesh with the pecorino cheese and 2 teaspoons of the fresh oregano and season to taste with salt and pepper. Add 1 tablespoon of the olive oil and mix thoroughly.

Crush the garlic and spread evenly over the bread slices. Heat 2 tablespoons of the olive oil in a large frying pan and fry the bread slices until they are crisp and golden.

Place the fried bread on a lightly oiled baking sheet and spoon on the tomato and cheese topping. Place a little mozzarella on top and place under the preheated grill for 3–4 minutes until golden and bubbling. Garnish with the remaining oregano, then arrange the bruschettas on a serving plate and serve immediately with the olives.

Health Rating: 3 points

Crostini with Chicken Livers

Serves 4

Ingredients

2 tbsp olive oil

25 g/1 oz/2 tbsp butter

1 shallot, peeled and finely chopped

1 garlic clove, peeled and crushed

150 g/5 oz/1½ cups chicken livers

1 tbsp plain/all-purpose flour

2 tbsp dry white wine

1 tbsp brandy

50 g/2 oz/¼ cup sliced mushrooms

salt and freshly ground black pepper

4 slices ciabatta or similar bread

To garnish:

fresh sage leaves

lemon wedges

Heat 1 tablespoon of the olive oil and 15 g/½ oz/1 tbsp of the butter in a frying pan, add the shallot and garlic and cook gently for 2–3 minutes.

Trim and wash the chicken livers thoroughly. Pat dry on absorbent paper towels. Cut into slices, then toss in the flour. Add the livers to the frying pan with the shallot and garlic. Continue to fry for another 2 minutes, stirring constantly.

Pour in the white wine and brandy and bring to the boil. Boil rapidly for 1–2 minutes to allow the alcohol to evaporate, then stir in the sliced mushrooms and cook gently for about 5 minutes until the chicken livers are cooked but just a little pink inside. Season to taste with salt and pepper.

Fry the ciabatta slices or similar-style bread in the remaining oil and butter, then place on individual serving dishes. Spoon over the liver mixture and garnish with a few sage leaves and lemon wedges. Serve immediately.

Health Rating: 2 points

Mushroom Sauté

Serves 4

Ingredients

1 fennel bulb
1 red pepper
2 courgettes/zucchini
125 g/4 oz/generous ³/₄ cup broad/fava beans
2–3 tbsp olive oil
2 medium onions, peeled and chopped
2–3 garlic cloves, peeled and chopped
225 g/8 oz field mushrooms, wiped
2 tbsp balsamic vinegar
salt and freshly ground black pepper

To serve:
2 tbsp fresh Parmesan cheese shavings
2 tbsp shredded basil leaves

Remove the feathery leaves from the fennel bulb and reserve. Trim the bulb, then slice. Cut the pepper into quarters and discard the seeds, then slice thinly. Trim the courgettes/zucchini, then slice and cut each slice in half to form half-moon shapes.

If using fresh broad/fava beans, cook in lightly salted water for 5 minutes, then drain and reserve. If using frozen broad beans, allow to thaw or cover with boiling water for 10 minutes, then drain and reserve.

Heat the oil in a large frying pan, add the onions, garlic and fennel and fry for 5 minutes, stirring frequently. Add the mushrooms and cook for a further 5–8 minutes until all the vegetables are tender.

Add the vinegar with seasoning to taste and heat through. Serve in a warm dish scattered with the Parmesan cheese shavings and shredded basil and garnished with the fennel leaves.

Health Rating: 4 points

Italian Baked Tomatoes with Curly Endive & Radicchio

Serves 4

Ingredients

1 tsp olive oil
4 beef tomatoes
50 g/2 oz/¹/₂ cup fresh white breadcrumbs
1 tbsp freshly snipped chives
1 tbsp freshly chopped parsley
125 g/4 oz/1 cup finely chopped button mushrooms
salt and freshly ground black pepper
25 g/1 oz/¹/₄ cup grated fresh Parmesan cheese

For the salad:
¹/₂ curly endive
¹/₂ small piece radicchio
2 tbsp olive oil
1 tsp balsamic vinegar
salt and freshly ground black pepper

Preheat the oven to 190°C/375°F/Gas Mark 5. Lightly oil a baking tray with the teaspoon of oil. Slice the tops off the tomatoes and remove all the tomato flesh and sieve into a large bowl. Sprinkle a little salt inside the tomato shells and then place them upside down on a plate while the filling is prepared.

Mix the sieved tomato with the breadcrumbs, fresh herbs and mushrooms and season well. Place the tomato shells on the baking tray and fill with the tomato and mushroom mixture. Sprinkle the cheese on the top and bake in the oven for 15–20 minutes until golden brown.

Meanwhile, prepare the salad. Arrange the endive and radicchio on individual serving plates and mix the remaining ingredients together in a small bowl to make the dressing. Season to taste. When the tomatoes are cooked, allow to rest for 5 minutes, then place on the plates and drizzle over a little dressing. Serve warm.

Health Rating: 4 points

Spaghettini with Lemon Pesto & Cheese & Herb Bread

Serves 4

Ingredients

1 small onion, peeled and grated

2 tsp freshly chopped oregano

1 tbsp freshly chopped parsley

75 g/3 oz/6 tbsp butter

125 g/4 oz/1¼ cups grated pecorino cheese

8 slices Italian flat bread

275 g/10 oz dried spaghettini

4 tbsp olive oil

1 large bunch basil, approximately 25 g/1 oz

75 g/3 oz/½ cup pine nuts

1 garlic clove, peeled and crushed

75 g/3 oz/¾ cup grated Parmesan cheese

finely grated zest and juice of 2 lemons

salt and freshly ground black pepper

4 tsp butter

Preheat the oven to 200°C/400°F/Gas Mark 6, 15 minutes before baking. Mix together the onion, oregano, parsley, butter and cheese.

Spread the bread with the cheese mixture, place on a lightly oiled baking tray and cover with kitchen foil. Bake in the preheated oven for 10–15 minutes, then keep warm.

Add the spaghettini with 1 tablespoon olive oil to a large saucepan of fast-boiling, lightly salted water and cook for 3–4 minutes until *al dente*. Drain, reserving 2 tablespoons of the cooking liquor.

Blend the basil, pine nuts, garlic, Parmesan cheese, lemon zest and juice and remaining olive oil in a food processor or blender until a purée is formed. Season to taste with salt and pepper, then place in a saucepan.

Heat the lemon pesto very gently until piping hot, then stir in the pasta together with the reserved cooking liquor. Add the butter and mix together well.

Add plenty of black pepper to the pasta and serve immediately with the warm cheese and herb bread.

Health Rating: 3 points

Mussels with Creamy Garlic & Saffron Sauce

Serves 4

Ingredients

700 g/1½ lb fresh live mussels

300 ml/½ pint/1¼ cups good-quality dry white wine

1 tbsp olive oil

1 shallot, peeled and finely chopped

2 garlic cloves, peeled and crushed

1 tbsp freshly chopped oregano

2 saffron strands

150 ml/¼ pint/⅔ cup single/light cream

salt and freshly ground black pepper

fresh crusty bread, to serve

Clean the mussels thoroughly in plenty of cold water and remove any beards and barnacles from the shells. Discard any mussels that are open or damaged. Place in a large bowl and cover with cold water and leave in the refrigerator until required if prepared earlier.

Pour the wine into a large saucepan and bring to the boil. Tip the mussels into the pan, cover and cook, shaking the saucepan periodically for 6–8 minutes until the mussels have opened completely.

Discard any mussels with closed shells, then, using a slotted spoon, carefully remove the remaining open mussels from the saucepan and keep them warm. Reserve the cooking liquor.

Heat the olive oil in a small frying pan and cook the shallot and garlic gently for 2–3 minutes until softened. Add the reserved cooking liquor and chopped oregano and cook for a further 3–4 minutes. Stir in the saffron and the cream and heat through gently. Season to taste with salt and pepper. Place a few mussels in individual serving bowls and spoon over the saffron sauce. Serve immediately with plenty of fresh crusty bread.

Health Rating: 2 points

Peperonata (Braised Mixed Peppers)

Serves 4

Ingredients

2 green peppers
1 red pepper
1 yellow pepper
1 orange pepper
1 onion, peeled
2 garlic cloves, peeled
2 tbsp olive oil
4 very ripe tomatoes
1 tbsp freshly chopped oregano
salt and freshly ground black pepper
150 ml/¼ pint/⅔ cup light chicken or vegetable stock
fresh oregano sprigs, to garnish
focaccia or flat bread, to serve

Remove the seeds from the peppers and cut into thin strips. Slice the onion into rings and chop the garlic cloves finely.

Heat the olive oil in a frying pan and fry the peppers, onion and garlic for 5–10 minutes until soft and lightly coloured. Stir constantly.

Make a cross on the tops of the tomatoes, then place in a bowl and cover with boiling water. Allow to stand for about 2 minutes. Drain, then remove the skins and seeds and chop the tomato flesh into cubes.

Add the tomatoes and oregano to the peppers and onion and season to taste with salt and pepper. Cover the pan and bring to the boil. Simmer gently for about 30 minutes until tender, adding the chicken or vegetable stock halfway through the cooking time.

Garnish with oregano sprigs and serve hot with plenty of freshly baked focaccia bread or lightly toasted slices of flat bread and pile a spoonful of peperonata onto each plate.

Health Rating: 5 points

Wild Garlic Mushrooms with Pizza Breadsticks

Serves 6

Ingredients

For the breadsticks:

1 tbsp easy-blend active dried yeast

400 g/14 oz/3½ cups strong white/bread flour

25 g/1 oz/½ cup finely grated Parmesan cheese

2 tbsp olive oil

2 tbsp tomato purée/paste

1 tsp salt

For the mushrooms:

125 ml/4 fl oz/½ cup olive oil

4 garlic cloves, peeled and crushed

450 g/1 lb/6½ cups wiped and dried mixed wild mushrooms

salt and freshly ground black pepper

1 tbsp freshly chopped parsley

1 tbsp freshly chopped basil

1 tsp fresh oregano leaves

juice of 1 lemon

Preheat the oven to 240°C/475°F/Gas Mark 9, 15 minutes before baking. Place the dried active yeast in 250 ml/8 fl oz/1 cup warm water for 10 minutes.

Place the flour in a large bowl and stir in the cheese. Blend 1 tablespoon of the olive oil, with the tomato purée/paste, dried yeast, salt and warm water, then stir into the flour and cheese mixture.

Knead on a lightly floured surface to form a smooth and pliable dough. Cover with plastic wrap and leave in a warm place for 15 minutes to allow the dough to rise, then roll out again and cut into sticks of equal length. Cover and leave to rise again for 10 minutes. Brush with the olive oil, sprinkle with salt and bake in the preheated oven for 10 minutes.

Pour 3 tablespoons of the oil into a frying pan and add the crushed garlic. Cook over a very low heat, stirring well, for 3–4 minutes to flavour the oil.

Cut the wild mushrooms into bite-size slices if very large, then add to the pan. Season well with salt and pepper and cook very gently for 6–8 minutes until tender.

Whisk the fresh herbs, the remaining olive oil and the lemon juice together. Pour over the mushrooms. Heat through, season to taste, place on individual dishes and serve with the breadsticks.

Health Rating: 3 points

Hot Tiger Prawns with Prosciutto

Serves 4

Ingredients

½ cucumber, peeled if preferred

4 ripe tomatoes

12 raw tiger prawns/jumbo shrimp

6 tbsp olive oil

4 garlic cloves, peeled and crushed

4 tbsp freshly chopped parsley

salt and freshly ground black pepper

6 slices Parma ham/prosciutto, cut in half

4 slices Italian flat bread

4 tbsp dry white wine

Preheat the oven to 180°C/350°F/Gas Mark 4. Slice the cucumber and tomatoes thinly, then arrange on four large plates and reserve. Peel the prawns/shrimp, leaving the tail shells intact and remove the thin black vein running down the back.

Whisk together 4 tablespoons of the olive oil, the garlic and chopped parsley in a small bowl and season to taste with plenty of salt and pepper. Add the prawns to the mixture and stir until they are well coated. Remove the prawns, then wrap each one in a piece of Parma ham/prosciutto and secure with a cocktail stick/toothpick.

Place the prepared prawns on a lightly oiled baking sheet or dish with the bread slices and cook in the preheated oven for 5 minutes.

Remove the prawns from the oven and spoon the wine over the prawns and bread. Return to the oven and cook for a further 10 minutes until piping hot.

Carefully remove the cocktail sticks and arrange three prawn rolls on each slice of bread. Place on top of the sliced cucumber and tomatoes and serve immediately.

Health Rating: 2 points

Fresh Tagliatelle with Courgettes

Serves 4–6

Ingredients

225 g/8 oz/2 cups strong plain bread flour or type '00' pasta flour,
  plus extra for rolling

1 tsp salt

2 medium/large eggs

1 medium egg yolk

3 tbsp extra virgin olive oil

2 small courgettes/zucchini, halved lengthways and thinly sliced

2 garlic cloves, peeled and thinly sliced

large pinch chilli flakes

zest of ½ lemon

1 tbsp freshly shredded basil

salt and freshly ground black pepper

freshly grated Parmesan cheese, to serve

Sift the flour and salt into a large bowl, make a well in the centre and add the eggs and yolk, 1 tablespoon oil and 1 teaspoon water. Gradually mix to form a soft but not sticky dough, adding a little more flour or water if necessary. Turn out on to a lightly floured surface and knead for 5 minutes, or until smooth and elastic. Wrap in plastic wrap and leave to rest at room temperature for about 30 minutes.

Divide the dough into eight pieces. Feed a piece of dough through a pasta machine. Gradually decrease the settings on the rollers, feeding the pasta through each time, until the sheet is very long and thin. If the pasta seems sticky, dust the work surface and both sides of the pasta generously with flour. Cut in half crossways and hang over a clean pole.

Repeat with the remaining dough. Leave to dry for about 5 minutes. Feed each sheet through the tagliatelle cutter, hanging the cut pasta over the pole. Leave to dry for a further 5 minutes. Wind a handful of pasta strands into nests and leave on a floured dish towel. Repeat with the remaining dough and leave to dry for 5 minutes. Cook the pasta in plenty of salted boiling water for 2–3 minutes until *al dente*.

Meanwhile, heat the remaining oil in a large frying pan and add the courgettes/zucchini, garlic, chilli and lemon zest. Cook over a medium heat for 3–4 minutes until the courgettes are lightly golden and tender.

Drain the pasta thoroughly, reserving 2 tablespoons of the cooking water. Add the pasta to the courgettes with the basil and seasoning. Mix well, adding the reserved cooking water. Serve with the Parmesan cheese.

Health Rating: 3 points

Mixed Antipasti with Roasted Pepper Salad

Serves 4–6

Ingredients

1 green pepper

1 orange pepper

1 red pepper

1 red onion

2–3 garlic cloves

2 tbsp olive oil

1 ripe Cantaloupe melon

4–6 fresh figs

few radicchio, rocket/arugula and chicory leaves

75 g/3 oz Italian salami, thinly sliced

125 g/4 oz Parma ham/prosciutto, thinly sliced

75 g/3 oz bresaola, thinly sliced

125 g/4 oz baby plum tomatoes

50 g/2 oz/generous ¼ cup pitted black olives

For the dressing:

50 ml/2 fl oz/¼ cup extra virgin olive oil

salt and freshly ground black pepper

2 tbsp balsamic vinegar

Preheat the oven to 200°C/400°F/Gas Mark 6, 15 minutes before cooking. Cut the peppers into quarters, deseed and cut into chunks. Peel and chop the onion and garlic, then place all the vegetables in a roasting tin/pan and drizzle over the olive oil. Roast for 15–20 minutes, turning the vegetables over occasionally, until tender. Remove and reserve. Cut the melon in half, scoop out and discard the seeds, peel if preferred, then slice thinly and reserve. Lightly rinse the figs, make a small cross on top of each fig, gently push to open and reserve.

Arrange the radicchio, rocket/arugula and chicory leaves on a large platter. Top with the meats, tomatoes, melon and olives. Spoon the roasted peppers into a separate serving dish. Just before serving, place the dressing ingredients in a screw-top jar and shake until blended. Drizzle over the meat platter and roasted peppers. Serve.

Health Rating: 4 points

Mozzarella Parcels with Cranberry Relish

Serves 4

Ingredients

125 g/4 oz/1 cup mozzarella cheese

8 slices thin white bread

2 medium/large eggs, beaten

salt and freshly ground black pepper

300 ml/½ pint/1¼ cups olive oil

For the relish:

125 g/4 oz/1¼ cups cranberries

2 tbsp fresh orange juice

grated zest of 1 small orange

50 g/2 oz/¼ cup soft light brown sugar

1 tbsp port

Slice the mozzarella thinly, remove the crusts from the bread and make sandwiches with the bread and cheese. Cut into 5 cm/2 inch squares and squash them quite flat. Season the eggs with salt and pepper, then soak the bread in the seasoned egg for 1 minute on each side until well coated.

Heat the oil in a wok or deep fryer to 190°C/375°F and deep-fry the bread squares for 1–2 minutes until crisp and golden brown. Drain on absorbent paper towels. Keep warm while the cranberry relish is prepared.

Place the cranberries, orange juice, zest, sugar and port into a small saucepan and add 5 tablespoons water. Bring to the boil, then simmer for 10 minutes until the cranberries have 'popped'. Sweeten with a little more sugar if necessary. Arrange the mozzarella parcels on individual serving plates and serve with a little of the cranberry relish.

Health Rating: 1 point

Beetroot Ravioli with Dill Cream Sauce

Serves 4–6

Ingredients

For the pasta:
225 g/8 oz/1⅛ cups strong plain bread flour or type '00' pasta flour, plus extra for rolling
1 tsp salt
2 medium/large eggs
1 medium/large egg yolk
1 tbsp extra virgin olive oil

For the filling:
1 tbsp olive oil
1 small onion, peeled and finely chopped
½ tsp caraway seeds
175 g/6 oz/1 cup chopped cooked beetroot
175 g/6 oz/¾ cup ricotta cheese
25 g/1 oz/½ cup fresh white breadcrumbs
1 medium/large egg yolk
2 tbsp grated Parmesan cheese
salt and freshly ground black pepper
4 tbsp walnut oil; 4 tbsp freshly chopped dill
1 tbsp drained and roughly chopped green peppercorns
6 tbsp crème fraîche

To make the pasta dough, sift the flour and salt into a large bowl, make a well in the centre and add the eggs and yolk, the oil and 1 teaspoon water. Gradually mix to form a soft but not sticky dough, adding a little more flour or water if necessary. Turn out onto a lightly floured surface and knead for 5 minutes, or until smooth and elastic. Wrap in plastic wrap and leave to rest at room temperature for about 30 minutes.

To make the filling, heat the olive oil in a large frying pan, add the onion and caraway seeds and cook over a medium heat for 5 minutes, or until the onion is softened and lightly golden. Stir in the beetroot and cook for 5 minutes. Blend the beetroot mixture in a food processor until smooth, then allow to cool. Stir in the ricotta cheese, breadcrumbs, egg yolk and Parmesan cheese. Season the filling to taste with salt and pepper and reserve.

Divide the pasta dough into eight pieces. Roll out as for tagliatelle, but do not cut the sheets in half. Lay one sheet on a floured surface and place 5 heaped teaspoons of the filling 2.5 cm/1 inch apart.

Dampen around the heaps of filling and lay a second sheet of pasta over the top. Press around the heaps to seal. Cut into squares using a pastry wheel or sharp knife. Put the filled pasta shapes onto a floured dish towel.

Bring a large pan of lightly salted water to a rolling boil. Drop the ravioli into the boiling water, return to the boil and cook for 3–4 minutes until *al dente*.

Meanwhile, heat the walnut oil in a small pan, then add the chopped dill and green peppercorns. Remove from the heat, stir in the crème fraîche and season well.

Drain the cooked pasta thoroughly and toss with the sauce. Tip into warmed serving dishes and serve immediately.

Health Rating: 2 points

Gnocchi with Grilled Cherry Tomato Sauce

Serves 4

Ingredients

450 g/1 lb floury potatoes, unpeeled

1 medium/large egg

1 tsp salt

75–100 g/3–3½ oz/¾ cup plain/all-purpose flour

450 g/1 lb mixed red and orange cherry tomatoes,
  halved lengthways

2 garlic cloves, peeled and finely sliced

finely grated zest of ½ lemon

1 tbsp freshly chopped thyme

1 tbsp freshly chopped basil

2 tbsp extra virgin olive oil, plus extra for drizzling

salt and freshly ground black pepper

pinch sugar

freshly grated Parmesan cheese, to serve

Preheat the grill/broiler just before required. Bring a large pan of salted water to the boil, add the potatoes and cook for 20–25 minutes until tender. Drain. Leave until cool enough to handle but still hot, then peel them and place in a large bowl. Mash until smooth, then work in the egg, salt and enough of the flour to form a soft dough.

With floured hands, roll a spoonful of the dough into a small ball. Flatten the ball slightly onto the back of a large fork, then roll it off the fork to make a little ridged dumpling. Place each gnocchi onto a floured dish towel as you work.

Place the tomatoes in a flameproof, shallow dish. Add the garlic, lemon zest, herbs and olive oil. Season to taste with salt and pepper and sprinkle over the sugar. Cook under the preheated grill for 10 minutes, or until the tomatoes are charred and tender, stirring once or twice.

Meanwhile, bring a large pan of lightly salted water to the boil, then reduce to a steady simmer. Dropping in 6–8 gnocchi at a time, cook in batches for 3–4 minutes until they begin bobbing up to the surface.

Remove with a slotted spoon and drain well on absorbent paper before towels transferring to a warmed serving dish. Toss the cooked gnocchi with the tomato sauce. Serve immediately with a little grated Parmesan cheese.

Health Rating: 3 points

Aubergine in Oil with Garlic Bread

Serves 4

Ingredients

450 g/1 lb aubergines/eggplants, trimmed
3 tsp coarsely ground sea salt
600 ml/1 pint/2½ cups white wine vinegar
1 garlic clove, peeled and crushed
1 medium-hot chilli, deseeded and finely chopped
few fresh oregano sprigs or 2 tsp dried oregano
about 300 ml/½ pint/1¼ cups olive oil

For the garlic bread:
50 g/2 oz/4 tbsp softened butter
2–3 garlic cloves, peeled and crushed
1–2 tsp lemon juice
1 ciabatta loaf

Slice the aubergines/eggplants into 1 cm/½ inch thick slices, layer in a colander, sprinkling each layer with a little salt. Leave for at least 30 minutes–1 hour (this helps to remove any bitterness from the aubergine). Rinse well and pat dry with paper towels.

Pour the vinegar and 300 ml/½ pint/1¼ cups water into a saucepan and bring to the boil. Add the aubergine slices and cook for 5 minutes, or until soft, then drain.

Layer the aubergine slices in a large, clean bowl or dish, sprinkling with the remaining salt, the garlic, chilli and oregano. Pour over the oil, pressing the aubergine slices down, making sure that they are under the oil and water. Add a little more oil if necessary. Cover with a dish towel and leave in a cool place for at least 2 weeks, longer if preferred. Serve with chunks of garlic bread.

For the garlic bread, preheat the oven to 200°C/400°F/Gas Mark 6. Beat the butter, garlic and lemon juice until blended. Slice the bread and spread with the flavoured butter. Place on a foil-lined baking tray and cook in the oven for 10–12 minutes. Serve hot.

Health Rating: 3 points

Spinach & Ricotta Gnocchi with Butter & Parmesan

Serves 2–4

Ingredients

125 g/4 oz/1 cup thawed frozen leaf spinach
225 g/8 oz ricotta cheese
2 small/medium eggs, lightly beaten
50 g/2 oz/½ cup freshly grated Parmesan cheese
salt and freshly ground black pepper
2 tbsp freshly chopped basil
50 g/2 oz /½ cup plain/all-purpose flour
50 g/2 oz/4 tbsp unsalted butter
2 garlic cloves, peeled and crushed
Parmesan cheese shavings, to serve

Squeeze the excess moisture from the spinach and chop finely. Blend in a food processor with the ricotta cheese, eggs, Parmesan cheese, seasoning and 1 tablespoon of the basil until smooth. Scrape into a bowl, then add sufficient flour to form a soft, slightly sticky dough.

Bring a large pan of salted water to a rolling boil. Transfer the spinach mixture to a piping bag fitted with a large, plain tip. As soon as the water is boiling, pipe 10–12 short lengths of the mixture into the water, using a sharp knife to cut the gnocchi as you go.

Bring the water back to the boil and cook the gnocchi for 3–4 minutes until they begin to rise to the surface. Remove with a slotted spoon, drain on absorbent paper towels and transfer to a warmed serving dish. Cook the gnocchi in batches if necessary.

Melt the butter in a small frying pan and, when foaming, add the garlic and remaining basil. Remove from the heat and immediately pour over the cooked gnocchi. Season well with salt and pepper and serve immediately with grated Parmesan.

Health Rating: 2 points

Tagliatelle with Brown Butter, Asparagus & Parmesan

Serves 6

Ingredients

350 g/12 oz asparagus, trimmed and cut into short lengths

75 g/3 oz/6 tbsp unsalted butter

1 garlic clove, peeled and sliced

25 g/1 oz/¼ cup roughly chopped flaked hazelnuts or
   whole hazelnuts

1 tbsp freshly chopped parsley

1 tbsp freshly snipped chives

450 g/1 lb fresh or dried tagliatelle nests, such as the white and
   green variety

salt and freshly ground black pepper

50 g/2 oz/½ cup freshly grated Parmesan cheese, to serve

Bring a pan of lightly salted water to the boil. Add the asparagus and cook for 1 minute. Drain immediately, refresh under cold running water and drain again. Pat dry and reserve.

Melt the butter in a large frying pan, then add the garlic and hazelnuts and cook over a medium heat until the butter turns golden. Immediately remove from the heat and add the parsley, chives and asparagus. Leave for 2–3 minutes until the asparagus is heated through.

Meanwhile, bring a large pan of lightly salted water to a rolling boil, then add the pasta nests. Cook until *al dente*: 2–3 minutes for fresh pasta and according to the packet instructions for dried pasta. Drain the pasta thoroughly and return to the pan.

Add the asparagus mixture and toss together. Season to taste with salt and pepper and tip into a warmed serving dish. Serve immediately with grated Parmesan cheese.

Health Rating: 2 points

Pasta with Raw Fennel, Tomato & Red Onions

Serves 6

Ingredients

1 fennel bulb
700 g/1½ lb tomatoes
1 garlic clove
¼ small red onion
small handful fresh basil
small handful fresh mint
100 ml/3½ fl oz/⅓ cup extra virgin olive oil, plus extra to serve
juice of 1 lemon
salt and freshly ground black pepper
450 g/1 lb/4 cups penne or pennette
freshly grated Parmesan cheese, to serve

Health Rating: 3 points

Trim the fennel and slice thinly. Stack the slices and cut into sticks, then cut crossways again into fine dice. Deseed the tomatoes and chop them finely. Peel and finely chop or crush the garlic. Peel and finely chop or grate the onion.

Stack the basil leaves, then roll up tightly. Slice crossways into fine shreds. Finely chop the mint.

Place the chopped vegetables and herbs in a medium bowl. Add the olive oil and lemon juice and mix together. Season well with salt and pepper, then leave for 30 minutes to allow the flavours to develop.

Bring a large pan of salted water to a rolling boil. Add the pasta and cook according to the packet instructions, or until *al dente*.

Drain the cooked pasta thoroughly. Transfer to a warmed serving dish, pour over the vegetable mixture and toss. Serve with the grated Parmesan cheese and extra olive oil to drizzle over.

Tagliatelle with Parma Ham, Pepper & Tomato

Serves 4

Ingredients

2 tbsp olive oil

1 red onion, peeled and thinly sliced

2–3 garlic cloves, peeled and crushed

1 yellow pepper, deseeded and chopped

125 g/4 oz assorted coloured baby plum tomatoes, halved

125 g/4 oz Parma ham/prosciutto, cut into small strips

125 ml/4 fl oz/$\frac{1}{2}$ cup single/light cream

225 g/8 oz tagliatelle, fresh or dried

2 tbsp shredded basil

freshly ground black pepper

Heat the oil in a large saucepan, add the onion, garlic and yellow pepper and fry for 5 minutes, or until beginning to soften. Add the tomatoes and cook, stirring occasionally, for a further 3 minutes until the tomatoes are starting to collapse. Add the Parma ham/prosciutto, then pour in the cream and stir lightly. Keep warm.

Bring a large saucepan of water to a rolling boil. Add the pasta and cook until *al dente*: 2–3 minutes for fresh and 8–10 minutes for dried. Drain, reserving 1 tablespoon of the pasta cooking water.

Return the pasta to the pan, together with the reserved pasta cooking water. Add the sauce with the basil and stir. Place over a gentle heat and heat for 2 minutes, or until piping hot. Serve sprinkled with black pepper.

Health Rating: 2 points

Spaghetti with Fresh Tomatoes, Chilli & Potatoes

Serves 6

Ingredients

2 medium potatoes, unpeeled

3 garlic cloves, peeled and crushed

1 small bunch basil, roughly chopped

6 tbsp olive oil

4 large ripe plum tomatoes, skinned, deseeded and chopped

1 small red chilli, deseeded and finely chopped

salt and freshly ground black pepper

450 g/1 lb spaghetti

4 tbsp freshly grated Parmesan cheese, to serve (optional)

Preheat the grill/broiler to high, 5 minutes before using. Cook the potatoes in plenty of boiling water until tender but firm. Allow to cool, then peel and cut into cubes.

Blend the garlic, basil and 4 tablespoons of the olive oil in a blender or food processor until the basil is finely chopped, then reserve.

Place the tomatoes, basil and oil mixture in a small bowl, add the chilli and season with salt and pepper to taste. Mix together and reserve the sauce.

Bring a large pan of salted water to a rolling boil, add the spaghetti and cook according to the packet instructions, or until *al dente*.

Meanwhile, toss the potato cubes with the remaining olive oil and transfer to a baking sheet. Place the potatoes under the preheated grill until they are crisp and golden, turning once or twice, then drain on absorbent paper towels.

Drain the pasta thoroughly and transfer to a warmed shallow serving bowl. Add the tomato sauce and the hot potatoes. Toss well and adjust the seasoning to taste. Serve immediately with the grated Parmesan cheese, if using.

Health Rating: 3 points

Pasta Genovese with Pesto, Green Beans & Potatoes

Serves 6

Ingredients

40 g/1½ oz/½ cup basil leaves

2 garlic cloves, peeled and crushed

2 tbsp pine nuts, lightly toasted

25 g/1 oz/¼ cup freshly grated Parmesan cheese

75 ml/3 fl oz/6 tbsp extra virgin olive oil

salt and freshly ground black pepper

175 g/6 oz new potatoes, scrubbed

125 g/4 oz/scant 1 cup fine French/green beans, trimmed

2 tbsp olive oil

450 g/1 lb/4 cups pasta shapes

extra freshly grated Parmesan cheese, to serve

Put the basil leaves, garlic, pine nuts and Parmesan cheese into a food processor and blend until finely chopped. Transfer the mixture into a small bowl and stir in the olive oil. Season the pesto to taste with salt and pepper and reserve.

Bring a pan of salted water to the boil and cook the potatoes for 12–14 minutes until tender. About 4 minutes before the end of the cooking time, add the beans. Drain well and refresh under cold water. Reserve the beans and slice the potatoes thickly, or halve them if small.

Heat the olive oil in a frying pan and add the potatoes. Fry over a medium heat for 5 minutes, or until golden. Add the reserved beans and pesto and cook for a further 2 minutes.

Meanwhile, bring a large pan of lightly salted water to a rolling boil. Cook the pasta shapes according to the packet instructions, or until *al dente*. Drain thoroughly, return to the pan and add the pesto mixture. Toss well and heat through for 1–2 minutes. Tip into a warmed serving bowl and serve immediately with Parmesan cheese.

Health Rating: 3 points

Tiny Pasta with Fresh Herb Sauce

Serves 6

Ingredients

375 g/13 oz/3¼ cups tripolini (small bows with rounded ends) or
 small farfalle
2 tbsp freshly chopped flat-leaf parsley
2 tbsp freshly chopped basil
1 tbsp freshly snipped chives
1 tbsp freshly chopped chervil
1 tbsp freshly chopped tarragon
1 tbsp freshly chopped sage
1 tbsp freshly chopped oregano
1 tbsp freshly chopped marjoram
1 tbsp freshly chopped thyme
1 tbsp freshly chopped rosemary
finely grated zest of 1 lemon
75 ml/3 fl oz/6 tbsp extra virgin olive oil
2 garlic cloves, peeled and finely chopped
½ tsp dried chilli flakes
salt and freshly ground black pepper
freshly grated Parmesan cheese, to serve

Bring a pan of lightly salted water to a rolling boil. Add the pasta
and cook according to the packet instructions, or until *al dente*.

Meanwhile, place all the herbs, the lemon zest, olive oil, garlic and
chilli flakes in a heavy-based pan. Heat gently for 2–3 minutes
until the herbs turn bright green and become very fragrant.
Remove from the heat and season to taste with salt and pepper.

Drain the pasta thoroughly, reserving 2–3 tablespoons of the
cooking water. Transfer the pasta to a large warmed bowl.

Pour the heated herb mixture over the pasta and toss together
until thoroughly mixed. Check and adjust the seasoning, adding
a little of the pasta cooking water if the pasta mixture seems a
bit dry. Transfer to warmed serving dishes and serve
immediately with grated Parmesan cheese.

Health Rating: 3 points

Angel Hair Pasta with Lemon & Olives

Serves 4

Ingredients

3 tbsp olive oil

1 red onion, peeled and thinly sliced

2–3 plump garlic cloves, peeled and chopped

1 tbsp finely grated lemon zest

2 tbsp lemon juice, strained

salt and freshly ground black pepper

225 g/8 oz fresh angel hair pasta, or bought dried pasta, such as spaghettini

50 g/2 oz/generous ¼ cup chopped and pitted black/ripe olives

1 tbsp freshly torn basil leaves

125 ml/4 fl oz/½ cup single/light cream or crème fraîche

freshly grated Parmesan cheese, to serve

Heat the oil in a medium saucepan, add the onion and garlic and fry gently for 5 minutes, or until softened. Add the lemon zest and juice together with seasoning to taste. Bring to the boil, then reduce the heat to a gentle simmer.

Meanwhile, bring a large saucepan of water to a rolling boil. Add the pasta and cook until *al dente*: 2–3 minutes for fresh and 8–10 minutes for dried. Drain, reserving 2 tablespoons of the pasta cooking water. Return the pasta to the saucepan.

Add the olives to the pasta together with the reserved pasta cooking water, the lemon sauce and torn basil and stir lightly. Add the cream or crème fraîche, stir, then serve sprinkled with freshly grated Parmesan cheese.

Health Rating: 2 points

Tagliarini with Broad Beans, Saffron & Crème Fraîche

Serves 4

Ingredients

225 g/8 oz fresh young broad/fava beans in pods or 100 g/3½ oz/1 cup thawed frozen broad/fava beans

1 tbsp olive oil

1 garlic clove, peeled and chopped

small handful shredded basil leaves

200 ml/7 fl oz/¾ cup crème fraîche

large pinch saffron strands

350 g/12 oz tagliarini

salt and freshly ground black pepper

1 tbsp freshly snipped chives

freshly grated Parmesan cheese, to serve

If using fresh broad/fava beans, bring a pan of lightly salted water to the boil. Pod the beans and drop them into the boiling water for 1 minute. Drain and refresh under cold water. Drain again. Remove the outer skin of the beans and discard. If using thawed frozen broad beans, remove and discard the skins. Reserve the peeled beans.

Heat the olive oil in a saucepan. Add the peeled broad beans and the garlic and cook gently for 2–3 minutes. Stir in the basil, the crème fraîche and the saffron strands and simmer for 1 minute.

Meanwhile, bring a large pan of lightly salted water to a rolling boil. Add the pasta and cook according to the packet instructions, or until *al dente*. Drain the pasta well and add to the sauce. Toss together and season to taste with salt and pepper.

Transfer the pasta and sauce to a warmed serving dish. Sprinkle with snipped chives and serve immediately with Parmesan.

Health Rating: 3 points

Spaghettini with Peas, Spring Onions & Mint

Serves 6

Ingredients

pinch saffron strands

700 g/1½ lb fresh peas or 350 g/12 oz/3 cups thawed
   petit pois

75 g/3 oz/6 tbsp unsalted butter, softened

6 spring onions/scallions, trimmed and finely sliced

salt and freshly ground black pepper

1 garlic clove, peeled and finely chopped

2 tbsp freshly chopped mint

450 g/1 lb spaghettini

freshly grated Parmesan cheese, to serve

Health Rating: 3 points

Soak the saffron in 2 tablespoons hot water while you prepare the sauce. Shell the peas if using fresh ones.

Heat 50 g/2 oz/4 tbsp of the butter in a medium frying pan, add the spring onions/scallions and a little salt and cook over a low heat for 2–3 minutes until the onions are softened. Add the garlic, then the peas and 100 ml/3½ fl oz water. Bring to the boil and cook for 5–6 minutes until the peas are just tender. Stir in the mint and keep warm.

Blend the remaining butter and the saffron water in a large, warmed serving bowl and reserve.

Meanwhile, bring a large pan of lightly salted water to a rolling boil and add the spaghettini. Cook according to the packet instructions, or until *al dente*.

Drain thoroughly, reserving 2–3 tablespoons of the pasta cooking water. Tip into a warmed serving bowl, add the pea sauce and toss together gently. Season to taste with salt and pepper. Serve immediately with extra black pepper and grated Parmesan.

Fusilli with Spicy Tomato & Chorizo Sauce with Roasted Peppers

Serves 6

Ingredients

1 red pepper, deseeded and quartered

1 yellow pepper, deseeded and quartered

4 tbsp olive oil

175 g/6 oz/³⁄₄ cup roughly chopped chorizo (outer skin removed)

2 garlic cloves, peeled and finely chopped

large pinch chilli flakes

700 g/1¹⁄₂ lb/3 cups skinned and roughly chopped ripe tomatoes

salt and freshly ground black pepper

450 g/1 lb fusilli

basil leaves, to garnish

freshly grated Parmesan cheese, to serve

Preheat the grill/broiler to high. Brush the pepper quarters with 1 tablespoon of the olive oil, then cook under the preheated grill, turning once, for 8–10 minutes until the skins have blackened and the flesh is tender. Place the peppers in a plastic bag until cool enough to handle. When cooled, peel the peppers, slice very thinly and reserve.

Heat the remaining oil in a frying pan and add the chorizo. Cook over a medium heat for 3–4 minutes until starting to brown. Add the garlic and chilli flakes and cook for a further 2–3 minutes.

Add the tomatoes, season lightly with salt and pepper, then cook gently for about 5 minutes until the tomatoes have broken down.

Lower the heat and cook for a further 10–15 minutes until the sauce has thickened. Add the peppers and heat gently for 1–2 minutes. Adjust the seasoning to taste.

Meanwhile, bring a large pan of lightly salted water to a rolling boil. Add the fusilli and cook according to the packet instructions, or until *al dente*.

Drain thoroughly and transfer to a warmed serving dish. Pour over the sauce, sprinkle with basil and serve with Parmesan.

Health Rating: 2 points

Fettuccine with Mixed Seafood

Serves 4

Ingredients

12 fresh clams
12 fresh mussels
125 g/4 oz raw prawns/shrimp
125 g/4 oz fresh squid
125 g/4 oz salmon fillet
4 tbsp olive oil
2–3 garlic cloves, peeled and chopped
1 medium-hot red chilli, deseeded and chopped
125 ml/4 fl oz/½ cup dry white wine
300 g/10 oz fresh fettuccine or use bought dried pasta
4 tbsp double/heavy cream
freshly chopped flat-leaf parsley, to garnish

Scrub the clams and mussels, removing any beards or barnacles and discarding any that are open. Place in a large bowl, cover with cold water and keep in a cool place. Peel the prawns/shrimp, then remove and discard the black vein that runs down the back of the prawns. Rinse, pat dry with absorbent paper towels and reserve. Clean the squid, removing any intestines, then rinse and slice. Skin the salmon, removing any fine bones, then cut into small pieces and reserve.

Heat the oil in a saucepan, add the garlic and chilli and fry for 3–4 minutes until beginning to soften. Add the prepared seafood and cook for 2 minutes before pouring in the wine. Cook for 5 minutes, or until the seafood is cooked, discarding any clams or mussels that do not open.

Bring a large saucepan of water to a rolling boil. Add the pasta and cook until *al dente*: 2–3 minutes for fresh and 8–10 minutes for dried. Drain, reserving 2 tablespoons of the pasta cooking water, then return the pasta and cooking water to the saucepan and add the seafood and cream. Stir lightly together, then serve garnished with the parsley.

Health Rating: 1 point

Pasta with Walnut Sauce

Serves 4

Ingredients

50 g/2 oz/½ cup walnuts, toasted
3 spring onions/scallions, trimmed and chopped
2 garlic cloves, peeled and sliced
1 tbsp freshly chopped parsley or basil
5 tbsp extra virgin olive oil
salt and freshly ground black pepper
450 g/1 lb broccoli, cut into florets
350 g/12 oz/3 cups pasta shapes
1 red chilli, deseeded and finely chopped

Place the toasted walnuts in a blender or food processor with the chopped spring onions/scallions, one of the garlic cloves and the parsley or basil. Blend to a fairly smooth paste, then gradually add 3 tablespoons of the olive oil, until it is well mixed into the paste. Season the walnut paste to taste with salt and pepper and reserve.

Bring a large pan of lightly salted water to a rolling boil. Add the broccoli, return to the boil and cook for 2 minutes. Remove the broccoli using a slotted draining spoon and refresh under cold running water. Drain again and pat dry on absorbent paper towels.

Bring the water back to a rolling boil. Add the pasta and cook according to the packet instructions, or until *al dente*.

Meanwhile, heat the remaining oil in a frying pan. Add the remaining garlic and the chilli. Cook gently for 2 minutes, or until softened. Add the broccoli and the walnut paste. Cook for a further 3–4 minutes until heated through.

Drain the pasta thoroughly and transfer to a large, warmed serving bowl. Pour over the walnut and broccoli sauce. Toss together, adjust the seasoning and serve immediately.

Health Rating: 4 points

Pasta & Bean Soup

Serves 4–6

Ingredients

3 tbsp olive oil

2 celery stalks, trimmed and finely chopped

100 g/3½ oz/¾ cup prosciutto or prosciutto di speck,
   cut into pieces

1 red chilli, deseeded and finely chopped

2 large potatoes, peeled and cut into 2.5 cm/1 in cubes

2 garlic cloves, peeled and finely chopped

3 ripe plum tomatoes, skinned and chopped

400 g/14 oz canned borlotti/cranberry beans, drained and rinsed

1 litre/1¾ pints/4 cups chicken or vegetable stock

100 g/3½ oz/1 cup pasta shapes

large handful basil leaves, torn

salt and freshly ground black pepper

shredded basil leaves, to garnish

crusty bread, to serve

Heat the olive oil in a heavy-based pan, add the celery and prosciutto and cook gently for 6–8 minutes until softened. Add the chopped chilli and potato cubes and cook for a further 10 minutes.

Add the garlic to the chilli and potato mixture and cook for 1 minute. Add the chopped tomatoes and simmer for 5 minutes. Stir in two thirds of the beans, then pour in the chicken or vegetable stock and bring to the boil.

Add the pasta shapes to the soup stock and return it to simmering point. Cook the pasta for about 10 minutes, or until *al dente*.

Meanwhile, place the remaining beans in a food processor or blender and blend with enough of the soup stock to make a smooth, thinnish purée.

When the pasta is cooked, stir in the puréed beans with the torn basil. Season the soup to taste with salt and pepper. Ladle into serving bowls, garnish with shredded basil and serve immediately with plenty of crusty bread.

Health Rating: 3 points

Gnocchetti with Broccoli & Bacon Sauce

Serves 6

Ingredients

450 g/1 lb broccoli florets

4 tbsp olive oil

50 g/2 oz/½ cup finely chopped smoked bacon or pancetta

1 small onion, peeled and finely chopped

3 garlic cloves, peeled and sliced

200 ml/7 fl oz/¾ cup milk

450 g/1 lb gnocchetti (little elongated ribbed shells)

50 g/2 oz/½ cup freshly grated Parmesan cheese, plus extra
   to serve

salt and freshly ground black pepper

Bring a large pan of salted water to the boil. Add the broccoli florets and cook for about 8–10 minutes until very soft. Drain thoroughly, allow to cool slightly, then chop finely and reserve.

Heat the olive oil in a heavy-based pan, add the pancetta or bacon and cook over a medium heat for 5 minutes, or until golden and crisp. Add the onion and cook for a further 5 minutes, or until soft and lightly golden. Add the garlic and cook for 1 minute.

Transfer the chopped broccoli to the bacon or pancetta mixture and pour in the milk. Bring slowly to the boil and simmer rapidly for about 15 minutes until reduced to a creamy texture.

Meanwhile, bring a large pan of lightly salted water to a rolling boil. Add the pasta and cook according to the packet instructions, or until *al dente*.

Drain the pasta thoroughly, reserving a little of the cooking water. Add the pasta and the Parmesan cheese to the broccoli mixture. Toss, adding enough of the reserved cooking water to make a creamy sauce. Season to taste with salt and pepper. Serve immediately with extra Parmesan cheese.

Health Rating: 3 points

Penne with Wild Mushrooms & Truffles

Serves 4

Ingredients

15 g/½ oz dried porcini mushrooms

3 tbsp olive oil

3 shallots, peeled and sliced into rings

2 garlic cloves, peeled and crushed

300 g/11 oz wild mushrooms, cleaned and sliced

1 red pepper, deseeded and cut into small slices

50 ml/2 fl oz/¼ cup dry white wine

50 g/2 oz Parma ham/prosciutto, cut into small pieces

salt and freshly ground black pepper

4 tbsp double/heavy cream or crème fraîche

1 tbsp freshly chopped oregano

225 g/8 oz fresh penne or use bought dried pasta

few fresh truffle shavings or 2–3 tsp truffle oil

Soak the dried mushrooms, in enough warm water to cover, for 20 minutes, then drain and reserve the soaking liquor. Chop the mushrooms, discarding any grit or tough stems.

Heat the oil in a saucepan, add the shallots and garlic and fry for 4–5 minutes until softened. Add the soaked dried mushrooms together with the wild mushrooms, red pepper and wine and fry gently, stirring occasionally, for 10 minutes, or until almost tender. Stir in the mushroom soaking liquor together with the Parma ham/prosciutto and season to taste. Stir in the cream or crème fraîche and oregano. Keep warm.

Meanwhile, bring a large saucepan of water to a rolling boil. Add the pasta and cook until al dente: 2–3 minutes for fresh and 8–10 minutes for dried. Drain, reserving 2 tablespoons of the pasta cooking water. Return the pasta to the saucepan, stir in the reserved cooking water and the mushroom mixture. Heat through gently for 2–3 minutes, then turn off the heat. Stir in the truffle shavings or truffle oil, then cover and leave for 3–4 minutes to allow the flavours to infuse before serving.

Health Rating: 2 points

Penne with Artichokes, Bacon & Mushrooms

Serves 6

Ingredients

2 tbsp olive oil

75 g/3 oz/¼ cup chopped smoked bacon or pancetta

1 small onion, peeled and finely sliced

125 g/4 oz/1⅓ cups wiped and sliced chestnut mushrooms

2 garlic cloves, peeled and finely chopped

400 g/14 oz canned artichoke hearts, drained and halved, or quartered if large

100 ml/3½ fl oz/7 tbsp dry white wine

100 ml/3½ fl oz/7 tbsp chicken stock

3 tbsp double/heavy cream

50 g/2 oz/½ cup freshly grated Parmesan cheese, plus extra to serve

salt and freshly ground black pepper

450 g/1 lb/4 cups penne

shredded basil leaves, to garnish

Heat the olive oil in a frying pan and add the bacon or pancetta and the onion. Cook over a medium heat for 8–10 minutes until the bacon is crisp and the onion is just golden.

Add the mushrooms and garlic and cook for a further 5 minutes, or until softened. Add the artichoke hearts to the mushroom mixture and cook for 3–4 minutes. Pour in the wine, bring to the boil, then simmer rapidly until the liquid is reduced and syrupy.

Pour in the chicken stock, bring to the boil, then simmer rapidly for about 5 minutes until slightly reduced. Reduce the heat slightly, then slowly stir in the double/heavy cream and Parmesan cheese. Season the sauce to taste with salt and pepper.

Meanwhile, bring a large pan of lightly salted water to a rolling boil. Add the pasta and cook according to the packet instructions, or until al dente. Drain the pasta thoroughly and transfer to a large, warmed serving dish. Pour over the sauce and toss together. Garnish with shredded basil and serve with extra Parmesan.

Health Rating: 2 points

Fettuccine with Wild Mushrooms & Prosciutto

Serves 6

Ingredients

15 g/½ oz dried porcini mushrooms

150 ml/¼ pint/⅔ cup chicken stock, heated

2 tbsp olive oil

1 small onion, peeled and finely chopped

2 garlic cloves, peeled and finely chopped

4 slices Parma ham/prosciutto, chopped or torn

225 g/8 oz mixed wild or cultivated mushrooms, wiped, sliced if necessary

450 g/1 lb fettuccine

3 tbsp crème fraîche

2 tbsp freshly chopped parsley

salt and freshly ground black pepper

freshly grated Parmesan cheese, to serve

Place the dried mushrooms in a small bowl and pour over the hot chicken stock. Leave to soak for 15–20 minutes until the mushrooms have softened.

Meanwhile, heat the olive oil in a large frying pan. Add the onion and cook for 5 minutes over a medium heat, or until softened. Add the garlic and cook for 1 minute. Add the Parma ham/prosciutto and cook for a further minute.

Drain the dried mushrooms, reserving the soaking liquid. Roughly chop and add to the frying pan together with the fresh mushrooms. Cook over a high heat for 5 minutes, stirring often, until softened. Strain the mushroom soaking liquid into the pan.

Bring a large pan of lightly salted water to a rolling boil. Add the pasta; cook according to the packet instructions, or until *al dente*.

Stir the crème fraîche and chopped parsley into the mushroom mixture and heat through gently. Season to taste. Drain the pasta well, transfer to a large, warmed serving dish and pour over the sauce. Serve immediately with grated Parmesan.

Health Rating: 3 points

Salmon & Roasted Red Pepper Pasta

Serves 6

Ingredients

225 g/8 oz skinned and boneless salmon fillet, thinly sliced

3 shallots, peeled and finely chopped

1 tbsp freshly chopped parsley

6 tbsp olive oil

juice of ½ lemon

2 red peppers, deseeded and quartered

handful fresh basil leaves, shredded

50 g/2 oz/1 cup fresh breadcrumbs

4 tbsp extra virgin olive oil

450 g/1 lb fettuccine or linguine

6 spring onions/scallions, trimmed and shredded

salt and freshly ground black pepper

Preheat the grill/broiler to high. Place the salmon in a bowl. Add the shallots, parsley, 3 tablespoons of the olive oil and the lemon juice. Reserve.

Brush the pepper quarters with a little olive oil. Cook them under the grill for 8–10 minutes until the skins have blackened and the flesh is tender. Place the peppers in a plastic bag until cool enough to handle.

When cooled, peel the peppers and cut into strips. Put the strips into a bowl with the basil and the remaining olive oil and reserve.

Toast the breadcrumbs until dry and lightly browned, then toss with the extra virgin olive oil and reserve.

Bring a large pan of salted water to a rolling boil and add the pasta. Cook according to the packet instructions, or until *al dente*.

Transfer the peppers and their marinade to a hot frying pan. Add the spring onions/scallions and cook for 1–2 minutes until they have just softened. Add the salmon and its marinade and cook for a further 1–2 minutes until the salmon is just cooked. Season to taste with salt and pepper.

Drain the pasta thoroughly and transfer to a warmed serving bowl. Add the salmon mixture and toss gently. Garnish with the breadcrumbs and serve immediately.

Health Rating: 4 points

Tagliatelle with Radicchio & Rocket

Serves 4

Ingredients

50 g/2 oz/4 tbsp unsalted butter

1 red onion, peeled and sliced

125 g/4 oz pancetta, chopped

75 g/3 oz radicchio, outer leaves discarded, then sliced

125 ml/4 fl oz/½ cup dry white wine

50 ml/2 fl oz/¼ cup double/heavy cream or crème fraîche

2–3 tbsp freshly grated Parmesan cheese, plus fresh
   Parmesan shavings

225 g/8 oz fresh tagliatelle or use bought pasta

25 g/1 oz rocket/arugula, lightly chopped if leaves are large, rinsed

Heat the butter in a saucepan, add the onion and pancetta and fry gently for 3–5 minutes until the onion is beginning to soften. Add the radicchio and continue to fry for 3 minutes.

Pour in the wine, bring to the boil and let it bubble for 2 minutes. Take the pan off the heat and slowly pour in the cream or crème fraîche. Stir in the grated Parmesan cheese and keep warm.

Meanwhile, bring a large saucepan of water to a rolling boil. Add the pasta and cook until *al dente*: 3–4 minutes for fresh and 8–10 minutes for dried. Drain, reserving 2 tablespoons of the pasta cooking water.

Return the cooked pasta to the saucepan, add the sauce and the cooking water, stir, then gently stir in the rocket/arugula. Serve immediately with fresh Parmesan shavings.

Health Rating: 2 points

Linguine with Fennel, Crab & Chervil

Serves 6

Ingredients

450 g/1 lb linguine

25 g/1 oz/2 tbsp butter

2 carrots, peeled and finely diced

2 shallots, peeled and finely diced

2 celery stalks, trimmed and finely diced

1 fennel bulb, trimmed and finely diced

6 spring onions/scallions, trimmed and finely chopped

300 ml/½ pint/1¼ cups double/heavy cream

3 tbsp freshly chopped chervil, plus extra to garnish

1 large cooked crab

salt and freshly ground black pepper

juice of ½ lemon, or to taste

dill sprig, to garnish

Bring a large pan of lightly salted water to a rolling boil. Add the pasta and cook according to the packet instructions, or until *al dente*.

Meanwhile, heat the butter in a large saucepan. Add the carrots, shallots, celery, fennel and three quarters of the chopped spring onions/scallions. Cook the vegetables gently for 8–10 minutes until tender, stirring frequently and ensuring that they do not brown.

Add the double/heavy cream and chopped chervil to the vegetable mixture. Scrape the crab meat over the sauce, then stir to mix the sauce ingredients.

Season the sauce to taste with salt and pepper and stir in the lemon juice. Drain the pasta thoroughly and transfer to a large, warmed serving dish. Pour over the sauce and toss. Garnish with extra chervil, the remaining spring onions and a sprig of dill. Serve immediately.

Health Rating: 3 points

Pizza Tricolour Wedges

Serves 2–4

Ingredients

1 quantity pizza dough (*see page 282*)

plain/all-purpose flour, for dusting

2 tbsp olive oil

2 medium onions, peeled and sliced

2–4 garlic cloves, peeled and chopped

2–3 tbsp tomato purée/paste

2 beefsteak tomatoes, sliced

225 g/8 oz/scant 2 cups sliced mozzarella cheese

freshly ground black pepper

large handful basil, torn

Preheat the oven to 230°C/450°F/Gas Mark 8, 15 minutes before cooking. Place a pizza stone or large baking sheet in the oven to heat 5 minutes before cooking. Roll the dough out on a lightly floured surface to form an oblong 25 x 20.5 cm/10 x 8 inches, cover lightly with plastic wrap and reserve.

Heat the oil in a frying pan, add the onions and garlic and fry for 5–8 minutes until softened. Drain with a slotted spoon and reserve.

Remove the plastic wrap from the pizza base. Spread the base with the tomato purée/paste and spoon the onions and garlic on top. Arrange the sliced tomatoes on top together with the sliced mozzarella cheese and season with black pepper.

Bake in the preheated oven for 15–20 minutes until the cheese has melted and is bubbly. Sprinkle with torn basil, cut into wedges and serve immediately.

Health Rating: 2 points

Beetroot Risotto

Serves 6

Ingredients

6 tbsp extra virgin olive oil

1 onion, peeled and finely chopped

2 garlic cloves, peeled and finely chopped

2 tsp freshly chopped thyme

1 tsp grated lemon zest

350 g/12 oz/2 cups Arborio/risotto rice

150 ml/¼ pint/⅔ cup dry white wine

900 ml/1½ pints/3¾ cups vegetable stock, heated

2 tbsp double/heavy cream

225 g/8 oz/1½ cups peeled and finely chopped cooked beetroot

2 tbsp freshly chopped parsley

75 g/3 oz/¾ cup freshly grated Parmesan cheese

salt and freshly ground black pepper

fresh thyme sprigs, to garnish

Heat half the oil in a large, heavy-based frying pan. Add the onion, garlic, thyme and lemon zest. Cook for 5 minutes, stirring frequently, until the onion is soft and transparent but not coloured. Add the rice and stir until it is well coated in the oil.

Add the wine, then bring to the boil and boil rapidly until the wine has almost evaporated. Reduce the heat.

Keeping the pan over a low heat, add a ladleful of the hot stock to the rice and cook, stirring constantly, until the stock is absorbed. Continue gradually adding the stock in this way until the rice is tender; this should take about 20 minutes. You may not need all the stock.

Stir in the cream, chopped beetroot, parsley and half the grated Parmesan cheese. Season to taste with salt and pepper. Garnish with sprigs of fresh thyme and serve immediately with the remaining grated Parmesan cheese.

Health Rating: 3 points

Fish & Seafood

Seafood is a healthy option for a main course, and one that features prominently in Italian cooking, especially in dishes that originated in coastal cities. Featuring many different types of fish and shellfish and a plethora of preparation methods, this chapter has recipes that will delight the seafood enthusiast and tempt even the most reluctant fish eater. Why not try Fish Lasagne or Pan-Fried Salmon with Herb Risotto for a delicious new dinner alternative?

Pea & Prawn Risotto

Serves 6

Ingredients

450 g/1 lb whole raw prawns/shrimp

125 g/4 oz/½ cup (1 stick) butter

1 red onion, peeled and chopped

4 garlic cloves, peeled and finely chopped

225 g/8 oz/1 heaping cup Arborio/risotto rice

150 ml/¼ pint/⅔ cup dry white wine

1.1 litres/2 pints/4⅔ cups vegetable or fish stock

375 g/13 oz/2½ cups frozen peas

4 tbsp freshly chopped mint

salt and freshly ground black pepper

Health Rating: 3 points

Peel the prawns/shrimp and reserve the heads and shells. Remove the black vein from the back of each prawn, then wash and dry on absorbent paper towels. Melt half the butter in a large frying pan, add the prawns' heads and shells and fry, stirring occasionally, for 3–4 minutes until golden. Strain the butter, discard the heads and shells and return the butter to the pan.

Add half of the remaining butter to the pan and fry the onion and garlic for 5 minutes until softened but not coloured. Add the rice and stir the grains in the butter for 1 minute until they are coated thoroughly. Add the white wine and boil rapidly until the wine is reduced by half.

Bring the stock to a gentle simmer and add to the rice, a ladleful at a time. Stir constantly, adding the stock as it is absorbed, until the rice is creamy but still has a bite in the centre.

Melt the remaining butter and stir-fry the prawns for 3–4 minutes. Stir into the rice, along with all the pan juices and the peas. Add the chopped mint and season to taste with salt and pepper. Cover the pan and leave the prawns to infuse for 5 minutes before serving.

Stuffed Squid with Romesco Sauce

Serves 4

Ingredients

8 small squid, about 350 g/12 oz

5 tbsp olive oil

50 g/2 oz/½ cup diced pancetta

1 onion, peeled and chopped

3 garlic cloves, peeled and finely chopped

2 tsp freshly chopped thyme

50 g/2 oz/½ cup drained and chopped sun-dried tomatoes in oil

75 g/3 oz/¾ cup fresh white breadcrumbs

2 tbsp freshly chopped basil

juice of ½ lime

salt and freshly ground black pepper

2 vine-ripened tomatoes, peeled and finely chopped

pinch dried chilli flakes

1 tsp dried oregano

1 large red pepper, skinned and chopped

assorted salad leaves, to serve

Preheat the oven to 230°C/450°F/Gas Mark 8, 15 minutes before cooking. Clean the squid if necessary, rinse lightly, pat dry with absorbent kitchen paper and finely chop the tentacles.

Heat 2 tablespoons of the olive oil in a large, nonstick frying pan and fry the pancetta for 5 minutes, or until crisp. Remove the pancetta and reserve. Add the tentacles, onion, 2 garlic cloves, thyme and sun-dried tomatoes to the oil remaining in the pan and cook gently for 5 minutes, or until softened.

Remove the pan from the heat and stir in the diced pancetta. Blend in a food processor if a smoother stuffing is preferred, then stir in the breadcrumbs, basil and lime juice. Season to taste with salt and pepper and reserve. Spoon the stuffing into the cavity of the squid and secure the tops with cocktail sticks/toothpicks.

Place the squid in a large roasting tin and sprinkle over 2 tablespoons each of oil and water. Place in the preheated oven and cook for 20 minutes.

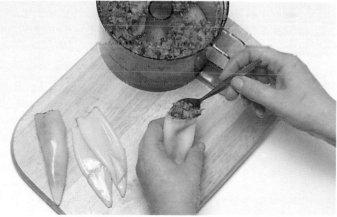

Heat the remaining oil in a saucepan and cook the remaining garlic for 3 minutes. Add the tomatoes, chilli flakes and oregano and simmer gently for 15 minutes before stirring in the red pepper. Cook gently for a further 5 minutes. Blend in a food processor to make a smooth sauce and season to taste. Pour the sauce over the squid and serve immediately with some assorted salad leaves.

Health Rating: 3 points

Sicilian Tuna with Tomato, Pepper & Olives

Serves 4

Ingredients

4 tuna steaks, each about 125 g/4 oz in weight

sea salt and freshly ground black pepper

2 tbsp olive oil

4 shallots, peeled and sliced

2–3 garlic cloves, peeled and chopped

1 medium-hot red chilli, deseeded and chopped

1 red pepper, deseeded and sliced

350 g/12 oz/scant 2 cups chopped plum tomatoes

1 fresh rosemary sprig

2 tbsp freshly chopped oregano

125 ml/4 fl oz/½ cup red wine

50 g/2 oz/generous ¼ cup pitted black olives

Lightly rinse the tuna, pat dry with absorbent paper towels, then season lightly. Heat the oil in a frying pan and cook the tuna for 1–2 minutes on each side until sealed. Remove and reserve.

Add the shallots, garlic and chilli to the oil remaining in the pan and fry for 5 minutes, or until beginning to soften. Add the red pepper, chopped tomatoes, rosemary sprig, 1 tablespoon of the chopped oregano and the wine. Bring to the boil, then reduce the heat and simmer for 12 minutes, or until the tomatoes have collapsed and formed a sauce.

Add the tuna and push the steaks down into the sauce. Cook for 5–8 minutes until the tuna is cooked to your personal preference. Add the olives and cook for a further 2 minutes. Serve sprinkled with the remaining chopped oregano.

Health Rating: 4 points

Parmesan & Garlic Lobster

Serves 2

Ingredients

1 large, cooked lobster

25 g/1 oz/2 tbsp unsalted butter

4 garlic cloves, peeled and crushed

1 tbsp plain/all-purpose flour

300 ml/½ pint/1¼ cups milk

125 g/4 oz/1¼ cups grated Parmesan cheese

sea salt and freshly ground black pepper

assorted salad leaves, to serve

Preheat the oven to 180°C/350°F/Gas Mark 4, 10 minutes before cooking. Halve the lobster and crack the claws. Remove the gills, the green sac behind the head and the black vein running down the body. Place the two lobster halves in a shallow, ovenproof dish.

Melt the butter in a small saucepan and gently cook the garlic for 3 minutes until softened. Add the flour and stir over a medium heat for 1 minute. Draw the saucepan off the heat, then gradually stir in the milk, stirring until the sauce thickens. Return to the heat and cook for 2 minutes, stirring throughout, until smooth and thickened. Stir in half the cheese and continue to cook for 1 minute, then season to taste with salt and pepper.

Pour the cheese sauce over the lobster halves and sprinkle with the remaining Parmesan cheese. Bake in the preheated oven for 20 minutes, or until heated through and the cheese sauce is golden brown. Serve with assorted salad leaves.

Health Rating: 3 points

Red Pesto & Clam Spaghetti

Serves 4

Ingredients

For the red pesto:
2 garlic cloves, peeled and finely chopped
50 g/2 oz/½ cup pine nuts
25 g/1 oz/¼ cup fresh basil leaves
4 sun-dried tomatoes in oil, drained
4 tbsp olive oil
4 tbsp grated Parmesan cheese
salt and freshly ground black pepper

For the clam sauce:
450 g/1 lb live clams, in their shells
1 tbsp olive oil
2 garlic cloves, peeled and crushed
1 small onion, peeled and chopped
5 tbsp/⅓ cup medium dry white wine
150 ml/¼ pint/⅔ cup fish or chicken stock
275 g/10 oz/3¾ cups spaghetti

To make the red pesto, place the garlic, pine nuts, basil leaves, sun-dried tomatoes and olive oil in a food processor and blend in short, sharp bursts until smooth. Scrape into a bowl, then stir in the Parmesan cheese and season to taste with salt and pepper. Cover and leave in the refrigerator until required.

Scrub the clams with a soft brush and remove any beards from the shells, discarding any shells that are open or damaged. Wash in plenty of cold water, then leave in a bowl covered with cold water in the refrigerator until required. Change the water frequently.

Heat the olive oil in a large saucepan and gently fry the garlic and onion for 5 minutes until softened but not coloured. Add the wine and stock and bring to the boil. Add the clams, cover and cook for 3–4 minutes until the clams have opened.

Discard any clams that have not opened and stir in the red pesto sauce. Bring a large saucepan of lightly salted water to the boil and cook the spaghetti for 5–7 minutes until *al dente*. Drain and return to the saucepan. Add the sauce to the spaghetti, mix well, then spoon into a serving dish and serve immediately.

Health Rating: 3 points

Sardines in Vine Leaves

Serves 4

Ingredients

8–16 vine leaves in brine, drained
2 spring onions/scallions
6 tbsp/½ cup olive oil
2 tbsp lime juice
2 tbsp freshly chopped oregano
1 tsp mustard powder
salt and freshly ground black pepper
8 sardines, cleaned
8 bay leaves
8 fresh dill sprigs

To garnish:
lime wedges
fresh dill sprigs

To serve:
olive salad
crusty bread

Preheat the grill/broiler and line the grill rack with foil just before cooking. Cut eight pieces of string about 25.5 cm/10 inches long, and leave to soak in cold water for about 10 minutes. Cover the vine leaves in almost-boiling water. Leave for 20 minutes, then drain and rinse thoroughly. Pat the vine leaves dry with absorbent paper towels.

Trim the spring onions/scallions and finely chop, then place into a small bowl. With a balloon whisk, beat in the olive oil, lime juice, oregano and mustard powder and season to taste with salt and pepper. Cover with plastic wrap and leave in the refrigerator until required. Stir the mixture before using.

Prepare the sardines by making two slashes on both sides of each fish and brush with a little of the lime juice mixture. Place a bay leaf and a dill sprig inside each sardine cavity and wrap with 1–2 vine leaves, depending on size. Brush with the lime mixture and tie the vine leaves in place with string

Grill the fish for 4–5 minutes on each side under a medium heat, brushing with a little more of the lime mixture if necessary. Leave the fish to rest, unwrap and discard the vine leaves. Garnish with lime wedges and sprigs of fresh dill and serve with the remaining lime mixture, olive salad and crusty bread.

Health Rating: 4 points

Scallops & Monkfish Kebabs with Fennel Sauce

Serves 4

Ingredients

700 g/1½ lb monkfish tail
8 large, fresh scallops
2 tbsp olive oil
1 garlic clove, peeled and crushed
freshly ground black pepper
1 fennel bulb, trimmed and thinly sliced
assorted salad leaves, to serve

For the sauce:
2 tbsp fennel seeds
pinch chilli flakes
4 tbsp olive oil
2 tsp lemon juice
salt and freshly ground black pepper

Place the monkfish on a chopping board and remove the skin and the bone that runs down the centre of the tail and discard. Lightly rinse and pat dry with absorbent paper towels. Cut the two fillets into 12 equal-sized pieces and place in a shallow bowl.

Remove the scallops from their shells if necessary, and clean thoroughly, discarding the black vein. Rinse lightly and pat dry with absorbent paper towels. Put in the bowl with the fish.

Blend the 2 tablespoons of olive oil, the crushed garlic and a pinch of black pepper in a small bowl. Pour the mixture over the monkfish and scallops, making sure they are well coated. Cover lightly and leave to marinate in the refrigerator for at least 30 minutes, or longer if time permits. Spoon over the marinade occasionally.

Lightly crush the fennel seeds and chilli flakes in a pestle and mortar. Stir in the 4 tablespoons of olive oil and the lemon juice and season to taste with salt and pepper. Cover and leave to infuse for 20 minutes. Drain the monkfish and scallops, reserving the marinade and thread onto four skewers.

Spray a griddle pan/ridged grill pan with a fine spray of oil, then heat until almost smoking and cook the kebabs for 5–6 minutes, turning halfway through, and brushing with the marinade throughout.

Brush the fennel slices with the fennel sauce and cook on the griddle pan for 1 minute on each side. Serve the fennel slices topped with the kebabs and drizzled with the fennel sauce. Serve with a few assorted salad leaves.

Health Rating: 4 points

Roasted Cod with Saffron Aïoli

Serves 4

Ingredients

For the saffron aïoli:
2 garlic cloves, peeled
¼ tsp saffron strands
sea salt, to taste
1 egg yolk
200 ml/7 fl oz/¾ cup extra virgin olive oil
2 tbsp lemon juice

For the marinade:
2 tbsp olive oil
4 garlic cloves, peeled and finely chopped
1 red onion, peeled and finely chopped
1 tbsp freshly chopped rosemary
2 tbsp freshly chopped thyme
4–6 fresh rosemary sprigs
1 lemon, sliced
4 thick cod fillets with skin, 175 g/6 oz each
freshly cooked vegetables, to serve

Preheat the oven to 180°C/350°F/Gas Mark 4, 10 minutes before cooking. Crush the garlic, saffron and a pinch of salt in a pestle and mortar to form a paste. Place in a blender with the egg yolk and blend for 30 seconds. With the motor running, slowly add the olive oil in a thin, steady stream until the mayonnaise is smooth and thick. Spoon into a small bowl and stir in the lemon juice. Cover and leave in the refrigerator until required. Combine the olive oil, garlic, red onion, rosemary and thyme for the marinade and leave to infuse for about 10 minutes.

Place the rosemary and lemon in the bottom of a lightly oiled roasting tin/pan. Add the cod, skin-side up. Pour over the marinade and leave to marinate in the refrigerator for 15–20 minutes. Bake in the oven for 15–20 minutes until the cod is cooked and the flesh flakes easily with a fork. Leave the cod to rest for 1 minute before serving with the saffron aïoli and vegetables.

Health Rating: 4 points

Foil-baked Fish

Serves 4

Ingredients

For the tomato sauce:
125 ml/4 fl oz/½ cup olive oil
4 garlic cloves, peeled and finely chopped
4 shallots, peeled and finely chopped
400 g/14 oz/2 cups canned chopped Italian tomatoes
2 tbsp freshly chopped flat-leaf parsley
3 tbsp basil leaves
salt and freshly ground black pepper

700 g/1½ lb red mullet, bass or haddock fillets
450 g/1 lb live mussels
4 squid
8 large, raw prawns/shrimp
2 tbsp olive oil
3 tbsp dry white wine
3 tbsp freshly chopped basil leaves
lemon wedges, to garnish

Preheat the oven to 180°C/350°F/Gas Mark 4, 10 minutes before cooking. Heat the olive oil and gently fry the garlic and shallots for 2 minutes. Stir in the tomatoes and simmer for 10 minutes, breaking the tomatoes down with a wooden spoon. Add the parsley and basil, season to taste with salt and pepper and cook for a further 2 minutes. Reserve and keep warm.

Lightly rinse the fish fillets and cut into four portions. Scrub the mussels thoroughly, removing the beard and any barnacles from the shells. Discard any mussels that are open. Clean the squid and cut into rings. Peel the prawns/shrimp and remove the thin black intestinal vein that runs down the back.

Cut four large pieces of foil, then place them on a large baking sheet and brush with olive oil. Place one fish portion in the centre of each piece of foil. Close the foil to form parcels and bake in the oven for 10 minutes, then remove.

Carefully open up the parcels and add the mussels, squid and prawns. Pour in the wine and spoon over a little of the

tomato sauce. Sprinkle with the basil leaves and return to the oven and bake for 5 minutes, or until cooked thoroughly. Discard any unopened mussels, then garnish with lemon wedges and serve with the extra tomato sauce.

Health Rating: 5 points

Roasted Monkfish with Prosciutto

Serves 4

Ingredients

700 g/1½ lb monkfish tail
sea salt and freshly ground black pepper
4 bay leaves
4 slices fontina cheese, rind removed
8 slices Parma ham/prosciutto
225 g/8 oz/3 cups angel hair pasta
50 g/2 oz/4 tbsp butter
zest and juice of 1 lemon
fresh coriander/cilantro sprigs, to garnish

To serve:
chargrilled courgettes/zucchini
chargrilled tomatoes

Preheat the oven to 200°C/400°F/Gas Mark 6, 15 minutes before cooking. Discard any skin from the monkfish tail and cut away and discard the central bone. Cut the fish into four equal pieces and season to taste. Lay a bay leaf on each fillet, along with a slice of cheese. Wrap each fillet with 2 slices of Parma ham/ prosciutto, so that the fish is covered completely. Tuck the ends of the Parma ham in, and secure with a cocktail stick/toothpick.

Lightly oil a baking tray/pan and place in the oven for a few minutes. Place the fish on the preheated tray, put in the oven and cook for 12–15 minutes.

Bring a large saucepan of lightly salted water to the boil, then slowly add the pasta and cook for 5 minutes until *al dente*, or according to packet instructions. Drain, reserving 2 tablespoons of the pasta cooking water. Return the pasta to the saucepan and add the reserved pasta water, the butter, lemon zest and juice. Toss until the pasta is well coated and glistening. Twirl the pasta into small nests on four warmed serving plates and top with the monkfish parcels. Garnish with sprigs of coriander/cilantro and serve with chargrilled courgettes/zucchini and tomatoes.

Health Rating: 2 points

Squid with Tomatoes & Spinach

Serves 4

Ingredients

700 g/1½ lb squid, cleaned
plain/all-purpose flour, for dusting
2 tbsp olive oil
3 shallots, peeled and sliced
2 celery stalks, trimmed and sliced
350 g/12 oz/scant 2 cups chopped ripe plum tomatoes
1 yellow pepper, deseeded and chopped
3 small courgettes/zucchini, trimmed and sliced
300 ml/½ pint/1¼ cups fish or vegetable stock
150 ml/¼ pint/²⁄₃ cup dry white wine, or use more stock
salt and freshly ground black pepper
350 g/12 oz fresh spinach
1 tbsp freshly chopped flat-leaf parsley

Rinse the squid and pat dry with absorbent paper towels. Slice into rings, then toss lightly in the flour. Reserve.

Heat the oil in a large frying pan, add the shallots and celery and fry for 5 minutes, or until beginning to soften. Add the tomatoes together with the yellow pepper and courgettes/zucchini and cook gently for 5–8 minutes until the tomatoes have collapsed. Add the stock and wine, then bring to the boil.

Reduce the heat and simmer for 10 minutes, then add seasoning to taste. Add the squid and stir lightly together before adding the fresh spinach. Cook gently for 3–4 minutes until the squid and spinach are cooked.

Spoon into a warmed serving dish, sprinkle with the chopped parsley and serve.

Health Rating: 5 points

Mussels Arrabbiata

Serves 4

Ingredients

1.8 kg/4 lb mussels
3–4 tbsp olive oil
1 large onion, peeled and sliced
4 garlic cloves, peeled and finely chopped
1 red chilli, deseeded and finely chopped
1.2 kg/2²⁄₃ lb/3 cups canned chopped tomatoes
150 ml/¼ pint/²⁄₃ cup white wine
175 g/6 oz/1 cup pitted and halved black/ripe olives
salt and freshly ground black pepper
2 tbsp freshly chopped parsley
warm crusty bread, to serve

Clean the mussels by scrubbing with a small, soft brush, removing the beard and any barnacles from the shells. Discard any mussels that are open or have damaged shells. Place in a large bowl and cover with cold water. Change the water frequently before cooking and leave in the refrigerator until required.

Heat the olive oil in a large saucepan and sweat the onion, garlic and chilli until soft but not coloured. Add the tomatoes and bring to the boil, then simmer for 15 minutes.

Add the white wine to the tomato sauce, bring the sauce to the boil and add the mussels. Cover and carefully shake the pan. Cook the mussels for 5–7 minutes until the shells have opened.

Add the olives to the pan and cook uncovered for about 5 minutes to warm through. Season to taste with salt and pepper and sprinkle in the chopped parsley. Discard any mussels that have not opened and serve immediately with lots of warm crusty bread.

Health Rating: 3 points

Tuna Cannelloni

Serves 4

Ingredients

1 tbsp olive oil

6 spring onions/scallions, trimmed and finely sliced

1 sweet Mediterranean red pepper, deseeded and finely chopped

200 g/7 oz canned tuna in brine

250 g/9 oz tub ricotta or quark cheese

zest and juice of 1 lemon

1 tbsp freshly snipped chives

salt and freshly ground black pepper

8 dried cannelloni tubes

1 medium/large egg, beaten

125 g/4 oz/¼ cup cottage cheese

150 ml/¼ pt/⅔ cup natural/plain yogurt

pinch freshly grated nutmeg

50 g/2 oz/¼ cup grated mozzarella cheese

tossed green salad, to serve

Preheat the oven to 190°C/375°F/Gas Mark 5, 10 minutes before cooking. Heat the olive oil in a frying pan and cook the spring onions/scallions and pepper until soft. Remove from the pan with a slotted draining spoon and place in a large bowl.

Drain the tuna, then stir into the spring onions and pepper. Beat the ricotta cheese with the lemon zest and juice and the snipped chives and season to taste with salt and pepper. Beat until soft and blended. Add to the tuna and mix together. If the mixture is still a little stiff, add a little extra lemon juice.

With a teaspoon, carefully spoon the mixture into the cannelloni tubes, then lay the filled tubes in a lightly oiled, shallow, ovenproof dish. Beat the egg, cottage cheese, yogurt and nutmeg together and pour over the cannelloni. Sprinkle with the grated mozzarella cheese and bake in the preheated oven for 15–20 minutes until the topping is golden brown and bubbling. Serve immediately with a tossed green salad.

Health Rating: 2 points

Seared Tuna with Italian Salsa

Serves 4

Ingredients

4 tuna or swordfish steaks, about 175 g/6 oz each

salt and freshly ground black pepper

3 tbsp Pernod

2 tbsp olive oil

zest and juice of 1 lemon

2 tsp fresh thyme leaves

2 tsp fennel seeds, lightly roasted

4 sun-dried tomatoes, chopped

1 tsp dried chilli flakes

assorted salad leaves, to serve

For the salsa:

1 white onion, peeled and finely chopped

2 tomatoes, deseeded and sliced

2 tbsp freshly shredded basil leaves

1 red chilli, deseeded and finely sliced

3 tbsp extra virgin olive oil

2 tsp balsamic vinegar

1 tsp caster/superfine sugar

Wipe the fish and season lightly with salt and pepper, then place in a shallow dish. Mix together the Pernod, olive oil, lemon zest and juice, thyme, fennel seeds, sun-dried tomatoes and chilli flakes and pour over the fish. Cover lightly and leave to marinate in a cool place for 1–2 hours, occasionally spooning over the marinade. Meanwhile, mix all the ingredients for the salsa together in a bowl. Season to taste with salt and pepper, then cover and leave for about 30 minutes to allow all the flavours to develop.

Lightly oil a griddle pan/ridged grill pan and heat until hot. When the pan is very hot, drain the fish, reserving the marinade. Cook the fish for 3–4 minutes on each side, taking care not to overcook – the tuna steaks should be a little pink inside. Pour any remaining marinade into a saucepan, bring to the boil and boil for 1 minute. Serve hot with the marinade, chilled salsa and a few salad leaves.

Health Rating: 3 points

Mediterranean Fish Stew

Serves 4–6

Ingredients

4 tbsp olive oil

1 onion, peeled and finely sliced

5 garlic cloves, peeled and finely sliced

1 fennel bulb, trimmed and finely chopped

3 celery stalks, trimmed and finely chopped

400 g/14 oz/2 cups canned chopped tomatoes with Italian herbs

1 tbsp freshly chopped oregano

1 bay leaf

zest and juice of 1 orange

1 tsp saffron strands

750 ml/1¼ pints/3¼ cups fish stock

3 tbsp dry vermouth

salt and freshly ground black pepper

225 g/8 oz/½ lb thick haddock fillets

225 g/8 oz/½ lb sea bass or bream fillets

225 g/8 oz/½ lb raw tiger prawns/jumbo shrimp, peeled

crusty bread, to serve

Heat the olive oil in a large saucepan. Add the onion, garlic, fennel and celery and cook over a low heat for 15 minutes, stirring frequently, until the vegetables are soft and just beginning to turn brown.

Add the canned tomatoes with their juice, the oregano, bay leaf, orange zest and juice with the saffron strands. Bring to the boil, then reduce the heat and simmer for 5 minutes. Add the fish stock and vermouth and season to taste with salt and pepper. Bring to the boil. Reduce the heat and simmer for 20 minutes.

Wipe or rinse the haddock and bass fillets and remove as many of the bones as possible. Place on a chopping board and cut into 5 cm/2 inch cubes. Add to the saucepan and cook for 3 minutes. Add the prawns/shrimp and cook for a further 5 minutes. Adjust the seasoning to taste and serve with crusty bread.

Health Rating: 4 points

Plaice with Parmesan & Anchovies

Serves 4

Ingredients

4 plaice/flounder fillets

4 anchovy fillets, finely chopped

450 g/1 lb/2½ cups spinach

3 firm tomatoes, sliced

200 ml/7 fl oz/¾ cup double/heavy cream

5 slices olive ciabatta bread

50 g/2 oz/2 cups wild rocket/arugula

8 tbsp grated Parmesan cheese

freshly cooked pasta, to serve

Preheat the oven to 220°C/425°F/Gas Mark 7, 15 minutes before cooking. Put the plaice/flounder on a chopping board and, holding the tail, strip off the skin from both sides. With a filleting knife, fillet the fish, then wipe with a clean, damp cloth or dampened paper towel.

Place the fillets on a large chopping board, skinned-side up, and halve lengthways along the centre. Dot each one with some of the chopped anchovies, then roll up from the thickest end and reserve.

Pour boiling water over the spinach, leave for 2 minutes, then drain, squeezing out as much moisture as possible. Place in the base of an ovenproof dish, and arrange the tomatoes on top of the spinach. Arrange the rolled-up fillets standing up in the dish and pour over the cream.

Place the ciabatta and rocket/arugula in a food processor and blend until finely chopped, then stir in the grated Parmesan cheese.

Sprinkle the topping over the fish and bake in the preheated oven for 8–10 minutes until the fish is cooked and has lost its translucency and the topping is golden brown. Serve with freshly cooked pasta.

Health Rating: 3 points

Angel Hair Pasta with Crab

Serves 4

Ingredients

450 g/1 lb angel hair pasta, fresh or dried

For the crab sauce:
1 small fennel bulb
4 tbsp olive oil
1 medium-hot red chilli, deseeded and chopped
1 green pepper, deseeded and thinly sliced
6 spring onions/scallions, trimmed and thinly sliced
150 ml/¼ pint/⅔ cup dry white wine
300 g/11 oz white and brown crab meat
150 ml/¼ pint/⅔ cup double/heavy cream
salt and freshly ground black pepper
1–2 tbsp freshly chopped flat-leaf parsley

To make the sauce, trim the fennel bulb and cut off and reserve the feathery fronds for the garnish. Discard the outer leaves, cut into quarters and slice thinly into thin sticks.

Heat the oil in a large saucepan, add the fennel, chilli and green pepper and fry gently for 5 minutes, stirring frequently. Stir in the spring onions/scallions, then pour in the wine. Bring to the boil, reduce the heat and simmer for 5 minutes. Stir in the crab meat and simmer for a further 2–3 minutes. Slowly stir in the cream, add seasoning to taste and keep warm.

Meanwhile, bring a large saucepan of water to a rolling boil. Add the pasta and cook until *al dente*: 3–4 minutes for fresh and 6–8 minutes for dried. Drain, reserving 2 tablespoons of the pasta cooking water.

Return the pasta to the saucepan together with the pasta cooking water and the crab sauce. Stir lightly, then serve sprinkled with the parsley.

Health Rating: 3 points

Grilled Red Mullet with Orange & Anchovy Sauce

Serves 4

Ingredients

2 oranges
4 x 175 g/6 oz red mullet, cleaned and descaled
salt and freshly ground black pepper
4 fresh rosemary sprigs
1 lemon, sliced
2 tbsp olive oil
2 garlic cloves, peeled and crushed
6 anchovy fillets in oil, drained and roughly chopped
2 tsp freshly chopped rosemary
1 tsp lemon juice

Preheat the grill/broiler and line the grill rack with foil just before cooking. Peel the oranges with a sharp knife, over a bowl in order to catch the juice. Cut into thin slices and reserve. If necessary, make up the juice to 150 ml/¼ pint/⅔ cup with extra juice.

Place the fish on a chopping board and make two diagonal slashes across the thickest part of both sides of the fish. Season well, both inside and out, with salt and pepper. Tuck a rosemary sprig and a few lemon slices inside the cavity of each fish. Brush the fish with a little of the olive oil and then cook under the preheated grill for 4–5 minutes on each side. The flesh should just fall away from the bone.

Heat the remaining oil in a saucepan and gently fry the garlic and anchovies for 3–4 minutes. Do not allow to brown. Add the chopped rosemary and plenty of black pepper. The anchovies will be salty enough, so do not add any salt. Stir in the orange slices with their juice and the lemon juice. Simmer gently until heated through. Spoon the sauce over the red mullet and serve immediately.

Health Rating: 3 points

Grilled Snapper with Roasted Pepper

Serves 4

Ingredients

1 medium red pepper

1 medium green pepper

4–8 snapper fillets, depending on size, about 450 g/1 lb

sea salt and freshly ground black pepper

1 tbsp olive oil

5 tbsp double/heavy cream

125 ml/4 fl oz/½ cup white wine

1 tbsp freshly chopped dill

fresh dill sprigs, to garnish

freshly cooked tagliatelle, to serve

Preheat the gril/broilerl to a high heat and line the grill rack with foil. Cut the tops off the peppers and divide into quarters. Remove the seeds and the membrane, then place on the foil-lined grill rack and cook for 8–10 minutes, turning frequently, until the skins have become charred and blackened. Remove from the grill rack, place in a plastic bag and leave until cool. When the peppers are cool, strip off the skin, slice thinly and reserve.

Cover the grill rack with another piece of foil, then place the snapper fillets skin-side up on the grill rack. Season to taste with salt and pepper and brush with a little of the olive oil. Cook for 10–12 minutes, turning over once and brushing again with a little olive oil.

Pour the cream and wine into a small saucepan, bring to the boil and simmer for about 5 minutes until the sauce has thickened slightly. Add the dill, season to taste and stir in the sliced peppers. Arrange the cooked snapper fillets on warmed serving plates and pour over the cream and pepper sauce. Garnish with sprigs of dill and serve immediately with freshly cooked tagliatelle.

Health Rating: 3 points

Pan-fried Salmon with Herb Risotto

Serves 4

Ingredients

4 x 175 g/6 oz salmon fillets

3–4 tbsp plain/all-purpose flour

1 tsp dried mustard powder

salt and freshly ground black pepper

2 tbsp olive oil

3 shallots, peeled and chopped

225 g/8 oz/1 cup Arborio/risotto rice

150 ml/¼ pint/⅔ cup dry white wine

1.4 litres/2½ pints/6⅓ cups vegetable or fish stock

50 g/2 oz/4 tbsp butter

2 tbsp freshly snipped chives

2 tbsp freshly chopped dill

2 tbsp freshly chopped flat-leaf parsley

knob/pat butter

To garnish:

lemon slices

fresh dill sprigs

tomato salad, to serve

Wipe the salmon fillets with a clean, damp cloth. Mix together the flour, mustard powder and seasoning on a large plate and use to coat the salmon fillets and reserve.

Heat half the olive oil in a large frying pan and fry the shallots for 5 minutes until softened but not coloured. Add the rice and stir for 1 minute, then slowly add the wine, bring to the boil and boil rapidly until reduced by half.

Bring the stock to a gentle simmer, then add to the rice, a ladleful at a time. Cook, stirring frequently, until all the stock has been added and the rice is cooked but still retains a bite. Stir in the butter and freshly chopped herbs and season to taste with salt and pepper.

Heat the remaining olive oil and the knob of butter in a large griddle pan/ridged grill pan, add the salmon fillets and cook for

2–3 minutes on each side until cooked. Arrange the herb risotto on warmed serving plates and top with the salmon. Garnish with slices of lemon and sprigs of dill and serve immediately with a tomato salad.

Health Rating: 2 points

Sea Bass in Creamy Watercress & Prosciutto Sauce

Serves 4

Ingredients

75 g/3 oz/2¹/₂ cups watercress

450 ml/³/₄ pint/1³/₄ cups fish or chicken stock

150 ml/¹/₄ pint/²/₃ cup dry white wine

225 g/8 oz/3 cups tagliatelle

40 g/1¹/₂ oz/3 tbsp butter

75 g/3 oz/³/₄ cup chopped prosciutto

2 tbsp plain/all-purpose flour

300 ml/¹/₂ pint/1¹/₄ cups single/light cream

salt and freshly ground black pepper

olive oil, for spraying

4 sea bass fillets, 175 g/6 oz each

fresh watercress, to garnish

Remove the leaves from the watercress stalks and reserve. Chop the stalks roughly and put in a large pan with the stock. Bring to the boil slowly, cover, and simmer for 20 minutes.

Strain, and discard the stalks. Make the stock up to 300 ml/¹/₂ pint/1¹/₄ cups with the wine. Bring a large saucepan of lightly salted water to the boil and cook the pasta for 8–10 minutes until *al dente*. Drain and reserve.

Melt the butter in a saucepan and cook the prosciutto gently for 3 minutes. Remove with a slotted spoon. Stir the flour into the saucepan and cook on a medium heat for 2 minutes.

Remove from the heat and gradually pour in the hot watercress stock, stirring constantly. Return to the heat and bring to the boil, stirring throughout. Simmer for 3 minutes, or until the sauce has thickened and is smooth.

Purée the watercress leaves and cream in a food processor, then add to the sauce with the prosciutto. Season to taste with salt and pepper, add the pasta, toss lightly and keep warm.

Meanwhile, spray a griddle pan/ridged grill pan lightly with olive oil, then heat until hot. When hot, cook the sea bass fillets for 3–4 minutes on each side until cooked. Arrange the fillets on a bed of pasta and drizzle with a little sauce. Garnish with watercress and serve immediately.

Health Rating: 2 points

Marinated Mackerel with Tomato & Basil Salad

Serves 3

Ingredients

3 mackerel, filleted

3 beefsteak tomatoes, sliced

50 g/2 oz/2 cups watercress

2 oranges, peeled and segmented

75 g/3 oz/³⁄₄ cup sliced mozzarella cheese

2 tbsp basil leaves, shredded

fresh basil sprig, to garnish

For the marinade:

juice of 2 lemons

4 tbsp olive oil

4 tbsp basil leaves

For the dressing:

1 tbsp lemon juice

1 tsp Dijon mustard

1 tsp caster/superfine sugar

salt and freshly ground black pepper

5 tbsp olive oil

Remove as many of the fine pin bones as possible from the mackerel fillets, lightly rinse and pat dry with absorbent paper towels and place in a shallow dish.

Blend the marinade ingredients together and pour over the mackerel fillets. Make sure the marinade has covered the fish completely. Cover and leave in a cool place for at least 8 hours, but preferably overnight. As the fillets marinate, they will lose their translucency and look as if they are cooked.

Place the tomatoes, watercress, oranges and mozzarella cheese in a large bowl and toss.

To make the dressing, whisk the lemon juice with the mustard, sugar, seasoning and oil in a bowl. Pour over half the dressing, toss again and then arrange on a serving platter.

Remove the mackerel from the marinade, cut into bite-size pieces and sprinkle with the shredded basil. Arrange on top of the salad, drizzle over the remaining dressing, scatter with basil leaves and garnish with a basil sprig. Serve.

Health Rating: 4 points

Open Ravioli with Seafood

Serves 4

Ingredients

450 g/1 lb mixed seafood
$^1/_2$ basic quantity of fresh pasta dough (*see page 268*)
2 tbsp olive oil
2 shallots, peeled and sliced
1 medium-hot chilli, deseeded and chopped
2 celery stalks, trimmed and finely chopped
300 ml/$^1/_2$ pint/1$^1/_4$ cups dry white wine
2 red peppers, deseeded and skinned
freshly ground black pepper
fresh flat-leaf parsley sprigs, to garnish

Prepare the seafood. If using any fish fillets, skin and remove any fine bones and cut into small pieces. Peel prawns/shrimp, discard the black intestinal vein that runs down the back, then rinse and pat dry with paper towels. Scrub mussels, removing any beards and barnacles, discard any that are open. Leave in a bowl covered with cold water. Clean squid. Slice then flake white crabmeat. Reserve all.

Roll the pasta out on a lightly floured surface, cut into 7.5 cm/3 inch squares; cover with a dish towel. Heat the oil in a saucepan or frying pan, add the shallots, chilli and celery and fry for 3 minutes. Pour in the wine and 150 ml/$^1/_4$ pint/$^2/_3$ cup water, then bring to the boil and allow to bubble gently for 5 minutes. Add all the seafood except the crab and cook for 4–5 minutes until the mussels have opened (discard any that are closed) and the prawns have turned pink. Keep warm while cooking the pasta, then drain just before serving, reserving 50 ml/2 fl oz/$^1/_4$ cup of the seafood cooking water.

Bring a frying pan half–filled with water to the boil. Cook the pasta squares for 2–3 minutes, then drain and keep warm. Place the cooked pasta layered with paper towels on a large plate placed over a pan of simmering water. Continue until all the pasta is cooked. Place 3–4 pasta squares on a plate and place a few strips of red pepper on top. Spoon over some crabmeat and top with the cooked shellfish. Spoon a little of the cooking water over, then season with black pepper and garnish with parsley sprigs.

Health Rating: 3 points

Seafood Special

Serves 4

Ingredients

2 tbsp olive oil
4 garlic cloves, peeled
125 g/4 oz squid, cut into rings
300 ml/$^1/_2$ pint/1$^1/_4$ cups medium-dry white wine
400 g/14 oz/2 cups canned chopped tomatoes
2 tbsp fresh parsley, finely chopped
225 g/8 oz/2 cups cleaned and debearded live mussels
125 g/4 oz/1 cup monkfish fillet
125 g/4 oz/1 cup fresh tuna
4 slices Italian bread

To garnish:
225 g/8 oz/2 cups cooked large, unpeeled prawns/shrimp
4 langoustines, cooked
3 tbsp freshly chopped parsley

Heat the olive oil in a saucepan. Chop half of the garlic, add to the saucepan and cook gently for 1–2 minutes. Add the squid. 150 ml/$^1/_4$ pint/$^2/_3$ cup of the wine together with the tomatoes and simmer for 10–15 minutes.

Chop the remaining garlic and place with the remaining wine and the 2 tablespoons of parsley in another saucepan. Add the cleaned mussels to the pan, cover and cook for 7–8 minutes. Discard any mussels that have not opened, then remove the remaining mussels with a slotted spoon and add to the squid and tomato mixture. Reserve the liquor.

Cut the monkfish and tuna into chunks and place in the saucepan with the mussels' cooking liquor. Simmer for about 5 minutes until the fish is just tender. Mix all the cooked fish and shellfish, with the exception of the prawns/shrimp and langoustines, with the tomato mixture and cooking liquor in a large saucepan. Heat everything through until piping hot. Toast the slices of bread and place in the base of a large, shallow serving dish. Pour the fish mixture over the toasted bread and garnish with the prawns, langoustines and chopped parsley. Serve immediately.

Health Rating: 3 points

Farfalle with Smoked Trout in a Dill & Vodka Sauce

Serves 4

Ingredients

400 g/14 oz/3½ cups farfalle

150 g/5 oz smoked trout

2 tsp lemon juice

200 ml/7 fl oz/¾ cup double/heavy cream

2 tsp wholegrain mustard

2 tbsp freshly chopped dill

4 tbsp vodka

salt and freshly ground black pepper

dill sprigs, to garnish

Bring a large pan of lightly salted water to a rolling boil. Add the pasta and cook according to the packet instructions, or until *al dente*.

Meanwhile, cut the smoked trout into thin slivers, using scissors. Sprinkle lightly with the lemon juice and reserve.

Place the cream, mustard, chopped dill and vodka in a small pan. Season lightly with salt and pepper. Bring the contents of the pan to the boil and simmer gently for 2–3 minutes until slightly thickened.

Drain the cooked pasta thoroughly, then return to the pan. Add the smoked trout to the dill and vodka sauce, then pour over the pasta. Toss gently until the pasta is coated and the trout evenly mixed.

Spoon into a warmed serving dish or onto individual plates. Garnish with sprigs of dill and serve immediately.

Health Rating: 3 points

Pappardelle with Smoked Haddock & Blue Cheese Sauce

Serves 4

Ingredients

350 g/12 oz smoked haddock

2 bay leaves

300 ml/$\frac{1}{2}$ pint/1$\frac{1}{4}$ cups milk

400 g/14 oz pappardelle or tagliatelle

25 g/1 oz/2 tbsp butter

25 g/1 oz/$\frac{1}{4}$ cup plain/all-purpose flour

150 ml/$\frac{1}{4}$ pint/$\frac{2}{3}$ cup single/light cream, or extra milk

125 g/4 oz Dolcelatte cheese or Gorgonzola, cut into small pieces

$\frac{1}{4}$ tsp freshly grated nutmeg

salt and freshly ground black pepper

40 g/1$\frac{1}{2}$ oz/$\frac{1}{3}$ cup toasted chopped walnuts

1 tbsp freshly chopped parsley

Place the smoked haddock in a saucepan with 1 bay leaf and pour in the milk. Bring to the boil slowly, cover and simmer for 6–7 minutes until the fish is opaque. Remove and roughly flake the fish, discarding the skin and any bones. Strain the milk and reserve.

Bring a pan of lightly salted water to a rolling boil. Add the pasta and cook according to the packet instructions, or until *al dente*.

Meanwhile, place the butter, flour and single cream, or milk if preferred, in a pan and stir to mix. Stir in the reserved warm milk and add the remaining bay leaf. Bring to the boil, whisking all the time, until smooth and thick. Gently simmer for 3–4 minutes, stirring frequently. Discard the bay leaf. Add the cheese to the sauce. Heat gently, stirring, until melted. Add the flaked haddock and season to taste with nutmeg and salt and pepper.

Drain the pasta thoroughly and return to the pan. Add the sauce and toss gently to coat, taking care not to break up the flakes of fish. Tip into a warmed serving bowl, sprinkle with toasted walnuts and parsley and serve immediately.

Health Rating: 2 points

Special Seafood Lasagne

Serves 4–6

Ingredients

450 g/1 lb fresh haddock fillet, skinned

150 ml/¹⁄₄ pint/²⁄₃ cup dry white wine

150 ml/¹⁄₄ pint/²⁄₃ cup fish stock

¹⁄₂ onion, peeled and thickly sliced

1 bay leaf

75 g/3 oz/6 tbsp butter

350 g/12 oz/2 cups trimmed and thickly sliced leeks

1 garlic clove, peeled and crushed

25 g/1 oz/¹⁄₄ cup plain/all-purpose flour

150 ml/¹⁄₄ pint/²⁄₃ cup single/light cream

2 tbsp freshly chopped dill

salt and freshly ground black pepper

8–12 sheets lasagne verde, dried and cooked

225 g/8 oz/1¹⁄₂ cups ready-cooked seafood cocktail

50 g/2 oz/¹⁄₂ cup grated Gruyère cheese

Preheat the oven to 200˚C/400˚F/Gas Mark 6, 15 minutes before cooking. Place the haddock in a pan with the wine, fish stock, onion and bay leaf. Bring to the boil slowly, cover and simmer gently for 5 minutes, or until the fish is opaque. Remove and flake the fish, discarding any bones. Strain the cooking juices and reserve.

Melt 50 g/2 oz/4 tbsp of the butter in a large saucepan. Add the leeks and garlic and cook gently for 10 minutes. Remove from the pan, using a slotted draining spoon, and reserve.

Melt the remaining butter in a small saucepan. Stir in the flour, then gradually whisk in the cream, off the heat, followed by the reserved cooking juices. Bring to the boil slowly, whisking until thickened. Stir in the dill and season to taste with salt and pepper.

Spoon a little of the sauce into the base of a buttered 2.8 litre/5 pint, shallow ovenproof dish. Top with a layer of lasagne, followed by the haddock, seafood cocktail and leeks. Spoon over enough sauce to cover. Continue layering up, finishing with sheets of lasagne topped with sauce.

Sprinkle over the grated Gruyère cheese and bake in the preheated oven for 40–45 minutes until golden brown and bubbling. Serve immediately.

Health Rating: 2 points

Tuna & Macaroni Timbales

Serves 4

Ingredients

125 g/4 oz/1 cup macaroni

200 g/7 oz canned tuna in brine, drained

150 ml/¼ pint/⅔ cup single/light cream

150 ml/¼ pint/⅔ cup double/heavy cream

50 g/2 oz/½ cup grated Gruyère cheese

3 medium/large eggs, lightly beaten

salt and freshly ground black pepper

fresh chives, to garnish

For the fresh tomato dressing:

1 tsp Dijon mustard

1 tsp red wine vinegar

2 tbsp sunflower oil

1 tbsp hazelnut or walnut oil

350 g/12 oz/1¼ cups skinned, deseeded and chopped firm
   ripe tomatoes

2 tbsp freshly snipped chives

Preheat the oven to 180°C/350°F/Gas Mark 4, 10 minutes
before cooking. Oil and line the bases of four individual 150 ml/
¼ pint/⅔ cup timbales or ovenproof cups with nonstick baking
parchment and stand in a small roasting tin.

Bring a large pan of lightly salted water to a rolling boil. Add the
macaroni and cook according to the packet instructions, or until
al dente. Drain the cooked pasta thoroughly. Flake the tuna and
mix with the macaroni. Divide between the timbales or cups.

Pour the single/light and double/heavy cream into a small
saucepan. Bring to the boil slowly, remove from the heat and
stir in the Gruyère cheese until melted. Allow to cool for 1–2
minutes, then whisk into the beaten egg and season lightly with
salt and pepper.

Pour the mixture over the tuna and macaroni and cover each
timbale with a small piece of foil. Pour enough hot water into
the roasting tin to come halfway up the timbales. Place in the
oven and cook for 25 minutes. Remove the timbales from the
water and allow to stand for 5 minutes.

For the tomato dressing, whisk together the mustard and
vinegar in a small bowl, using a fork. Gradually whisk in the
sunflower and nut oils, then stir in the chopped tomatoes and
the snipped chives.

Unmould the timbales onto warmed serving plates and spoon
the tomato dressing over the top and around the bottom.
Garnish with fresh chives and serve immediately.

Health Rating: 2 points

Saucy Cod & Pasta Bake

Serves 4

Ingredients

450 g/1 lb cod fillets, skinned

2 tbsp sunflower/corn oil

1 onion, peeled and chopped

4 rashers smoked streaky bacon, rind removed and chopped

150 g/5 oz/1½ cups wiped baby button mushrooms

2 celery stalks, trimmed and thinly sliced

2 small courgettes/zucchini, halved lengthways and sliced

400 g/14 oz/2 cups canned chopped tomatoes

100 ml/3½ fl oz/7 tbsp fish stock or dry white wine

1 tbsp freshly chopped tarragon

salt and freshly ground black pepper

For the pasta topping:

225–275 g/8–10 oz/2–2½ cups pasta shells

25 g/1 oz/2 tbsp butter

4 tbsp plain/all-purpose flour

450 ml/¾ pint/1¾ cups milk

Preheat the oven to 200°C/400°F/Gas Mark 6, 15 minutes before cooking. Cut the cod into bite-size pieces and reserve. Heat the sunflower/corn oil in a large saucepan, add the onion and bacon and cook for 7–8 minutes. Add the mushrooms and celery and cook for 5 minutes, or until fairly soft.

Add the courgettes/zucchini and tomatoes to the bacon mixture and pour in the fish stock or wine. Bring to the boil, then simmer uncovered for 5 minutes, or until the sauce has thickened slightly. Remove from the heat and stir in the cod pieces and the tarragon. Season to taste with salt and pepper, then spoon into a large, oiled baking dish.

Meanwhile, bring a large pan of lightly salted water to a rolling boil. Add the pasta shells and cook according to the packet instructions, or until *al dente*.

For the topping, place the butter and flour in a saucepan and pour in the milk. Bring to the boil slowly, whisking, until thickened and smooth.

Drain the pasta thoroughly and stir into the sauce. Spoon carefully over the fish and vegetables. Place in the preheated oven and bake for 20–25 minutes until the top is lightly browned and bubbling. Serve.

Health Rating: 3 points

Seared Salmon & Lemon Linguine

Serves 4

Ingredients

4 small, skinless salmon fillets, each about 75 g/3 oz

2 tsp sunflower oil

½ tsp crushed mixed/black peppercorns

400 g/14 oz linguine

15 g/½ oz/1 tbsp unsalted butter

1 bunch spring onions/scallions, trimmed and shredded

300 ml/½ pint/1¼ cups sour cream

finely grated zest of 1 lemon

50 g/2 oz/½ cup freshly grated Parmesan cheese

1 tbsp lemon juice

To garnish:

dill sprigs

lemon slices

Brush the salmon fillets with the sunflower oil, sprinkle with crushed peppercorns and press on firmly and reserve.

Bring a large pan of lightly salted water to a rolling boil. Add the linguine and cook according to the packet instructions, or until *al dente*.

Meanwhile, melt the butter in a saucepan and cook the shredded spring onions/scallions gently for 2–3 minutes until soft. Stir in the sour cream and the lemon zest and remove from the heat.

Preheat a griddle/ridged grill pan or heavy-based frying pan until very hot. Add the salmon and sear for 1½–2 minutes on each side. Remove from the pan and allow to cool slightly.

Bring the sour cream sauce to the boil and stir in the Parmesan cheese and lemon juice. Drain the pasta thoroughly and return to the pan. Pour over the sauce and toss gently to coat. Spoon the pasta onto warmed serving plates and top with the salmon fillets. Serve immediately with dill sprigs and lemon slices.

Health Rating: 2 points

Vermicelli with Clams

Serves 4

Ingredients

900 g/2 lb fresh clams
2 tbsp olive oil
4 garlic cloves, peeled and chopped
1 small red chilli, deseeded and finely chopped
125 ml/4 fl oz/½ cup dry white wine
4 plum tomatoes, peeled and chopped
450 g/1 lb vermicelli or spaghetti, fresh or dried
1 tbsp freshly chopped parsley
freshly ground black pepper

Scrub the clams and discard any that are open. Place in salted water to cover, then drain when ready to cook.

Heat the oil in a large saucepan, add the garlic and chilli and fry for 2 minutes. Pour in the wine and cook for a further 2 minutes, then add the chopped tomatoes. Add the clams and cook, stirring frequently, for 3–5 minutes until the clams have opened.

Meanwhile, bring a large saucepan of water to a rolling boil. Add the pasta and cook until *al dente*: 4 minutes for fresh and 7–8 minutes for dried. Drain and return the pasta to the saucepan. Stir in the cooked clams with 4–6 tablespoons of the pasta cooking water. Discard any clams that are closed. Sprinkle with parsley and black pepper and serve.

Health Rating: 3 points

Tagliatelle with Tuna & Anchovy Tapenade

Serves 4

Ingredients

400 g/14 oz tagliatelle
125 g/4 oz canned tuna in oil, drained
50 g/2 oz canned anchovy fillets, drained
150 g/5 oz/1½ cup pitted black/ripe olives
2 tbsp capers in brine, drained
2 tsp lemon juice
100 ml/3½ fl oz/7 tbsp olive oil
2 tbsp freshly chopped parsley
freshly ground black pepper
flat-leaf parsley sprigs, to garnish

Bring a large pan of lightly salted water to a rolling boil. Add the tagliatelle and cook according to the packet instructions, or until *al dente*.

Meanwhile, place the tuna, anchovy fillets, olives and capers in a food processor with the lemon juice and 2 tablespoons of the olive oil and blend for a few seconds until roughly chopped. With the motor running, pour in the remaining olive oil in a steady stream; the resulting mixture should be slightly chunky rather than smooth.

Spoon the sauce into a bowl, stir in the chopped parsley and season to taste with black pepper. Check the taste of the sauce and add a little more lemon juice if required.

Drain the pasta thoroughly. Pour the sauce into the pan and cook over a low heat for 1–2 minutes to warm through.

Return the drained pasta to the pan and mix together with the sauce. Tip into a warmed serving bowl or spoon onto warmed individual plates. Garnish with sprigs of flat-leaf parsley and serve immediately.

Health Rating: 3 points

Pan–fried Scallops & Pasta

Serves 4

Ingredients

16 large scallops, shelled

1 tbsp olive oil

1 garlic clove, peeled and crushed

1 tsp freshly chopped thyme

400 g/14 oz/3½ cups penne

4 sun-dried tomatoes in oil, drained and thinly sliced thyme or
   oregano sprigs, to garnish

For the tomato dressing:

2 sun-dried tomatoes in oil, drained and chopped

1 tbsp red wine vinegar

2 tsp balsamic vinegar

1 tsp sun-dried tomato paste

1 tsp caster sugar

salt and freshly ground black pepper

2 tbsp oil from a jar of sun-dried tomatoes

2 tbsp olive oil

Rinse the scallops and pat dry on paper towels. Place in a bowl and add the olive oil, crushed garlic and thyme. Cover and chill in the refrigerator until ready to cook.

Bring a large pan of lightly salted water to a rolling boil. Add the penne and cook according to the packet instructions, or until *al dente*.

Meanwhile, make the dressing. Place the sun-dried tomatoes into a small bowl or glass jar and add the vinegars, tomato paste, sugar, salt and pepper. Whisk well, then pour into a food processor.

With the motor running, pour in the sun-dried tomato oil and olive oil in a steady stream to make a thick, smooth dressing.

Preheat a large, dry, cast-iron griddle pan/ridged grill pan over a high heat for about 5 minutes. Lower the heat to medium, then add the scallops to the pan. Cook for 1½ minutes on each side. Remove from the pan.

Drain the pasta thoroughly and return to the pan. Add the sliced sun-dried tomatoes and dressing and toss. Divide between individual serving plates, top each portion with 4 scallops, garnish with fresh thyme or oregano sprigs and serve immediately.

Health Rating: 3 points

Smoked Mackerel & Pasta Frittata

Serves 4

Ingredients

25 g/1 oz/¼ cup tricolore pasta spirals or shells

225 g/8 oz smoked mackerel (or salmon)

6 medium/large eggs; 3 tbsp milk

2 tsp wholegrain mustard; 2 tbsp freshly chopped parsley

salt and freshly ground black pepper

25 g/1 oz/2 tbsp unsalted butter

6 spring onions/scallions, trimmed and diagonally sliced

50 g/2 oz/⅓ cup thawed frozen peas

75 g/3 oz/¾ cup grated mature Cheddar cheese

To serve:

green salad

warm crusty bread

Preheat the grill/broiler to high just before cooking. Bring a pan of lightly salted water to a rolling boil. Add the pasta and cook according to the packet instructions, or until *al dente*. Drain thoroughly and reserve.

Remove the skin from the mackerel and break the fish into large flakes, discarding any bones, and reserve.

Place the eggs, milk, mustard and parsley in a bowl and whisk together. Season with just a little salt and plenty of freshly ground black pepper and reserve.

Melt the butter in a large, heavy-based frying pan. Cook the spring onions/scallions gently for 3–4 minutes until soft. Pour in the egg mixture, add the drained pasta, peas and half of the mackerel. Gently stir the mixture in the pan for 1–2 minutes until beginning to set. Stop stirring and cook for about 1 minute until the underside is golden brown. Scatter the remaining mackerel over the frittata, followed by the grated cheese. Place under the grill for about 1½ minutes until golden brown and set. Cut into wedges and serve immediately with salad and crusty bread.

Health Rating: 2 points

Crispy Cod Cannelloni

Serves 4

Ingredients

1 tbsp olive oil

8 dried cannelloni tubes

25 g/1 oz/2 tbsp unsalted butter

225 g/8 oz/2½ cups thinly sliced button/white mushrooms

175 g/6 oz/2 cups trimmed and finely chopped leeks

175 g/6 oz cod, skinned and diced

175 g/6 oz/1 cup cream cheese

salt and freshly ground black pepper

15 g/½ oz/2 tbsp grated Parmesan cheese

50 g/2 oz/1 cup fine, fresh white breadcrumbs

3 tbsp plain/all-purpose flour

1 medium/large egg, lightly beaten

oil for deep frying

fresh herbs or salad leaves, to serve

Add 1 teaspoon of the olive oil to a large pan of lightly salted water and bring to a rolling boil. Add the cannelloni tubes and cook, uncovered, for 5 minutes. Drain and leave in a bowl of cold water.

Melt the butter with the remaining oil in a saucepan. Add the mushrooms and leeks and cook gently for 5 minutes. Turn up the heat and cook for 1–2 minutes until the mixture is fairly dry. Add the cod and cook, stirring, for 2–3 minutes until the fish is opaque.

Add the cream cheese to the pan and stir until melted. Season to taste with salt and pepper, then leave the cod mixture to cool.

Drain the cannelloni. Using a decoratng bag without a nozzle/tip, or a spoon, fill the cannelloni with the cod mixture.

Mix the Parmesan cheese and breadcrumbs together on a plate. Dip the filled cannelloni into the flour, then into the beaten egg and finally into the breadcrumb mixture. Dip the ends twice to ensure they are thoroughly coated. Chill in the refrigerator for 30 minutes.

Heat the oil for deep frying to 180˚C/350˚F. Fry the stuffed cannelloni in batches for 2–3 minutes until the coating is crisp and golden brown. Drain on paper towels and serve immediately with fresh herbs or salad leaves.

Health Rating: 2 points

Spaghetti alle Vongole

Serves 4

Ingredients

1.8 kg/4 lb small, fresh clams
6 tbsp dry white wine
2 tbsp olive oil
1 small onion, peeled and finely chopped
2 garlic cloves, peeled and crushed
400 g/14 oz spaghetti
2 tbsp freshly chopped parsley
2 tbsp freshly chopped or torn basil
salt and freshly ground black pepper
oregano leaves, to garnish

Soak the clams in lightly salted, cold water 8 hours before required, changing the water once or twice. Scrub the clams and remove any that have broken shells or remain open when tapped.

Place clams in a large saucepan and pour in the wine. Cover with a tight-fitting lid and cook over a medium heat for 5–6 minutes, shaking the pan occasionally, until the shells have opened.

Strain the clams and cooking juices through a sieve lined with muslin and reserve. Discard clams that have remained unopened.

Heat the olive oil in a saucepan and fry the onion and garlic gently for 10 minutes, or until very soft.

Meanwhile, bring a large pan of lightly salted water to a rolling boil. Add the spaghetti and cook according to the packet instructions, or until *al dente*.

Add the cooked clams to the onions and garlic and pour in the reserved cooking juices. Bring to the boil, then add the parsley and basil and season to taste with salt and black pepper.

Drain the spaghetti thoroughly. Return to the pan and add the clams with their sauce. Toss together gently, then tip into a large, warmed serving bowl or into individual bowls. Serve immediately, sprinkled with oregano leaves.

Health Rating: 2 points

Seafood Parcels with Pappardelle & Coriander Pesto

Serves 4

Ingredients

300 g/11 oz pappardelle or tagliatelle

8 raw tiger prawns/jumbo shrimp, peeled

12 raw queen/bay scallops

225 g/8oz baby squid, cleaned and cut into rings

4 tbsp dry white wine

4 thin slices lemon

For the pesto:

50 g/2 oz/1 cup fresh coriander/cilantro leaves

1 garlic clove, peeled

25 g/1 oz/¼ cup toasted pine nuts

1 tsp lemon juice

5 tbsp olive oil

1 tbsp grated Parmesan cheese

salt and freshly ground black pepper

Preheat the oven to 180°C/350°F/Gas Mark 4, 10 minutes before cooking.

To make the pesto, blend the coriander/cilantro leaves, garlic, pine nuts and lemon juice with 1 tablespoon of the olive oil to a smooth paste in a food processor. With the motor running slowly, add the remaining oil. Stir the Parmesan cheese into the pesto and season to taste with salt and pepper.

Bring a pan of lightly salted water to a rolling boil. Add the pasta and cook for 3 minutes only. Drain thoroughly, return to the pan and spoon over two thirds of the pesto. Toss to coat.

Cut out four circles about 30 cm/12 inches in diameter from nonstick baking parchment. Spoon the pasta onto one half of each circle. Top each pile of pasta with 2 prawns/shrimp, 3 scallops and a few squid rings. Spoon 1 tablespoon of the wine over each serving, then drizzle with the remaining coriander pesto and top with a slice of lemon.

Close the parcels by folding over the other half of the paper to make a semicircle, then turn and twist the edges of the paper to secure.

Place the parcels on a baking tray/pan and bake in the preheated oven for 15 minutes, or until cooked. Serve immediately, allowing each person to open their own parcel.

Health Rating: 3 points

Pasta & Mussels in Tomato & Wine Sauce

Serves 4

Ingredients

900 g/2 lb fresh live mussels
1 bay leaf
150 ml/¼ pint/⅔ cup light red wine
15 g/½ oz/1 tbsp unsalted butter
1 tbsp olive oil
1 red onion, peeled and thinly sliced
2 garlic cloves, peeled and crushed
550 g/1 lb 3 oz/3 cups skinned, deseeded and chopped
    ripe tomatoes
400 g/14 oz/2½ cups fiochetti or penne
3 tbsp freshly chopped or torn basil
salt and freshly ground black pepper
basil leaves, to garnish
crusty bread, to serve

Scrub the mussels and remove any beards. Discard any that do not close when lightly tapped. Place in a large pan with the bay leaf and pour in the wine. Cover with a tight-fitting lid and steam, shaking the pan occasionally, for 3–4 minutes until the mussels open. Remove the mussels with a slotted spoon, discarding any that have not opened, and reserve. Strain the cooking liquid through a muslin-lined sieve and reserve.

Melt the butter with the oil in a large saucepan and gently cook the onion and garlic for 10 minutes until soft. Add the reserved cooking liquid and the tomatoes and simmer, uncovered, for 6–7 minutes until very soft and the sauce has reduced slightly.

Meanwhile, bring a large pan of lightly salted water to a rolling boil. Add the pasta and cook according to the packet instructions, or until al dente. Drain the pasta thoroughly and return to the pan. Add the mussels, removing the shells if you prefer, with the tomato sauce. Stir in the basil and season to taste with salt and pepper. Toss together gently. Tip into warmed serving bowls, garnish with basil leaves and serve with crusty bread.

Health Rating: 3 points

Pasta & Seafood Salad

Serves 4

Ingredients

300 g/11 oz pasta shapes, such as farfalle, penne or rigatoni

For the seafood:
75 g/3 oz fresh salmon fillet
75 g/3 oz squid, cleaned
1 tbsp olive oil
75 g/3 oz cooked, peeled prawns/shrimp, thawed if frozen
½ cucumber
50 g/2 oz smoked salmon, cut into small pieces
grated zest and juice ½ lemon
salt and freshly ground black pepper
6 spring onions/scallions, trimmed and diagonally sliced
2 tbsp freshly chopped dill
4–6 tbsp extra virgin olive oil

Bring a large saucepan of water to a rolling boil. Add the pasta and cook for 8–10 minutes until *al dente* or until tender but still firm to the bite, then drain and reserve. Discard the skin from the salmon and discard any fine bones. Cut into small pieces. Slice the squid into rings, then rinse and reserve.

Heat the olive oil in a frying pan, add the salmon and cook, stirring, for 3–5 minutes until just cooked. Remove and reserve. Add the squid to the oil remaining in the pan and cook for 2–3 minutes until just cooked. Drain and add to the salmon.

Check that the prawns/shrimp are thoroughly thawed and pat dry with absorbent paper towels. Peel the cucumber and cut in half lengthways. Remove the seeds and slice thinly.

Place the pasta into a large bowl and stir in all the fish with the cucumber, lemon zest, juice, salt and pepper, spring onions/scallions and chopped dill. Spoon into a serving bowl and sprinkle with the extra virgin olive oil just before serving.

Health Rating: 3 points

Salmon & Spaghetti in a Creamy Egg Sauce

Serves 4

Ingredients

3 eggs
1 tbsp freshly chopped parsley
1 tbsp freshly chopped dill
40 g/1½ oz/⅓ cup freshly grated Parmesan cheese
40 g/1½ oz/⅓ cup freshly grated pecorino cheese
2 tbsp dry white wine
freshly ground black pepper
400 g/14 oz spaghetti
350 g/12 oz salmon fillet, skinned
25 g/1 oz/2 tbsp butter
1 tsp olive oil
flat-leaf parsley sprigs, to garnish

Beat the eggs in a bowl with the parsley, dill, half of the Parmesan and pecorino cheeses and the white wine. Season to taste with freshly ground black pepper and reserve.

Bring a large pan of lightly salted water to a rolling boil. Add the spaghetti and cook according to the packet instructions, or until *al dente*.

Meanwhile, cut the salmon into bite-size pieces. Melt the butter in a large frying pan with the oil and cook the salmon pieces for 3–4 minutes until opaque.

Drain the spaghetti thoroughly, return to the pan and immediately add the egg mixture. Remove from the heat and toss well – the eggs will cook in the heat of the spaghetti to make a creamy sauce.

Stir in the remaining cheeses and the cooked pieces of salmon and toss again. Tip into a warmed serving bowl, or onto individual plates. Garnish with sprigs of flat-leaf parsley and serve immediately.

Health Rating: 2 points

Fettuccine with Sardines & Spinach

Serves 4

Ingredients

100 g/3½ oz canned sardines in olive oil

400 g/14 oz fettuccine or tagliarini

40 g/1½ oz/3 tbsp butter

2 tbsp olive oil

50 g/2 oz/1 cup one-day-old white breadcrumbs

1 garlic clove, peeled and finely chopped

50 g/2 oz/½ cup pine nuts

125 g/4 oz/1½ cups chestnut mushrooms, wiped and sliced

125 g/4 oz/1½ cups baby spinach leaves, rinsed

150 ml/¼ pint/⅔ cup crème fraîche/sour cream

finely grated zest of 1 lemon

salt and freshly ground black pepper

Health Rating: 3 points

Drain the sardines and cut in half lengthways. Remove the bones, then cut the fish into 2.5 cm/1 inch pieces and reserve.

Bring a large pan of lightly salted water to a rolling boil. Add the pasta and cook according to the packet instructions, or until *al dente*.

Melt half the butter with the olive oil in a large saucepan, add the breadcrumbs and fry, stirring, until they begin to turn crisp. Add the garlic and pine nuts and continue to cook until golden brown. Remove from the pan and reserve. Wipe the pan clean.

Melt the remaining butter in the pan, add the mushrooms and cook for 4–5 minutes until soft. Add the spinach and cook, stirring, for 1 minute, or until beginning to wilt. Stir in the crème fraîche/sour cream and lemon zest and bring to the boil. Simmer gently until the spinach is just cooked. Season the sauce to taste with salt and pepper.

Drain the pasta thoroughly and return to the pan. Add the spinach sauce and sardine pieces and gently toss together. Tip into a warmed serving dish. Sprinkle with the toasted breadcrumbs and pine nuts and serve immediately.

Fish Lasagne

Serves 4

Ingredients

75 g/3 oz/³/₄ cup mushrooms

1 tsp sunflower/corn oil

1 small onion, peeled and finely chopped

1 tbsp freshly chopped oregano

400 g/14 oz/2 cups canned chopped tomatoes

1 tbsp tomato purée/paste

salt and freshly ground black pepper

450 g/1 lb cod or haddock fillets, skinned

9–12 sheets precooked lasagne verde

For the topping:

1 egg, beaten

125 g/4 oz/¹/₂ cup cottage cheese

150 ml/¹/₄ pint/²/₃ cup natural/plain yogurt

50 g/2 oz/¹/₂ cup grated Cheddar cheese

To serve:

mixed salad leaves

cherry tomatoes

Preheat the oven to 190°C/375°F/Gas Mark 5. Wipe the mushrooms, trim the stalks and chop. Heat the oil in a large, heavy-based pan, add the onion and cook gently for 3–5 minutes until soft. Stir in the mushrooms, oregano and chopped tomatoes.

Blend the tomato purée/paste with 1 tablespoon water. Stir into the pan and season to taste with salt and pepper. Bring the sauce to the boil, then simmer, uncovered, for 5–10 minutes. Remove as many of the tiny pin bones as possible from the fish and cut into cubes. Add to the tomato sauce mixture and stir gently, then remove the pan from the heat.

Cover the base of an ovenproof dish with 2–3 sheets of the lasagne verde. Top with half of the fish mixture. Repeat the layers, finishing with the lasagne sheets.

For the topping, mix together the beaten egg, cottage cheese and yogurt. Pour over the lasagne and sprinkle with the cheddar.

Cook the lasagne in the preheated oven for 35–40 minutes until the topping is golden brown and bubbling. Serve the lasagne immediately with the mixed salad leaves and cherry tomatoes.

Health Rating: 3 points

Seafood Risotto

Serves 4

Ingredients

50 g/2 oz/4 tbsp butter

2 shallots, peeled and finely chopped

1 garlic clove, peeled and crushed

350 g/12 oz/2 cups Arborio/risotto rice

150 ml/¼ pint/⅔ cup white wine

600 ml/1 pint/2½ cups fish or vegetable stock, heated

125 g/4 oz/¾ cup large prawns/shrimp

275 g/10 oz canned baby clams

50 g/2 oz/½ cup smoked salmon trimmings

2 tbsp freshly chopped parsley

freshly grated Parmesan cheese

To serve:

green salad

crusty bread

Melt the butter in a large, heavy-based saucepan, add the shallots and garlic and cook for 2 minutes until slightly softened. Add the rice and cook for 1–2 minutes, stirring constantly, then pour in the wine and boil for 1 minute.

Pour in half the hot stock, bring to the boil, cover the saucepan and simmer gently for 15 minutes, adding the remaining stock a little at a time. Continue to simmer for 5 minutes, or until the rice is cooked and all the liquid is absorbed.

Meanwhile, prepare the fish by peeling the prawns/shrimp and removing the heads and tails. Remove the black vein from the back of each prawn, then wash and dry on absorbent paper towels. Drain the clams and discard the liquid. Cut the smoked salmon trimmings into thin strips.

When the rice is cooked, stir in the prawns, smoked salmon strips, clams and half the chopped parsley, then heat through for 1–2 minutes until everything is piping hot. Turn into a serving dish, sprinkle with the remaining parsley and the Parmesan cheese and serve immediately with a green salad and crusty bread.

Health Rating: 3 points

Sole Florentine

Serves 4

Ingredients

8 sole or small plaice fillets, skinned, or 450 g/1 lb

few fresh dill sprigs

125 g/4 oz peeled prawns/shrimp, thawed if frozen

freshly ground black pepper

350 g/12 oz fresh spinach, rinsed

3 medium tomatoes, sliced

25 g/1 oz/2 tbsp unsalted butter or margarine

25 g/1 oz/¼ cup plain/all-purpose flour

300 ml/½ pint/1¼ cups milk, warmed

1 tsp ready-made mustard

salt to taste

40 g/1½ oz/⅓ cup grated mature Cheddar cheese

boiled new potatoes, carrots and broccoli, to serve

Preheat the oven to 180 C/350 F/Gas Mark 4, 10 minutes before required. Lightly rinse the fish and pat dry with paper towels. Place the fillets skin-side down on a chopping board and place a couple of dill sprigs on top. Divide the peeled prawns/shrimp between the fillets and sprinkle with a little pepper. Fold the fish over to form small parcels. Reserve.

Remove any tough outer leaves or stems from the spinach and shake off any excess water. Place in the base of a 1.1 litre/2 pint ovenproof dish. Place the fish parcels on the spinach and arrange the tomato slices on top.

Melt the butter or margarine in a saucepan over a low heat and sprinkle in the flour. Stir frequently for 2 minutes, then remove the pan from the heat and gradually stir in the milk. Return to the heat and cook, stirring, until the mixture is thick enough to coat the back of a wooden spoon.

Stir in the mustard. Season to taste and then add half of the cheese. Stir until melted, then spoon over the fish. Sprinkle with the remaining cheese. Cook in the oven for 20–25 minutes until the top is golden brown and bubbling. Serve with freshly cooked new potatoes, carrots and broccoli.

Health Rating: 3 points

Meat

No Italian cookbook would be complete without favourite recipes such as Spaghetti & Meatballs. This section features many well-loved classic Italian recipes, such as Traditional Lasagne and Spaghetti Bolognese, hearty and familiar dishes that you, your family and your guests will love. It also includes a number of equally delicious but less-familiar recipes, such as Prosciutto & Gruyère Carbonara and Roasted Lamb with Rosemary & Garlic that will soon become new favourites.

Oven-roasted Vegetables with Sausages

Serves 4

Ingredients

2 medium aubergines/eggplants, trimmed

3 medium courgettes/zucchini, trimmed

4 tbsp olive oil

6 garlic cloves

8 Tuscany-style sausages

4 plum tomatoes

650 g/1 lb 7 oz canned cannellini beans

salt and freshly ground black pepper

1 bunch fresh basil, torn into coarse pieces

4 tbsp Parmesan cheese, grated

Health Rating: 3 points

Preheat the oven to 200°C/400°F/Gas Mark 6, 15 minutes before cooking. Cut the aubergines/eggplants and courgettes/zucchini into bite-size chunks. Place the olive oil in a large roasting tin/pan and heat in the preheated oven for 3 minutes, or until very hot. Add the aubergines, courgettes and garlic cloves, then stir until coated in the hot oil and cook in the oven for 10 minutes.

Remove the roasting tin from the oven and stir. Lightly prick the sausages, add to the roasting tin and return to the oven. Continue to roast for a further 20 minutes, turning once during cooking, until the vegetables are tender and the sausages are golden brown.

Meanwhile, roughly chop the plum tomatoes and drain the cannellini beans. Remove the sausages from the oven and stir in the tomatoes and cannellini beans. Season to taste with salt and pepper, then return to the oven for 5 minutes, or until heated thoroughly.

Scatter over the basil leaves and sprinkle with plenty of Parmesan cheese and extra freshly ground black pepper. Serve immediately.

Hot Salami & Vegetable Gratin

Serves 4

Ingredients

350 g/12 oz/2 cups carrots

175 g/6 oz/1½ cups fine green beans

250 g/9 oz/1½ cups asparagus tips

175 g/6 oz/1½ cups frozen peas

225 g/8 oz/2 cups Italian salami

1 tbsp olive oil

1 tbsp freshly chopped mint

25 g/1 oz/2 tbsp butter

150 g/5 oz/3 cups baby spinach leaves

150 ml/¼ pint/⅔ cup double/heavy cream

salt and freshly ground black pepper

1 small or ½ an olive ciabatta loaf

75 g/3 oz/¾ cup Parmesan cheese, grated

green salad, to serve

Preheat the oven to 200°C/400°F/Gas Mark 6. Peel and slice the carrots, trim the beans and asparagus and reserve. Cook the carrots in a saucepan of lightly salted, boiling water for 5 minutes. Add the remaining vegetables, except the spinach, and cook for a further 5 minutes, or until tender. Drain; place in an ovenproof dish.

Discard any skin from the outside of the salami if necessary, then chop roughly. Heat the oil in a frying pan and fry the salami for 4–5 minutes, stirring occasionally, until golden. Using a slotted spoon, transfer the salami to the ovenproof dish and scatter over the mint.

Add the butter to the frying pan and cook the spinach for 1–2 minutes until just wilted. Stir in the double/heavy cream and season well. Spoon the mixture over the vegetables.

Whizz the ciabatta loaf in a food processor to make breadcrumbs. Stir in the Parmesan cheese and sprinkle over the vegetables. Bake in the preheated oven for 20 minutes until golden and heated through. Serve with a green salad.

Health Rating: 2 points

Asparagus Risotto with Prosciutto

Serves 4

Ingredients

450 g/1 lb fresh asparagus spears
1.5 litres/2½ pints/6⅓ cups vegetable or chicken stock, kept warm on the hob
125 g/4 oz/1 cup shelled fresh peas, or use thawed frozen peas
3 tbsp olive oil
1 onion, peeled and chopped
2–4 garlic cloves, peeled and crushed
350 g/12 oz/scant 1¾ cups Arborio/risotto rice
salt and freshly ground black pepper
25 g/1 oz/2 tbsp butter
125 g/4 oz Parma ham/prosciutto, cut into strips
freshly grated Parmesan cheese, to serve

Trim the asparagus and shave the spears to remove any woody bits. Cut off the tips, then cut the stalks into 2–5 cm/¾–2 inch lengths. Cook the stalks in 300 ml/½ pint/1¼ cups of the stock for 10 minutes, or until tender. Strain and return the stock to the stock pan and keep warm on the hob. Cook the asparagus tips in gently simmering water for 3–4 minutes, drain and reserve. If using fresh shelled peas, cook in a separate pan for 5 minutes, drain and reserve separately from the asparagus tips.

Heat the oil in a large frying pan, add the onion and garlic and fry for 5 minutes. Add the rice and fry, stirring, until the rice is lightly coated in the oil. Add a ladleful of the stock and stir. When the stock is absorbed, add another ladleful and stir until it has been absorbed. Continue adding the stock at intervals and stir as before. When most has been added, stir in the asparagus stalks and peas with seasoning to taste. Continue cooking, adding more stock if necessary until the rice is creamy with just a slight bite to it.

Remove from the heat and stir in the butter. When that has been absorbed, stir in the Parma ham/prosciutto and asparagus tips. Cover with a clean dishtowel and leave for 10 minutes for the flavours to infuse. Serve with grated Parmesan cheese.

Health Rating: 3 points

Antipasto Penne

Serves 4

Ingredients

3 courgettes/zucchini, trimmed
4 plum tomatoes
175 g/6 oz/1½ cups Italian ham
2 tbsp olive oil
salt and freshly ground black pepper
350 g/12 oz/4½ cups dried penne
285 g/10 oz jar antipasto
125 g/4½ oz/1 cup mozzarella cheese, drained and diced
125 g/4½ oz/1 cup Gorgonzola cheese, crumbled
3 tbsp freshly chopped flat-leaf parsley

Preheat the grill/broiler just before cooking. Cut the courgettes/zucchini into thick slices. Wash the tomatoes and cut into quarters. Cut the ham into strips. Pour the oil into a baking dish and place under the grill for 2 minutes, or until almost smoking. Remove from the grill and stir in the courgettes. Return to the grill and cook for 8 minutes, stirring occasionally. Remove from the grill, add the tomatoes and cook for a further 3 minutes.

Add the ham to the baking dish and cook under the grill for 4 minutes, or until all the vegetables are charred and the ham is brown. Season to taste with salt and pepper.

Plunge the pasta into a large saucepan of lightly salted boiling water and return to a rolling boil. Stir and cook for 8 minutes, or until *al dente*. Drain well and return to the saucepan.

Stir the antipasto into the vegetables. Cook under the grill for 2 minutes, or until heated through. Add the cooked pasta and toss together gently with the remaining ingredients. Grill for a further 4 minutes, then serve immediately.

Health Rating: 2 points

Italian Risotto

Serves 4

Ingredients

1 onion, peeled
2 garlic cloves, peeled
1 tbsp olive oil
125 g/4 oz/2 cups chopped Italian salami or speck
125 g/4 oz/½ cup asparagus tips
350 g/12 oz/1¼ cups Arborio/risotto rice
300 ml/½ pint/1¼ cups dry white wine
1 litre/1¾ pints/4 cups chicken stock, warmed
125 g/4 oz/¾ cup thawed frozen broad/fava beans
125 g/4 oz/1 cup diced Dolcelatte cheese
3 tbsp freshly chopped mixed herbs, such as parsley and basil
salt and freshly ground black pepper

Health Rating: 3 points

Chop the onion and garlic and reserve. Heat the olive oil in a large frying pan and cook the salami for 3–5 minutes until golden. Using a slotted spoon, transfer to a plate and keep warm. Add the asparagus and stir–fry for 2–3 minutes, until just wilted. Transfer to the plate with the salami. Add the onion and garlic to the pan and cook for 5 minutes, or until softened.

Add the rice to the pan and cook for about 2 minutes. Add the wine, bring to the boil, then simmer, stirring, until the wine has been absorbed. Add half the stock and return to the boil. Simmer, stirring, until the liquid has been absorbed.

Add half of the remaining stock and the broad/fava beans to the rice mixture. Bring to the boil, then simmer for a further 5–10 minutes until all of the liquid has been absorbed.

Add the remaining stock, bring to the boil, then simmer until all the liquid is absorbed and the rice is tender. Stir in the remaining ingredients until the cheese has just melted. Serve immediately.

Oven-baked Pork Balls with Peppers

Serves 4

Ingredients

For the garlic bread:
2–4 garlic cloves, peeled
50 g/2 oz/4 tbsp butter, softened
1 tbsp freshly chopped parsley
2–3 tsp lemon juice
1 focaccia loaf

For the pork balls:
450 g/1 lb fresh minced/ground pork
4 tbsp freshly chopped basil
2 garlic cloves, peeled and chopped
3 sun-dried tomatoes, chopped
salt and freshly ground black pepper
3 tbsp olive oil
1 medium red pepper, deseeded and cut into chunks
1 medium green pepper, deseeded and cut into chunks
1 medium yellow pepper, deseeded and cut into chunks
225 g/8 oz/2 cups cherry tomatoes
2 tbsp balsamic vinegar

Preheat the oven to 200°C/400°F/Gas Mark 6, 15 minutes before cooking. Crush the garlic, then blend with the softened butter, the parsley and enough lemon juice to give a soft consistency. Shape into a roll, wrap in baking parchment and chill for at least 30 minutes.

Mix together the pork, basil, 1 chopped garlic clove, sun-dried tomatoes and seasoning until well combined. With damp hands, divide the mixture into 16, roll into balls and reserve.

Spoon the olive oil into a large roasting tin/pan and place in the preheated oven for about 3 minutes until very hot. Remove from the heat and stir in the pork balls, the remaining chopped garlic and the peppers. Bake for about 15 minutes. Remove from the oven and stir in the cherry tomatoes and season to taste with plenty of salt and pepper. Bake again for about 20 minutes.

Just before the pork balls are ready, slice the bread, toast lightly and spread with the prepared garlic butter. Remove the pork balls from the oven, stir in the vinegar and serve immediately with the garlic bread.

Health Rating: 3 points

Calzone with Mushroom, Peppers & Smoked Bacon

Serves 4

Ingredients

1 basic quantity pizza dough (*see* page 282)
plain/all-purpose flour, for dusting

For the filling:
2 tbsp olive oil
1 medium red onion, peeled and thinly sliced
225 g/8 oz smoked bacon, trimmed and sliced
1 large red pepper, deseeded and thinly sliced
1 large yellow pepper, deseeded and thinly sliced
225 g/8 oz mixed mushrooms such as field, chestnut/cremini
    and button/white, wiped and sliced
1 tbsp freshly chopped oregano
salt and freshly ground black pepper

Preheat the oven to 230°C/450°F/Gas Mark 8, 15 minutes before cooking and place a pizza stone or large baking sheet in the oven 5 minutes before cooking. Divide the dough into four pieces, then wrap in plastic wrap while preparing the filling.

Heat the oil in a frying pan, add the onion and bacon and cook, stirring, for 5 minutes, or until the onion has softened and the bacon is lightly cooked. Add the peppers and mushrooms and continue to fry for a further 5 minutes, or until the peppers have softened slightly. Add the chopped oregano with seasoning. Remove from the heat and leave to cool.

Unwrap one piece of the dough and roll out on a lightly floured surface to form a 20.5 cm/8 inch round. Divide the filling into four portions, then place one portion on half the rolled out dough, about 1 cm/½ inch from the edge. Brush lightly with water and fold over to encase the filling completely. Pinch the edges firmly together. Repeat with the remaining dough and filling. Place the calzones on the baking stone or baking sheet and bake in the oven for 20–25 minutes until golden brown. Serve warm.

Health Rating: 2 points

Pan–fried Beef with Creamy Mushrooms

Serves 4

Ingredients

2 tbsp olive oil
225 g/8 oz/1 cup peeled and halved shallots
2 garlic cloves, peeled and chopped
4 beef medallions
4 plum tomatoes, cut into eighths
125 g/4 oz/1¾ cups sliced flat mushrooms
3 tbsp brandy
150 ml/¼ pint/⅔ cup red wine
salt and freshly ground black pepper
4 tbsp double/heavy cream

To serve:
baby new potatoes
French/green beans

Heat the oil in a large frying pan and cook the shallots for about 8 minutes, stirring occasionally, until almost softened. Add the garlic and beef and cook for 8–10 minutes, turning once during cooking, until the meat is browned all over. Using a slotted spoon, transfer the beef to a plate. Keep warm.

Add the tomatoes and mushrooms to the pan and cook for 5 minutes, stirring frequently, until the mushrooms have softened.

Pour in the brandy and heat through. Draw the pan off the heat and carefully ignite. Allow the flames to subside. Pour in the wine, return to the heat and bring to the boil. Boil until reduced by one third. Draw the pan off the heat, season to taste with salt and pepper, add the cream and stir.

Arrange the beef on serving plates and spoon over the sauce. Serve with baby new potatoes and a few French/green beans.

Health Rating: 2 points

Pork Chop Hotpot

Serves 4

Ingredients

4 pork chops
flour, for dusting
8–12 shallots, peeled
2 garlic cloves, peeled
50 g/2 oz (about 20) sun-dried tomatoes
2 tbsp olive oil
400 g/14 oz/2 cups canned plum tomatoes
150 ml/¼ pint/⅔ cup red wine
150 ml/¼ pint/⅔ cup chicken stock
3 tbsp tomato purée/paste
2 tbsp freshly chopped oregano
salt and freshly ground black pepper
fresh oregano leaves, to garnish

To serve:
freshly cooked new potatoes
French/green beans

Preheat the oven to 190°C/375°F/Gas Mark 5, 10 minutes before cooking. Trim the pork chops, removing any excess fat, wipe with a clean, damp cloth, then dust with a little flour and reserve.

Cut the shallots in half if large. Chop the garlic and slice the sun-dried tomatoes.

Heat the olive oil in a large casserole dish and cook the pork chops for about 5 minutes, turning occasionally during cooking, until browned all over. Using a slotted spoon, carefully lift out of the dish and reserve. Add the shallots and cook for 5 minutes, stirring occasionally.

Return the pork chops to the casserole dish and scatter with the garlic and sun-dried tomatoes, then pour over the can of tomatoes.

Blend the red wine, stock and tomato purée/paste together and add the chopped oregano. Season to taste with salt and pepper, then pour over the pork chops and bring to a

gentle boil. Cover with a close-fitting lid and cook in the preheated oven for 1 hour, or until the pork chops are tender. Adjust the seasoning to taste, then scatter with a few oregano leaves and serve immediately with freshly cooked potatoes and French/green beans.

Health Rating: 3 points

Rabbit Italian

Serves 4

Ingredients

450 g/1 lb diced rabbit, thawed if frozen

6 rashers/slices streaky/fatty bacon

1 garlic clove, peeled

1 onion, peeled

1 carrot, peeled

1 celery stalk

25 g/1 oz/2 tbsp butter

2 tbsp olive oil

400 g/14 oz/2 cups canned chopped tomatoes

150 ml/¼ pint/⅔ cup red wine

salt and freshly ground black pepper

125 g/4 oz/1¾ cups mushrooms

To serve:

freshly cooked pasta

green salad

Trim the rabbit if necessary. Chop the bacon and reserve. Chop the garlic and onion and slice the carrot thinly, then trim the celery and chop.

Heat the butter and 1 tablespoon of the oil in a large saucepan and brown the rabbit for 5 minutes, stirring frequently, until sealed all over. Transfer the rabbit to a plate and reserve.

Add the garlic, bacon, celery, carrot and onion to the saucepan and cook for a further 5 minutes, stirring occasionally, until softened, then return the rabbit to the saucepan and pour over the tomatoes with their juice and the wine. Season to taste with salt and pepper. Bring to the boil, cover, reduce the heat and simmer for 45 minutes.

Meanwhile, wipe the mushrooms and, if large, cut in half. Heat the remaining oil in a small frying pan and sauté the mushrooms for 2 minutes. Drain, then add to the rabbit and cook for 15 minutes, or until the rabbit is tender. Season to taste and serve immediately with freshly cooked pasta and a green salad.

Health Rating: 3 points

Calzone with Meat & Peppers

Serves 4

Ingredients

1 basic quantity pizza dough (*see* page 282)

For the filling:
2 tbsp olive oil
4 shallots, peeled and thinly sliced
2 garlic cloves, peeled and sliced
1 red pepper, deseeded and thinly sliced
1 yellow pepper, deseeded and thinly sliced
125 g/4 oz cherry tomatoes
salt and freshly ground black pepper
175 g/6 oz assorted sliced meat, such as salami, prosciutto
   and speck

Divide the dough into four pieces, then wrap in plastic wrap while preparing the filling. Preheat the oven to 230°C/450°F/Gas Mark 8, 15 minutes before cooking and place a pizza stone or large baking sheet in the oven 5 minutes before cooking.

Heat the oil in a frying pan and add the shallots and garlic and cook, stirring, for 5 minutes or until the shallots have softened. Add the peppers and continue to fry for a further 5 minutes, or until the peppers have softened slightly. Add the tomatoes with seasoning and cook for a further 3 minutes, or until the tomatoes are beginning to soften. Remove from the heat and cool.

Unwrap one piece of the dough and roll out on a lightly floured surface to form a 20.5 cm/8 inch round. Place a quarter of the meat on one side of the dough and top with a quarter of the pepper and tomato mixture. Brush the edges lightly with water and fold over to encase the filling completely. Pinch the edges firmly together.

Repeat with the remaining dough and filling. Place on the hot baking stone or baking sheet. Cook for 20–25 minutes until golden brown. Serve warm.

Health Rating: 3 points

Roasted Lamb with Rosemary & Garlic

Serves 4

Ingredients

1.6 kg/3½ lb leg of lamb
8 garlic cloves, peeled
few fresh rosemary sprigs
salt and freshly ground black pepper
4 slices pancetta
4 tbsp olive oil
4 tbsp red wine vinegar
6 potatoes, peeled and cut into large dice
1 large onion, peeled and cut into wedges
fresh rosemary sprigs, to garnish
freshly cooked ratatouille, to serve

Preheat the oven to 200°C/400°F/Gas Mark 6, 15 minutes before roasting. Wipe the leg of lamb with a clean, damp cloth, then place the lamb in a large roasting tin/pan. With a sharp knife, make small, deep incisions into the meat. Cut 2–3 garlic cloves into small slivers, then insert with a few small sprigs of rosemary into the lamb. Season to taste with salt and pepper and cover the lamb with the slices of pancetta.

Drizzle over 1 tablespoon of the olive oil and lay a few more rosemary sprigs across the lamb. Roast in the preheated oven for 30 minutes, then pour over the vinegar.

Arrange the potatoes, onion and remaining garlic around the lamb. Pour the remaining olive oil over the potatoes, then reduce the oven temperature to 180°C/350°F/Gas Mark 4 and roast for a further 1 hour, or until the lamb is tender. Garnish with fresh rosemary sprigs and serve immediately with the roast potatoes and ratatouille.

Health Rating: 2 points

Braised Lamb with Broad Beans

Serves 4

Ingredients

700 g/1½ lb lamb, cut into large chunks

1 tbsp plain/all-purpose flour

1 onion

2 garlic cloves

1 tbsp olive oil

400 g/14 oz/2 cups canned chopped tomatoes with basil

300 ml/½ pint/1¼ cups lamb stock

2 tbsp freshly chopped thyme

2 tbsp freshly chopped oregano

salt and freshly ground black pepper

150 g/5 oz/1 cup frozen broad/fava beans

fresh oregano, to garnish

creamy mashed potatoes, to serve

Trim the lamb, discarding any fat or gristle, then place the flour in a plastic bag, add the lamb and toss until coated thoroughly. Peel and slice the onion and garlic and reserve.

Heat the olive oil in a heavy-based saucepan and, when hot, add the lamb and cook, stirring, until the meat is sealed and browned all over. Using a slotted spoon, transfer the lamb to a plate and reserve.

Add the onion and garlic to the saucepan and cook for 3 minutes, stirring frequently, until softened, then return the lamb to the saucepan.

Add the chopped tomatoes with their juice, the stock, the chopped thyme and oregano to the pan and season to taste with salt and pepper. Bring to the boil, then cover with a close-fitting lid, reduce the heat and simmer for 1 hour.

Add the broad/fava beans to the lamb and simmer for 20–30 minutes until the lamb is tender. Garnish with fresh oregano and serve with creamy mashed potatoes.

Health Rating: 3 points

Lasagne

Serves 4

Ingredients

75 g/3 oz/6 tbsp butter

4 tbsp plain/all-purpose flour

750 ml/1¼ pints/3 cups milk

1 tsp wholegrain mustard

salt and freshly ground black pepper

¼ tsp freshly grated nutmeg

9 sheets lasagne

1 quantity of prepared Bolognese sauce (see page 150)

75g/3oz/¾ cup freshly grated Parmesan cheese

freshly chopped parsley, to garnish

garlic bread, to serve

Preheat the oven to 200°C/400°F/Gas Mark 6, 15 minutes before cooking. To make the white sauce, melt the butter in a small heavy-based pan, add the flour and cook gently, stirring, for 2 minutes. Remove from the heat and gradually stir in the milk. Return to the heat and cook, stirring, for 2 minutes, or until the sauce thickens. Bring to the boil, remove from the heat and stir in the mustard. Season to taste with salt, pepper and nutmeg.

Butter a rectangular ovenproof dish and spread a thin layer of the white sauce over the base. Cover completely with 3 sheets of lasagne.

Spoon a quarter of the prepared Bolognese sauce over the lasagne. Spoon over a quarter of the remaining white sauce, then sprinkle with a quarter of the grated Parmesan cheese. Repeat the layers, finishing with Parmesan cheese.

Bake in the preheated oven for 30 minutes, or until golden-brown. Garnish with chopped parsley and serve immediately with warm garlic bread.

Health Rating: 2 points

Lamb Fillet with Artichokes & Capers

Serves 4

Ingredients

25 g/1 oz capers
4 globe artichokes
1 lemon slice, if using fresh artichokes
450 g/1 lb neck of lamb fillet
2 tbsp olive oil
1 medium onion, peeled and chopped
2 plump garlic cloves, peeled and chopped
1 small red chilli, deseeded and chopped
50 g/2 oz pancetta, chopped
300 ml/½ pint/1¼ cups lamb or chicken stock
3 spring onions/scallions, trimmed and chopped
salt and freshly ground black pepper

Soak the capers in enough cold water to cover for 10 minutes to remove the salt. Drain when ready to use.

Prepare the artichokes as described on page 228 and cover with cold water. Add a slice of lemon, if using.

Trim the lamb fillet, discarding any excess fat, then cut into small pieces and reserve.

Heat the oil in a frying pan, add the onion and garlic and fry for 5 minutes, or until beginning to soften. Add the chilli and pancetta and cook for a further 2 minutes. Remove the onion mixture with a slotted spoon and reserve. Add the lamb to the frying pan and fry, stirring frequently, until browned, then return the onion mixture to the pan with the stock. Bring to the boil, then reduce the heat to a simmer and cook for 15–20 minutes until the lamb is almost tender.

Drain the capers and add to the pan with the prepared artichoke hearts. Continue to cook for a further 5 minutes, or until the lamb is tender. Add the chopped spring onions/scallions and seasoning to taste, then serve.

Health Rating: 2 points

Meatballs with Olives

Serves 4

Ingredients

250 g/9 oz/1 cup peeled shallots
2–3 garlic cloves, peeled
450 g/1 lb minced/ground beef
2 tbsp fresh white or wholemeal breadcrumbs
3 tbsp freshly chopped basil
salt and freshly ground black pepper
2 tbsp olive oil
5 tbsp ready-made pesto
5 tbsp mascarpone cheese
50 g/2 oz/5 tbsp pitted and halved black/ripe olives
275 g/10 oz/3¼ cups thick pasta noodles
freshly chopped flat-leaf parsley
fresh flat-leaf parsley sprigs, to garnish
freshly grated Parmesan cheese, to serve

Chop 2 of the shallots finely and place in a bowl with the garlic, beef, breadcrumbs, basil and seasoning to taste. With damp hands, bring the mixture together and shape into small balls about the size of an apricot. Heat the olive oil in a frying pan and cook the meatballs for 8–10 minutes, turning occasionally, until browned and the beef is tender. Remove and drain on absorbent paper towels.

Slice the remaining shallots, add to the pan and cook for 5 minutes until softened. Blend the pesto and mascarpone together, then stir into the pan with the olives. Bring to the boil, reduce the heat and return the meatballs to the pan. Simmer for 5–8 minutes until the sauce has thickened and the meatballs are cooked thoroughly.

Meanwhile, bring a large saucepan of lightly salted water to the boil and cook the noodles for 8–10 minutes, or until *al dente*. Drain the noodles, reserving 2 tablespoons of the cooking liquor. Return the noodles to the pan with the cooking liquor and pour in the sauce. Stir the noodles, then sprinkle with chopped parsley. Garnish with a few sprigs of parsley and serve immediately with grated Parmesan cheese.

Health Rating: 2 points

Fillet Steaks with Tomato & Garlic Sauce

Serves 4

Ingredients

700 g/1½ lb ripe tomatoes
2 garlic cloves
2 tbsp olive oil
2 tbsp freshly chopped basil
2 tbsp freshly chopped oregano
2 tbsp red wine
salt and freshly ground black pepper
75 g/3 oz/½ cup pitted and chopped black/ripe olives
4 fillet steaks, about 175 g/6 oz each
freshly cooked vegetables, to serve

Health Rating: 3 points

Make a small cross on the top of each tomato and place in a large bowl. Cover with boiling water and leave for 2 minutes. Using a slotted spoon, remove the tomatoes and skin carefully. Repeat until all the tomatoes are skinned. Place on a chopping board, cut into quarters, remove the seeds and roughly chop, then reserve.

Peel and chop the garlic. Heat half the olive oil in a saucepan and cook the garlic for 30 seconds. Add the chopped tomatoes with the basil, oregano and red wine and season to taste with salt and pepper. Bring to the boil, then reduce the heat, cover and simmer for 15 minutes, stirring occasionally, or until the sauce is reduced and thickened. Stir the olives into the sauce and keep warm while cooking the steaks.

Meanwhile, lightly oil a griddle pan/ridged grill pan or heavy-based frying pan with the remaining olive oil and cook the steaks for 2 minutes on each side to seal. Continue to cook the steaks for a further 2–4 minutes, depending on personal preference. Serve the steaks immediately with the garlic sauce and freshly cooked vegetables.

Veal Escalopes with Marsala Sauce

Serves 6

Ingredients

6 veal escalopes, about 125 g/4 oz each

lemon juice, for sprinkling

salt and freshly ground black pepper

6 sage leaves

6 slices prosciutto

2 tbsp olive oil

25 g/1 oz/2 tbsp butter

1 onion, peeled and sliced

1 garlic clove, peeled and chopped

2 tbsp Marsala wine

4 tbsp double/heavy cream

2 tbsp freshly chopped parsley

selection of freshly cooked vegetables, to serve

Place the veal escalopes between sheets of non-pvc plastic wrap and, using a mallet or rolling pin, pound lightly to flatten out to about 5 mm/¼ inch thickness. Remove the plastic wrap and sprinkle the veal escalopes with lemon juice, salt and black pepper.

Place a sage leaf in the centre of each escalope. Top with a slice of prosciutto, making sure it fits, then roll up the escalopes enclosing the prosciutto and sage leaves. Secure with a cocktail stick/toothpick.

Heat the olive oil and butter in a large, nonstick frying pan and fry the onion for 5 minutes, or until softened. Add the garlic and rolled escalopes and cook for about 8 minutes, turning occasionally, until the escalopes are browned all over.

Add the Marsala wine and cream to the pan and bring to the boil, cover and simmer for 10 minutes, or until the veal is tender. Season to taste, then sprinkle with the parsley. Discard the cocktail sticks and serve immediately with a selection of freshly cooked vegetables.

Health Rating: 2 points

Kidneys in Garlic, Wine & Oregano

Serves 4

Ingredients

450 g/1 lb lambs' kidneys
2 tbsp plain/all-purpose flour
2 tbsp olive oil
1 medium onion, peeled and chopped
4 garlic cloves, peeled and crushed
300 ml/$\frac{1}{2}$ pint/1$\frac{1}{4}$ cups red wine or lamb stock
3 medium tomatoes, chopped
2 tbsp fresh oregano leaves
salt and freshly ground black pepper

Remove and discard the transparent membrane from the kidneys and cut in half. Discard the tubes, then rinse and pat dry with absorbent paper towels. Toss in the flour and reserve both the kidneys and flour.

Heat the oil in a frying pan, add the onion and garlic and fry for 5 minutes. Add the kidneys and fry until sealed, then sprinkle in the reserved flour. Cook for 2 minutes, stirring, before pouring in the wine or stock. Bring to the boil and let it bubble for 2–3 minutes.

Add the tomatoes with the oregano and seasoning to taste. Reduce the heat to a simmer and cook for 6–8 minutes until the kidneys are tender. Check the seasoning and serve.

Health Rating: 3 points

Cannelloni

Serves 4

Ingredients

2 tbsp olive oil
175 g/6 oz/$\frac{3}{4}$ cup fresh minced/ground pork
75 g/3 oz/$\frac{2}{3}$ cup chopped chicken livers
1 small onion, peeled and chopped
1 garlic clove, peeled and chopped
175 g/6 oz/1 cup thawed and chopped frozen spinach
1 tbsp freeze-dried oregano
pinch freshly grated nutmeg
salt and freshly ground black pepper
175 g/6 oz/$\frac{3}{4}$ cup ricotta or quark cheese
25 g/1 oz/2 tbsp butter
25 g/1 oz/$\frac{1}{4}$ cup plain/all-purpose flour
600 ml/1 pint/2$\frac{1}{2}$ cups milk
600 ml/1 pint/2$\frac{1}{2}$ cups ready-made tomato sauce
16 precooked cannelloni tubes
50 g/2 oz/$\frac{1}{2}$ cup grated Parmesan cheese
green salad, to serve

Preheat the oven to 190°C/375°F/Gas Mark 5, 10 minutes before cooking. Heat the olive oil in a frying pan and cook the mince and livers for about 5 minutes, stirring occasionally, until browned all over. Add the onion and garlic and cook for 4 minutes until softened. Add the spinach, oregano and nutmeg and season to taste. Cook until all the liquid has evaporated, then remove the pan from the heat and allow to cool. Stir in the ricotta or quark cheese. Melt the butter in a saucepan and stir in the flour to form a roux. Cook for 2 minutes, stirring occasionally. Remove from the heat and blend in the milk until smooth. Return to the heat and bring to the boil, stirring, until the sauce has thickened. Reserve.

Spoon a thin layer of the tomato sauce on the base of a large, ovenproof dish. Divide the pork filling between the cannelloni tubes. Arrange on top of the tomato sauce. Spoon over the remaining tomato sauce. Pour over the white sauce and sprinkle with the Parmesan. Bake in the oven for 30–35 minutes until the cannelloni is tender and the top is golden brown. Serve immediately with a green salad.

Health Rating: 2 points

Vitello Tonnato (Veal in Tuna Sauce)

Serves 6–8

Ingredients

900 g/2 lb boned, rolled leg or loin of veal

300 ml/$\frac{1}{2}$ pint/1$\frac{1}{4}$ cups dry white wine

1 onion, peeled and chopped

1 carrot, peeled and chopped

2 celery stalks, trimmed and chopped

1 bay leaf

2 garlic cloves

few parsley sprigs

salt and freshly ground black pepper

200 g/7 oz canned tuna in oil

2 tbsp capers, drained

6 anchovy fillets

200 ml/7 fl oz/$\frac{3}{4}$ cup mayonnaise

juice of $\frac{1}{2}$ lemon

To garnish:
lemon wedges
capers
black olives

To serve:
fresh green salad leaves
tomato wedges

Place the veal in a large bowl and pour over the wine. Add the onion, carrot, celery, bay leaf, garlic cloves, parsley, salt and pepper. Cover tightly and chill overnight in the refrigerator. Transfer the contents of the bowl to a large saucepan, adding just enough water to cover the meat. Bring to the boil, cover and simmer for 1–1$\frac{1}{4}$ hours until the veal is tender.

Remove from the heat and allow the veal to cool in the juices. Using a slotted spoon, transfer the veal to a plate, pat dry with paper towels and reserve.

Place the tuna, capers, anchovy fillets, mayonnaise and lemon juice in a food processor or liquidiser and blend until smooth, adding a few spoonfuls of the pan juices, if necessary, to make the sauce of a coating consistency. Season to taste with salt and pepper.

Using a sharp knife, slice the veal thinly and arrange on a large serving platter. Spoon the sauce over the veal. Cover with plastic wrap and chill in the refrigerator overnight. Garnish with lemon wedges, capers and olives. Serve with salad and tomato wedges.

Health Rating: 3 points

Italian Beef Pot Roast

Serves 6

Ingredients

1.8 kg/4 lb brisket of beef

225 g/8 oz small onions, peeled

3 garlic cloves, peeled and chopped

2 celery stalks, trimmed and chopped

2 carrots, peeled and sliced

450 g/1 lb ripe tomatoes

300 ml/½ pint/1¼ cups Italian red wine

2 tbsp olive oil

300 ml/½ pint/1¼ cups beef stock

1 tbsp tomato purée/paste

2 tsp freeze-dried mixed herbs

salt and freshly ground black pepper

25 g/1 oz/2 tbsp butter

3 tbsp plain/all-purpose flour

freshly cooked vegetables, to serve

Preheat the oven to 150°C/300°F/Gas Mark 2, 10 minutes before cooking. Place the beef in a bowl. Add the onions, garlic, celery and carrots.

Make a small cross on the top of each tomato. Pace in a bowl and cover with boiling water. Allow to stand for 2 minutes and drain. Peel away the skins, discard the seeds and chop, then add to the beef mixture along with the red wine. Cover tightly and marinate in the refrigerator overnight.

Lift the marinated beef from the bowl and pat dry with absorbent paper towels. Heat the olive oil in a large casserole dish and cook the beef until it is browned all over, then remove from the dish.

Drain the vegetables from the marinade, reserving the marinade. Add the vegetables to the casserole dish and fry gently for 5 minutes, stirring occasionally, until all the vegetables are browned.

Return the beef to the casserole dish with the marinade, beef stock, tomato purée/paste and mixed herbs and season with salt and pepper. Bring to the boil, then cover and cook in the preheated oven for 3 hours.

Using a slotted spoon, transfer the beef and any large vegetables to a plate and leave in a warm place. Blend the butter and flour to form a paste. Bring the casserole juices to the boil, then gradually stir in small spoonfuls of the paste. Cook until thickened. Serve with the sauce and a selection of vegetables.

Health Rating: 3 points

Lamb Shanks with Tomatoes & Olives

Serves 4

Ingredients

4 small lamb shanks
2 tbsp olive oil
1 medium onion, peeled and chopped
3–4 garlic cloves, peeled and chopped
1/2 small celeriac, peeled and chopped
1–2 tbsp tomato purée/paste
300 ml/1/2 pint/1 1/4 cups lamb or chicken stock
150 ml/1/4 pint/2/3 cup red wine
300 g/11 oz/1 2/3 cups chopped plum tomatoes
2 fresh bay leaves
50 g/2 oz/generous 1/4 cup pitted olives
salt and freshly ground black pepper

To serve:
few fresh oregano sprigs
1 tbsp freshly chopped parsley
freshly cooked vegetables

Preheat the oven to 160°C/325°F/Gas Mark 3, 10 minutes before cooking. Wipe or rinse the lamb shanks and pat dry with absorbent paper towels. Heat 1 tablespoon of the oil in a frying pan and fry the shanks until sealed all over. Place in a large casserole dish.

Add the remaining oil to the frying pan and fry the onion, garlic and celeriac for 5–8 minutes until softened. Blend the tomato purée/paste with the stock and red wine and pour into the frying pan. Add the chopped tomatoes with the bay leaves and bring to the boil. Pour over the lamb shanks. Cover with the lid and cook in the preheated oven for 2 hours.

Discard the bay leaves and then stir in the olives and seasoning to taste. Continue to cook for a further 30 minutes, or until the lamb shanks are really tender. Serve sprinkled with the fresh herbs and freshly cooked vegetables.

Health Rating: 3 points

Spaghetti Bolognese

Serves 4

Ingredients

3 tbsp olive oil
50 g/2 oz/1/4 cup chopped unsmoked streaky/fatty bacon, rind removed
1 small onion, peeled and finely chopped
1 carrot, peeled and chopped
1 celery stalk, trimmed and chopped
2 garlic cloves, peeled and crushed
1 bay leaf
500 g/1 lb 1 oz minced/ground beef
400 g/14 oz/2 cups canned chopped tomatoes
2 tbsp tomato purée/paste
150 ml/1/4 pint/2/3 cup red wine
150 ml/1/4 pint/2/3 cup beef stock
salt and freshly ground black pepper
450 g/1 lb spaghetti
freshly grated Parmesan cheese, to serve

Heat the olive oil in a large heavy-based pan, add the bacon and cook for 5 minutes, or until slightly coloured. Add the onion, carrot, celery, garlic and bay leaf and cook, stirring, for 8 minutes, or until the vegetables are soft.

Add the minced/ground beef to the pan and cook, stirring with a wooden spoon to break up any lumps, for 5–8 minutes until browned.

Stir the tomatoes and tomato purée/paste into the beef and pour in the wine and stock. Bring to the boil, then lower the heat and simmer for at least 40 minutes, stirring occasionally. The longer you cook the sauce, the more intense the flavour will be. Season to taste with salt and pepper and remove the bay leaf.

Meanwhile, bring a large pan of lightly salted water to a rolling boil, add the spaghetti and cook for about 8 minutes, or until *al dente*. Drain and arrange on warmed serving plates. Top with the prepared Bolognese sauce and serve immediately, sprinkled with grated Parmesan cheese.

Health Rating: 2 points

Italian Calf Liver

Serves 4

Ingredients

450 g/1 lb calf liver, trimmed
1 onion, peeled and sliced
2 fresh bay leaves, coarsely torn
fresh parsley sprigs
fresh sage leaves
5 black peppercorns, lightly crushed
1 tbsp redcurrant jelly, warmed
4 tbsp walnut or olive oil
4 tbsp red wine vinegar
3 tbsp plain/all-purpose flour
salt and freshly ground black pepper
2 garlic cloves, peeled and crushed
1 red pepper, deseeded and sliced
1 yellow pepper, deseeded and sliced
3 tbsp chopped sun-dried tomatoes
150 ml/¼ pint/⅔ cup chicken stock
fresh sage leaves, to garnish
diced sauté potatoes, to serve

Cut the liver into very thin slices and place in a shallow dish. Sprinkle over the onion, bay leaves, parsley, sage and peppercorns. Blend the jelly with 1 tablespoon of the oil and the vinegar. Pour over the liver, cover and leave to marinate for at least 30 minutes. Turn the liver occasionally, or spoon over the marinade. Remove the liver from the marinade, strain the liquor and reserve. Season the flour with salt and pepper, then use to coat the liver. Add the remaining oil to a heavy-based frying pan, then sauté the garlic and peppers for 5 minutes. Using a slotted spoon, remove from the pan.

Add the liver to the pan, turn the heat up to high and cook until the meat is browned on all sides. Return the garlic and peppers to the pan and add the reserved marinade, the sun-dried tomatoes and stock. Bring to the boil, then reduce the heat and simmer for 3–4 minutes until the liver is cooked. Add more seasoning, then garnish with a few sage leaves and serve immediately with diced sauté potatoes.

Health Rating: 3 points

Italian Meatballs in Tomato Sauce

Serves 4

Ingredients

For the tomato sauce:
4 tbsp olive oil
1 large onion, peeled and finely chopped
2 garlic cloves, peeled and chopped
400 g/14 oz/2 cups canned chopped tomatoes
1 tbsp sun-dried tomato paste
1 tbsp dried mixed herbs
150 ml/¼ pint/⅔ cup water
salt and freshly ground black pepper

For the meatballs:
450 g/1 lb fresh minced/ground pork
50 g/2 oz/1 cup fresh breadcrumbs
1 egg yolk
75 g/3 oz/¾ cup grated Parmesan cheese
20 small, stuffed green olives

freshly snipped chives, to garnish
freshly cooked pasta, to serve

To make the tomato sauce, heat half the olive oil in a saucepan and cook half the chopped onion for 5 minutes until softened. Add the garlic, chopped tomatoes, sun-dried tomato paste, mixed herbs and water to the pan and season to taste with salt and pepper. Stir well until blended. Bring to the boil, then cover and simmer for 15 minutes.

To make the meatballs, place the pork, breadcrumbs, remaining onion, the egg yolk and half the Parmesan in a large bowl. Season well and mix together with your hands. Divide into 20 balls.

Flatten one ball out in the palm of your hands, place an olive in the centre, then squeeze the meat around the olive to enclose completely. Repeat with the remaining mixture and olives. Place the meatballs on a baking sheet, cover with plastic wrap and chill for 30 minutes.

Heat the remaining oil in a large frying pan and cook the meatballs for 8–10 minutes, turning occasionally, until golden brown. Pour in the sauce and heat through. Sprinkle with chives and the remaining Parmesan. Serve immediately with the freshly cooked pasta.

Health Rating 3 points

Lamb Ragout

Serves 4

Ingredients

4–6 tbsp olive oil

350 g/12 oz freshly minced/ground lean lamb

1 large onion, peeled and chopped

2–4 garlic cloves, peeled and chopped

2 celery stalks, trimmed and chopped

700 g/1½ lb bottle passata/tomato purée or crushed tomatoes

300 g/11 oz/1⅔ cups chopped ripe plum tomatoes

2 tbsp tomato purée/paste

300 ml/½ pint/1¼ cups red wine

1 fresh bay leaf

2 fresh basil leaves

salt and freshly ground black pepper

few fresh thyme sprigs, leaves picked and chopped

350 g/12 oz rigatoni pasta

freshly grated Parmesan cheese, to serve

Heat the oil in a heavy-based saucepan, add the minced/ground lamb and fry, stirring frequently, for 10–12 minutes until sealed all over. Add the onion, garlic and celery and continue to fry for a further 10 minutes. Add the passata/tomato purée or crushed tomatoes and chopped tomatoes with the tomato purée/paste. Pour in the red wine, add the bay leaf and basil leaves. Bring to the boil, then reduce the heat to a gentle simmer and cook, uncovered, for 1 hour, stirring occasionally and adding a little water if the sauce is evaporating quickly. Add seasoning to taste.

Add the thyme leaves, then stir and continue to simmer gently for at least 30 minutes, or longer if time permits.

When ready to eat, bring a large saucepan of water to a rolling boil. Add the pasta and cook for 9–12 minutes until *al dente*. Drain and serve with spoonfuls of the prepared sauce on top and plenty of freshly grated Parmesan cheese.

Health Rating: 2 points

Pasta & Pork Ragout

Serves 4

Ingredients

1 tbsp sunflower oil

1 leek, trimmed and thinly sliced

225 g/8 oz/2½ cups diced pork fillet

1 garlic clove, peeled and crushed

2 tsp paprika

¼ tsp cayenne pepper

150 ml/¼ pint/⅔ cup white wine

600 ml/1 pint/2½ cups vegetable stock

400 g/14 oz canned borlotti beans, drained and rinsed

2 carrots, peeled and diced

salt and freshly ground black pepper

225 g/8 oz fresh egg tagliatelle

1 tbsp freshly chopped parsley, to garnish

crème fraîche, to serve

Heat the sunflower oil in a large frying pan. Add the sliced leek and cook, stirring frequently, for 5 minutes, or until softened. Add the pork and cook, stirring, for 4 minutes, or until sealed.

Add the crushed garlic and the paprika and cayenne pepper to the pan and stir until all the pork is lightly coated in the garlic and pepper mixture.

Pour in the wine and 450 ml/¾ pint/1¾ cups of the vegetable stock. Add the borlotti beans and carrots and season to taste with salt and pepper. Bring the sauce to the boil, then lower the heat and simmer for 5 minutes.

Meanwhile, place the egg tagliatelle in a large saucepan of lightly salted boiling water, cover and simmer for 5 minutes, or until the pasta is cooked *al dente*.

Drain the pasta, then add to the pork ragout; toss well. Adjust the seasoning, then tip into a warmed serving dish. Sprinkle with chopped parsley and serve with a little crème fraîche.

Health Rating: 3 points

Spaghetti & Meatballs

Serves 4

Ingredients

400 g/14 oz/2 cups canned chopped tomatoes

1 tbsp tomato purée/paste

1 tsp chilli sauce

¼ tsp brown sugar

salt and freshly ground black pepper

350 g/12 oz spaghetti

freshly chopped parsley, to garnish

grated Cheddar cheese, to serve

For the meatballs:

450 g/1 lb/5 cups lean minced/ground pork or beef

125 g/4½ oz/2 cups fresh breadcrumbs

1 large onion, peeled and finely chopped

1 egg, beaten

1 tbsp tomato purée/paste

2 tbsp freshly chopped parsley

1 tbsp freshly chopped oregano

Preheat the oven to 200°C/400°F/Gas Mark 6, 15 minutes before using. Place the chopped tomatoes, tomato purée/paste, chilli sauce and sugar in a saucepan. Season to taste with salt and pepper and bring to the boil.

Cover and simmer for 15 minutes, then cook, uncovered, for a further 10 minutes, or until the sauce has reduced and thickened.

Meanwhile, make the meatballs. Place the meat, breadcrumbs and onion in a food processor. Blend until all the ingredients are well mixed. Add the beaten egg, tomato purée, parsley and oregano and season to taste. Blend again.

Shape the mixture into small balls, about the size of a plum, and place on an oiled baking tray. Cook in the preheated oven for 25–30 minutes until browned and cooked.

Meanwhile, bring a large pan of lightly salted water to a rolling boil. Add the pasta and cook according to the packet instructions, or until *al dente*. Drain the pasta and return to

the pan. Pour over the tomato sauce and toss gently to coat the spaghetti. Tip into a warmed serving dish and top with the meatballs. Garnish with chopped parsley and serve immediately with grated cheese.

Health Rating: 2 points

Cannelloni with Spicy Bolognese Filling

Serves 6

Ingredients

12 dried cannelloni tubes
300 ml/½ pint/1¼ cups double/heavy cream
75 g/3 oz/¾ cup freshly grated Parmesan cheese
¼ tsp freshly grated nutmeg
crisp green salad, to serve

For the spicy bolognese filling:
2 tbsp olive oil
1 small onion, peeled and finely chopped
2 garlic cloves, peeled and crushed
500 g/1 lb 1 oz minced/ground beef
¼ tsp crushed chilli flakes
1 tsp fennel seeds
2 tbsp freshly chopped oregano
400 g/14 oz/2 cups canned chopped tomatoes
1 tbsp sun-dried tomato paste
150 ml/¼ pint/⅔ cup red wine
salt and freshly ground black pepper

Preheat the oven to 200°C/400°F/Gas Mark 6, 15 minutes before cooking the stuffed cannelloni.

For the Bolognese sauce, heat the oil in a large, heavy-based pan, add the onion and garlic and cook for 8 minutes, or until soft. Add the minced/ ground beef and cook, stirring with a wooden spoon to break up lumps, for 5–8 minutes until the meat is browned. Stir in the chilli flakes, fennel seeds, oregano, tomatoes and tomato paste and pour in the wine. Season well with salt and pepper.

Bring to the boil, cover and lower the heat, then simmer for at least 30 minutes, stirring occasionally. Remove the lid and simmer for a further 10 minutes. Allow to cool slightly.

With a teaspoon, fill the cannelloni tubes with the meat filling. Lay the stuffed cannelloni side by side in a lightly oiled, ovenproof dish.

Mix the double/heavy cream with three-quarters of the Parmesan and the nutmeg. Pour over the cannelloni and sprinkle with the remaining cheese. Bake in the preheated oven for 30 minutes, or until golden brown and bubbling. Serve immediately with a green salad.

Health Rating: 2 points

Farfalle with Sausages in Spicy Tomato Sauce

Serves 4

Ingredients

2 tbsp olive oil

8 spicy Italian sausages

1 medium onion, peeled and sliced

50 g/2 oz pancetta, chopped

2 garlic cloves, peeled and crushed

1 chilli, deseeded and chopped

1 celery stalk, trimmed and chopped

1 yellow pepper, deseeded and chopped

2 tbsp tomato purée/paste

300 ml/$\frac{1}{2}$ pint/1$\frac{1}{4}$ cups good-quality meat stock, such as beef

400 g/14 oz/2 cups canned chopped tomatoes

150 ml/$\frac{1}{4}$ pint/$\frac{2}{3}$ cup red wine

few oregano sprigs

1 fresh bay leaf

salt and freshly ground black pepper

50 g/2 oz/generous $\frac{1}{4}$ cup black/ripe olives

1 tbsp freshly chopped parsley, to garnish

freshly cooked pasta, such as farfalle, to serve

Heat the oil in a frying pan and fry the sausages on all sides, or until browned, then remove and reserve.

Add the onion, pancetta, garlic, chilli and celery to the frying pan and fry for 10 minutes, or until the vegetables have softened slightly. Add the yellow pepper with the tomato purée/paste blended with the stock to the pan with the canned tomatoes, the wine and herbs. Bring to the boil, then reduce the heat to a simmer and cook for 5 minutes, stirring frequently. Return the sausages to the pan and simmer for 15 minutes, then add seasoning to taste and the black olives.

Bring a large saucepan of water to a rolling boil. Add the pasta and cook for 8–10 minutes until al dente. Place the sausages in a warmed dish and pour over the sauce. Garnish with parsley and serve with freshly cooked pasta.

Health Rating: 3 points

Pappardelle Pork with Brandy Sauce

Serves 4

Ingredients

4 pork fillets, each weighing about 175 g/6 oz

1 tbsp freshly chopped sage, plus whole leaves to garnish

salt and freshly ground black pepper

4 slices Parma ham/prosciutto

1 tbsp olive oil

6 tbsp brandy

300 ml/$\frac{1}{2}$ pint/1$\frac{1}{4}$ cups chicken stock

200 ml/7 fl oz/$\frac{3}{4}$ cup double/heavy cream

350 g/12 oz pappardelle

1–2 tsp butter

2 tbsp freshly chopped flat-leaf parsley

Preheat the oven to 200°C/400°F/Gas Mark 6, 15 minutes before cooking. Using a sharp knife, cut two slits in each pork fillet, then stuff each slit with chopped sage. Season well and wrap each fillet with a slice of Parma ham/prosciutto. Heat the olive oil in a large frying pan. Add the wrapped pork fillets and cook, turning once, for 1–2 minutes until the Parma ham is golden brown. Transfer to a roasting tin/pan and cook in the oven for 10–12 minutes.

Return the frying pan to the heat and add the brandy, scraping the bottom of the pan with a spoon to release all the flavours. Boil for 1 minute, then pour in the chicken stock. Boil for a further 2 minutes, then pour in the cream and boil again for 2–3 minutes until the sauce has thickened slightly. Season the brandy sauce to taste.

Bring a pan of lightly salted water to a rolling boil. Add the pasta and cook according to the packet instructions, or until al dente. Drain the pasta thoroughly and return to the pan. Add the butter and chopped parsley and toss together. Keep the pasta warm.

Remove the pork from the oven and pour any juices into the brandy sauce. Pile the pasta onto individual plates, season with pepper, spoon over the brandy sauce and serve with the fillets.

Health Rating: 2 points

Tagliatelle with Spicy Sausage Ragout

Serves 4

Ingredients

3 tbsp olive oil

6 spicy sausages

1 small onion, peeled and finely chopped

1 tsp fennel seeds

175 g/6 oz/2¼ cups fresh minced/ground pork

225 g/8 oz/heaping 1 cup canned chopped tomatoes with garlic

1 tbsp sun-dried tomato paste

2 tbsp red wine or port

salt and freshly ground black pepper

350 g/12 oz tagliatelle

300 ml/½ pint/1¼ cups prepared white sauce (see page 141)

50 g/2 oz/½ cup freshly grated Parmesan cheese

Preheat the oven to 200°C/400°F/Gas Mark 6, 15 minutes before cooking. Heat 1 tablespoon of the olive oil in a large frying pan. Prick the sausages, add to the pan and cook for 8–10 minutes until browned and cooked through. Remove and cut into thin diagonal slices. Reserve.

Return the pan to the heat and pour in the remaining olive oil. Add the onion and cook for 8 minutes, or until softened. Add the fennel seeds and minced pork and cook, stirring, for 5–8 minutes until the meat is sealed and browned. Stir in the tomatoes, tomato paste and the wine or port. Season to taste. Bring to the boil, cover and simmer for 30 minutes, stirring occasionally. Remove the lid and simmer for 10 minutes.

Bring a large pan of lightly salted water to a rolling boil. Add the pasta and cook according to the packet instructions, or until *al dente*. Drain thoroughly and toss with the meat sauce. Place half the pasta in an ovenproof dish and cover with 4 tablespoons of the white sauce. Top with half the sausages and grated Parmesan. Repeat the layering, finishing with white sauce and Parmesan. Bake in the oven for 20 minutes until golden brown. Serve immediately.

Health Rating: 2 points

Pasta with Beef, Capers & Olives

Serves 4

Ingredients

2 tbsp olive oil

300 g/11 oz rump steak, trimmed and cut into strips

4 spring onions/scallions, trimmed and sliced

2 garlic cloves, peeled and chopped

2 courgettes/zucchini, trimmed and cut into strips

1 red pepper/bell pepper, deseeded and cut into strips

2 tsp freshly chopped oregano

2 tbsp capers, drained and rinsed

4 tbsp pitted black olives, sliced

400 g/14 oz/2 cups canned chopped tomatoes

salt and freshly ground black pepper

450 g/1 lb fettuccine

1 tbsp freshly chopped parsley, to garnish

Heat the olive oil in a large frying pan over a high heat. Add the steak and cook, stirring, for 3–4 minutes until browned. Remove from the pan using a slotted spoon and reserve.

Lower the heat, add the spring onions/scallions and garlic to the pan and cook for 1 minute. Add the courgettes/zucchini and pepper and cook for 3–4 minutes.

Add the oregano, capers and olives to the pan with the chopped tomatoes. Season to taste with salt and pepper, then simmer for 7 minutes, stirring occasionally. Return the beef to the pan and simmer for 3–5 minutes until the sauce has thickened slightly.

Meanwhile, bring a large pan of lightly salted water to a rolling boil. Add the pasta and cook according to the packet instructions, or until *al dente*. Drain the pasta thoroughly. Return to the pan and add the beef sauce. Toss gently until the pasta is lightly coated. Tip into a warmed serving dish or onto individual plates. Sprinkle with chopped parsley and serve immediately.

Health Rating: 3 points

Rigatoni with Lamb in a Rich Tomato Sauce

Serves 4

Ingredients

1 large onion, peeled and thinly sliced

2 tbsp olive oil

3–4 garlic cloves, peeled and chopped

3 celery stalks, trimmed and chopped

1 chilli, deseeded and chopped

350 g/12 oz lean fresh minced/ground lamb

300 g/11 oz ripe plum tomatoes

2 fresh bay leaves

2 tbsp freshly chopped oregano

2 tbsp tomato purée/paste

150 ml/¼ pint/⅔ cup red wine

salt and freshly ground black pepper

350 g/12 oz rigatoni pasta, fresh or dried

freshly grated Parmesan cheese, to serve

Cut the onion slices in half to form half moons. Heat the oil in a frying pan, add the onion, garlic, celery and chilli and fry for 5 minutes, stirring frequently.

Add the lamb and continue to fry, breaking up any lumps with the wooden spoon. Fry for a further 5 minutes, or until the lamb is browned. Add the chopped tomatoes, bay leaves and oregano.

Blend the tomato purée/paste with the wine and pour into the pan. Bring to the boil, then reduce the heat to a simmer and cook for 15 minutes, or until the sauce has thickened. Add seasoning to taste, discard the bay leaves and keep warm.

Bring a large saucepan of water to a rolling boil. Add the pasta and cook until *al dente*. Drain, reserving 2–3 tablespoons of the pasta cooking water.

Return the pasta to the saucepan together with the cooking water, tip in the sauce and stir lightly. Serve sprinkled with the grated Parmesan cheese.

Health Rating: 3 points

Gnocchi & Parma Ham Bake

Serves 4

Ingredients

3 tbsp olive oil

1 red onion, peeled and sliced

2 garlic cloves, peeled

3 plum tomatoes, skinned and quartered

2 tbsp sun-dried tomato paste

250 g tub/1 cup mascarpone cheese

salt and freshly ground black pepper

1 tbsp freshly chopped tarragon

300 g/11 oz fresh gnocchi

125 g/4 oz/1 cup grated Cheddar or Parmesan cheese

50 g/2 oz/1 cup fresh white breadcrumbs

50 g/2 oz sliced Parma ham/prosciutto

10 green olives, pitted and halved

flat-leaf parsley sprigs, to garnish

Preheat the oven to 180°C/350°F/Gas Mark 4, 10 minutes before cooking. Heat 2 tablespoons of the olive oil in a large frying pan and cook the onion and garlic for 5 minutes, or until softened. Stir in the tomatoes, sun-dried tomato paste and mascarpone cheese. Season to taste with salt and pepper. Add half the tarragon. Bring to the boil, then lower the heat immediately and simmer for 5 minutes.

Meanwhile, bring 1.7 litres/3 pints/7 cups water to the boil in a large pan. Add the remaining olive oil and a good pinch of salt. Add the gnocchi and cook for 1–2 minutes until they rise to the surface.

Drain the gnocchi thoroughly and transfer to a large, ovenproof dish. Add the tomato sauce and toss gently to coat the pasta. Combine the Cheddar or Parmesan cheese with the breadcrumbs and remaining tarragon and scatter over the pasta mixture. Top with the Parma ham/prosciutto and olives and season again. Cook in the oven for 20–25 minutes until golden and bubbling. Serve immediately, garnished with parsley sprigs.

Health Rating: 2 points

Lamb Arrabbiata

Serves 4

Ingredients

4 tbsp olive oil

450 g/1 lb lamb fillets, cubed

1 large onion, peeled and sliced

4 garlic cloves, peeled and finely chopped

1 red chilli, deseeded and finely chopped

400 g/14 oz/2 cups canned chopped tomatoes

175 g/6 oz/1½ cups pitted black olives, halved

150 ml/¼ pint/⅔ cup white wine

salt and freshly ground black pepper

275 g/10 oz/2½ cups farfalle pasta

knob/pat butter

4 tbsp freshly chopped parsley, plus 1 tbsp to garnish

Health Rating: 3 points

Heat 2 tablespoons of the olive oil in a large frying pan and cook the lamb for 5–7 minutes until sealed. Remove from the pan using a slotted spoon and reserve.

Heat the remaining oil in the pan, add the onion, garlic and chilli and cook until softened. Add the tomatoes, bring to the boil, then simmer for 10 minutes.

Return the browned lamb to the pan with the olives and pour in the wine. Bring the sauce back to the boil, reduce the heat, then simmer, uncovered, for 15 minutes until the lamb is tender. Season to taste with salt and pepper.

Meanwhile, bring a large pan of lightly salted water to a rolling boil. Add the pasta and cook according to the packet instructions, or until *al dente*. Drain the pasta, toss in the butter, then add to the sauce and mix lightly. Stir in 4 tablespoons of the chopped parsley, then tip into a warmed serving dish. Sprinkle with the remaining parsley and serve immediately.

Creamed Lamb & Wild Mushroom Pasta

Serves 4

Ingredients

25 g/1 oz/²⁄₃ cup dried porcini

450 g/1 lb/4 cups pasta shapes

25 g/1 oz/2 tbsp butter

1 tbsp olive oil

350 g/12 oz lamb neck fillet, thinly sliced

1 garlic clove, peeled and crushed

225 g/8 oz/2½ cups chestnut/cremini mushrooms, wiped and sliced

4 tbsp white wine

125 ml/4 fl oz/½ cup double/heavy cream

salt and freshly ground black pepper

1 tbsp freshly chopped parsley, to garnish

freshly grated Parmesan cheese, to serve

Place the porcini in a small bowl and cover with almost-boiling water. Leave to soak for 30 minutes. Drain the porcini, reserving the soaking liquid. Chop the porcini finely. Bring a large pan of lightly salted water to a rolling boil. Add the pasta and cook according to the packet instructions, or until *al dente*.

Meanwhile, melt the butter with the olive oil in a large frying pan and fry the lamb to seal. Add the garlic, mushrooms and prepared porcini and cook for 5 minutes, or until just soft. Add the wine and the reserved porcini soaking liquid, then simmer for 2 minutes. Stir in the cream with the seasoning and simmer for 1–2 minutes until just thickened.

Drain the pasta thoroughly, reserving about 4 tablespoons of the cooking water. Return the pasta to the pan. Pour over the mushroom sauce and toss lightly together, adding the pasta water if the sauce is too thick. Tip into a warmed serving dish or spoon onto individual plates. Garnish with the chopped parsley and serve immediately with grated Parmesan cheese.

Health Rating: 2 points

Neapolitan Style Macaroni

Serves 4

Ingredients

4 tbsp olive oil

1 medium onion, peeled and chopped

3–4 plump garlic cloves, peeled and chopped

1 red chilli, deseeded and finely chopped, or ½–1 tsp according to taste, dried crushed chilli

175 g/6 oz fresh minced/ground beef (optional)

1.5 litres/2½ pints/6⅓ cups passata/tomato purée or crushed tomatoes

3 tbsp freshly chopped parsley

salt and freshly ground black pepper

450 g/1 lb dried macaroni

freshly grated Parmesan cheese, to serve

Heat the oil in a medium saucepan, add the onion, garlic and chilli and fry gently for 5 minutes. Add the minced/ground beef, if using, and continue to fry, stirring frequently, for 10 minutes. Pour in the passata/tomato purée or crushed tomatoes and bring to the boil. Reduce the heat to a simmer and cook for 10 minutes. Add the parsley with salt to taste and simmer while cooking the pasta.

Bring a large saucepan of water to a rolling boil. Add the macaroni and cook for 8–10 minutes until *al dente*. Drain and return the pasta to the saucepan. Stir in the sauce. Heat for 2 minutes, then serve sprinkled with black pepper and Parmesan.

Health Rating: 2 points

Tagliatelle with Creamy Liver & Basil

Serves 4

Ingredients

25 g/1 oz/2 tbsp plain/all-purpose flour

salt and freshly ground black pepper

450 g/1 lb lambs' liver, thinly sliced and cut into bite-size pieces

25 g/1 oz/2 tbsp butter

1 tbsp olive oil

2 red onions, peeled and sliced

1 garlic clove, peeled and sliced

150 ml/¼ pint/⅔ cup chicken stock

1 tbsp tomato purée/paste

2 sun-dried tomatoes, finely chopped

350 g/12 oz tagliatelle verdi

1 tbsp freshly chopped basil

150 ml/¼ pint/⅔ cup double/heavy cream

fresh basil leaves, to garnish

Season the flour lightly with salt and pepper and place in a large plastic bag. Add the liver and toss gently to coat. Remove the liver from the bag and reserve.

Melt the butter with the olive oil in a large frying pan. Add the onions and garlic and fry for 6–8 minutes until the onions begin to colour. Add the liver and fry until brown on all sides. Stir in the stock, tomato purée/paste and sun-dried tomatoes. Bring to the boil, reduce the heat and simmer very gently for 10 minutes.

Meanwhile, bring a large pan of lightly salted water to a rolling boil. Add the pasta and cook according to the packet instructions, or until *al dente*.

Stir the chopped basil and cream into the liver sauce and season to taste. Drain the pasta thoroughly, reserving 2 tablespoons of the cooking water. Tip the pasta into a warmed serving dish or pile onto individual plates. Stir the reserved cooking water into the liver sauce and pour over the pasta. Toss lightly to coat the pasta. Garnish with basil leaves and serve immediately.

Health Rating: 2 points

Gammon with Red Wine Sauce & Pasta

Serves 2

Ingredients

25 g/1 oz/2 tbsp butter
150 ml/¼ pint/⅔ cup red wine
4 red onions, peeled and sliced
4 tbsp orange juice
1 tsp soft brown sugar
225 g/8 oz gammon/ham steak, trimmed
175 g/6 oz/1½ cups fusilli pasta
freshly ground black pepper
3 tbsp wholegrain mustard
2 tbsp freshly chopped flat-leaf parsley, plus sprigs to garnish

Preheat the grill/broiler to a medium heat before cooking. Heat the butter with the red wine in a large, heavy-based pan. Add the onions, cover with a tight-fitting lid and cook over a very low heat for 30 minutes, or until softened and transparent. Remove the lid from the pan, stir in the orange juice and sugar, then increase the heat and cook for about 10 minutes until the onions are golden.

Meanwhile, cook the gammon/ham steak under the preheated grill, turning at least once, for 4–6 minutes until tender. Cut the cooked gammon/ham steak into bite-size pieces. Reserve and keep warm.

Meanwhile, bring a large pan of very lightly salted water to a rolling boil. Add the pasta and cook according to the packet instructions, or until *al dente*. Drain the pasta thoroughly, return to the pan, season with a little pepper and keep warm.

Stir the mustard and chopped parsley into the onion sauce, then pour over the pasta. Add the gammon pieces to the pan and toss lightly to coat the pasta thoroughly with the sauce. Pile the pasta mixture onto two warmed serving plates. Garnish with sprigs of flat-leaf parsley and serve immediately.

Health Rating: 2 points

Gnocchi with Tuscan Beef Ragout

Serves 4

Ingredients

25 g/1 oz/²/₃ cup dried porcini

3 tbsp olive oil

1 small onion, peeled and finely chopped

1 carrot, peeled and finely chopped

1 celery stalk, trimmed and finely chopped

1 fennel bulb, trimmed and sliced

2 garlic cloves, peeled and crushed

450 g/1 lb fresh minced/ground beef

4 tbsp red wine

50 g/2 oz/½ cup pine nuts

1 tbsp freshly chopped rosemary

2 tbsp tomato purée/paste

400 g/14 oz/2 cups canned chopped tomatoes

225 g/8 oz fresh gnocchi

125 g/4 oz mozzarella cheese, cubed

Preheat the oven to 200°C/400°F/Gas Mark 6, 15 minutes before cooking. Place the porcini in a small bowl and cover with almost-boiling water. Leave to soak for 30 minutes.

Drain, reserving the soaking liquid and straining it through a muslin/ cheesecloth-lined sieve. Chop the porcini.

Heat the olive oil in a large, heavy-based pan. Add the onion, carrot, celery, fennel and garlic and cook for 8 minutes, stirring, or until soft. Add the beef and cook, stirring, for 5–8 minutes until sealed and any lumps are broken up. Pour in the wine, then add the porcini with half the pine nuts, the rosemary and tomato purée/paste.

Stir in the porcini soaking liquid, then simmer for 5 minutes. Add the chopped tomatoes and simmer gently for about 40 minutes, stirring occasionally.

Bring 1.7 litres/3 pints/7 cups of lightly salted water to a rolling boil in a pan. Add the gnocchi and cook for 1–2 minutes until they rise to the surface. Drain and place in an ovenproof dish. Stir in three

quarters of the mozzarella with the beef sauce. Top with the remaining mozzarella and the pine nuts, then bake for about 20 minutes until golden brown. Serve immediately.

Health Rating: 2 points

Stuffed Pork Roll with Prosciutto & Sun-dried Tomatoes

Serves 6–8

Ingredients

450 g/1 lb pork tenderloin
125 g/4 oz prosciutto
fresh herbs, to garnish; seasonal vegetables or salad, to serve

For the stuffing:
2 tbsp olive oil
2 shallots, peeled and sliced
2 plump garlic cloves, peeled and crushed
2 tbsp pine nuts
¹⁄₂ tsp, or to taste, crushed chillies
50 g/2 oz/scant 1 cup fresh white breadcrumbs
25 g/1 oz/scant ¹⁄₄ cup drained and chopped sun-dried
    tomatoes in oil
2 tbsp freshly grated Parmesan cheese
salt and freshly ground black pepper
1 medium/large egg, beaten

Preheat the oven to 190°C/375°F/Gas Mark 5, 10 minutes before cooking. Trim the pork of fat or sinew, then cut a pocket down the entire length of the meat. Cover and reserve.

Heat the oil in a saucepan, add the shallots and garlic and fry for 3 minutes, stirring occasionally. Add the pine nuts and chillies and fry for a further 2 minutes. Remove from the heat. Mix in all the remaining stuffing ingredients, with seasoning to taste and adding enough egg to hold the mixture together. Leave to cool slightly.

Stuff the pork pockets with the stuffing, pushing the sides together. Wrap the pork in the Parma ham/prosciutto using cocktail sticks/ toothpicks if necessary to hold the meat together. Place the pork in a roasting tin/pan and roast in the oven for 50–55 minutes until tender. Garnish with herbs and serve with seasonal vegetables or salad.

Health Rating: 3 points

Prosciutto & Gruyère Carbonara

Serves 4

Ingredients

3 medium/large egg yolks
50 g/2 oz/¹⁄₂ cup grated Gruyère cheese
2 tbsp olive oil
2 garlic cloves, peeled and crushed
2 shallots, peeled and finely chopped
200 g/7 oz/1¹⁄₂ cups julienned Parma ham/prosciutto
4 tbsp dry vermouth
salt and freshly ground black pepper
450 g/1 lb spaghetti
15 g/¹⁄₂ oz/1 tbsp butter
1 tbsp freshly shredded basil leaves
basil sprigs, to garnish

Place the egg yolks with 6 tablespoons of the Gruyère cheese in a bowl and mix lightly until well blended, then reserve.

Heat the olive oil in a large pan and cook the garlic and shallots for 5 minutes, or until golden brown. Add the Parma ham /prosciutto, then cook for a further 1 minute. Pour in the dry vermouth and simmer for 2 minutes, then remove from the heat. Season to taste with salt and pepper and keep warm.

Meanwhile, bring a large pan of lightly salted water to a rolling boil. Add the pasta and cook according to the packet instructions, or until *al dente*. Drain thoroughly, reserving 4 tablespoons of the water, and return the pasta to the pan.

Remove from the heat, then add the egg and cheese mixture with the butter to the pasta; toss lightly until coated. Add the prosciutto mixture and toss again, adding the reserved pasta water, if needed, to moisten. Season to taste and sprinkle with the remaining Gruyère cheese and the shredded basil leaves. Garnish with basil sprigs and serve immediately.

Health Rating: 2 points

Leek & Ham Risotto

Serves 4

Ingredients

1 tbsp olive oil
25 g/1 oz/2 tbsp butter
1 medium onion, peeled and finely chopped
4 leeks, trimmed and thinly sliced
1½ tbsp freshly chopped thyme
350 g/12 oz/1¾ cups Arborio/risotto rice
1.4 litres/2½ pints/5½ cups vegetable or chicken stock, heated
225 g/8 oz/1⅔ cups chopped or finely shredded cooked ham
175 g/6 oz/1¼ cups fresh or thawed peas
50 g/2 oz/½ cup grated Parmesan cheese
salt and freshly ground black pepper

Heat the oil and half the butter together in a large saucepan. Add the onion and leeks and cook over a medium heat for 6–8 minutes, stirring occasionally, until soft and beginning to colour. Stir in the thyme and cook briefly.

Add the rice and stir well. Continue stirring over a medium heat for about 1 minute until the rice is glossy. Add a ladleful or two of the stock and stir well until the stock is absorbed. Continue adding stock, a ladleful at a time and stirring well between additions, until about two thirds of the stock has been added. (Risotto should take about 15 minutes to cook, so taste it after this time – the rice should be creamy with just a slight bite to it. If it is not quite ready, continue adding the stock, a little at a time, and cook for a few more minutes. Stop as soon as it tastes ready, as you do not have to add all of the liquid.)

Add the ham and peas to the saucepan of rice. Continue adding ladlefuls of stock, as described in step 2, until the rice is tender and the ham is heated through thoroughly.

Add the remaining butter, sprinkle over the Parmesan cheese and season to taste with salt and pepper. When the butter has melted and the cheese has softened, stir well to incorporate. Taste and adjust the seasoning, then serve immediately.

Health Rating: 2 points

Red Wine Risotto with Lambs' Kidneys & Caramelised Shallots

Serves 4

Ingredients

8 lambs' kidneys, halved and cores removed

150 ml/¼ pint/⅔ cup milk

2 tbsp olive oil

50 g/2 oz/4 tbsp butter

275 g/10 oz/¾ lb shallots, peeled, and halved if large

1 onion, peeled and finely chopped

2 garlic cloves, peeled and finely chopped

350 g/12 oz/2 cups Arborio/risotto rice

225 ml/8 fl oz/1 cup red wine

1 litre/1¾ pints/4 cups chicken or vegetable stock, heated

1 tbsp fresh thyme sprigs

50 g/2 oz/½ cup grated Parmesan cheese

salt and freshly ground black pepper

fresh herbs, to garnish

Place the lambs' kidneys in a bowl and pour the milk over. Leave to soak for 15–20 minutes, then drain and pat dry on paper towels. Discard the milk.

Heat 1 tablespoon of the oil with 25 g/1 oz/2 tbsp of the butter in a medium saucepan. Add the shallots, cover and cook for 10 minutes over a gentle heat. Remove the lid and cook for a further 10 minutes, or until tender and golden.

Meanwhile, heat the remaining oil with the remaining butter in a deep-sided frying pan. Add the onion and cook over a medium heat for 5–7 minutes until starting to brown. Add the garlic and cook briefly.

Stir in the rice and cook for a further minute until glossy and well coated in oil and butter. Add half the red wine and stir until absorbed. Add a ladleful or two of the stock and stir well until the stock is absorbed. Continue adding the stock, a ladleful at a time, and stirring well between additions, until all of the stock is added and the rice is just tender but still firm. Remove from the heat.

Meanwhile, when the rice is nearly cooked, increase the heat under the shallots, then add the thyme and kidneys. Cook for 3–4 minutes, then add the remaining wine.

Bring to the boil, then simmer rapidly until the red wine is reduced and syrupy. Stir the cheese into the rice with the caramelised shallots and kidneys. Season to taste, garnish with fresh herbs and serve.

Health Rating: 2 points

Calves' Liver with Butter & Sage

Serves 4

Ingredients

450 g/1 lb calves' liver
2 tbsp plain/all-purpose flour
salt and freshly ground black pepper
about 50 g/2 oz/4 tbsp butter
few fresh sage leaves, plus a few extra to garnish
1–2 tbsp lemon juice

Cut away any sinew from the liver and slice thinly. Rinse lightly and pat dry with absorbent paper towels. Reserve.

Place the flour on a large plate and add seasoning. Stir lightly. Dip both sides of the sliced liver in the seasoned flour, shaking off any excess, then reserve.

Melt half the butter in a large frying pan, add the liver and cook on both sides for 2 minutes. Add the remaining butter together with the sage leaves and lemon juice, and leave in the pan while the butter melts.

Check the liver is cooked to your personal preference, and is not bloody. If not, cook a little longer (calves' liver is best eaten slightly pink). Place the cooked liver on warmed serving plates, pour over the butter and serve garnished with fresh sage leaves.

Calves' liver is normally eaten pink or medium. To cook the liver pink, cook on both sides for 2–3 minutes. The thinner the liver, the less cooking time required. To cook the liver to medium, cook for 3–4 minutes on both sides.

Health Rating: 2 points

Roquefort, Parma & Rocket Pizza

Serves 2–4

Ingredients

1 quantity pizza dough (*see* page 282)

For the basic tomato sauce:
400 g/14 oz/2 cups canned chopped tomatoes
2 garlic cloves, peeled and crushed
grated zest of ½ lime
2 tbsp extra virgin olive oil
2 tbsp freshly chopped basil
½ tsp sugar
salt and freshly ground black pepper

For the topping:
125 g/4 oz/1 cup Roquefort cheese, cut into chunks
6 slices Parma ham/prosciutto
50 g/2 oz/1 bunch rocket/arugula leaves, rinsed
1 tbsp extra virgin olive oil
50 g/2 oz/8 tbsp freshly grated Parmesan cheese

Preheat the oven to 220°C/425°F/Gas Mark 7. Roll the pizza dough out on a lightly floured board to form a 25.5 cm/10 inch round. Lightly cover the dough and reserve while making the sauce. Place a baking sheet in the preheated oven to heat up.

Place all of the tomato sauce ingredients in a large, heavy-based saucepan and slowly bring to the boil. Cover and simmer for 15 minutes, uncover and cook for a further 10 minutes until the sauce has thickened and reduced by half.

Spoon the tomato sauce over the shaped pizza dough. Place on the hot baking sheet and bake for 10 minutes. Remove the pizza from the oven and top with the Roquefort and Parma ham/prosciutto, then bake for a further 10 minutes.

Toss the rocket/arugula in the olive oil and pile onto the pizza. Sprinkle with the Parmesan cheese and serve immediately.

Health Rating: 2 points

Chilli Beef Calzone

Serves 4

Ingredients

1 tbsp sunflower/corn oil
1 onion, peeled and finely chopped
1 green pepper, deseeded and chopped
225 g/8 oz/1 cup minced/ground beef
450 g/15 oz canned chilli beans
225 g/8 oz/heaping 1 cup canned chopped tomatoes
1 quantity pizza dough (see page 282)
mixed salad leaves, to serve

Health Rating: 3 points

Preheat the oven to 220°C/425°F/Gas Mark 7, 15 minutes before baking. Heat the oil in a large saucepan and gently cook the onion and pepper for 5 minutes. Add the beef to the saucepan and cook for 10 minutes, or until browned.

Add the chilli beans and tomatoes and simmer gently for 30 minutes, or until the beef is tender. Place a baking sheet into the preheated oven to heat up.

Divide the pizza dough into four equal pieces. Cover three pieces of the dough with plastic wrap and roll out the other piece on a lightly floured board to a 20.5 cm/8 inch round.

Spoon a quarter of the chilli mixture onto half of the dough round and dampen the edges with a little water. Fold over the empty half of the dough and press the edges together well to seal.

Repeat this process with the remaining dough. Place on the hot baking sheet and bake for 15 minutes. Serve with the salad leaves.

Ossobuco with Saffron Risotto

Serves 4

Ingredients

125 g/4 oz/½ cup (1 stick) butter

2 tbsp olive oil

4 large pieces shin of veal (often sold as ossobuco)

2 onions, peeled and roughly chopped

2 garlic cloves, peeled and finely chopped

300 ml/½ pint/1¼ cups white wine

5 plum tomatoes, peeled and chopped

1 tbsp tomato purée/paste

salt and freshly ground black pepper

2 tbsp freshly chopped parsley

grated zest of 1 small lemon

few crushed saffron strands

350 g/12 oz/2 cups Arborio/risotto rice

1.3 litres/2⅓ pints/5¼ cups chicken stock, heated

50 g/2 oz/½ cup grated Parmesan cheese

Heat 50 g/2 oz/4 tbsp butter with half the oil in a saucepan and add the pieces of veal. Brown lightly on both sides, then transfer to a plate. Add half the onion and garlic and cook gently for about 10 minutes until the onion is just golden. Return the veal to the saucepan along with the white wine, tomatoes and tomato purée/paste. Season lightly, cover and bring to a gentle simmer. Cook very gently for 1 hour.

Uncover and cook for a further 30 minutes until the meat is cooked and the sauce is reduced and thickened. Season to taste. Mix together the remaining garlic, the parsley and lemon zest and reserve.

Slowly melt the remaining butter and oil in a large, deep-sided frying pan. Add the remaining onion and cook gently for 5–7 minutes until just brown. Add the saffron, stir for a few seconds, then add the rice. Cook for a further minute until the rice is well coated in oil and butter.

Begin adding the stock a ladleful at a time, stirring well after each addition of stock and waiting until it is absorbed before adding the next. Continue in this way until all the stock is used. Remove from the heat and stir in the grated Parmesan and the seasoning.

Spoon a little of the saffron risotto onto each of four serving plates. Top with the ossobuco and sauce and sprinkle over the reserved garlic and parsley mixture. Serve immediately.

Health Rating: 2 points

Poultry & Game

Who says that poultry has to be boring? In this section, there are many excellent recipes that will prove how delicious and exciting poultry can be. From Chicken Cacciatore to Turkey Escalopes Marsala with Wilted Watercress, you are sure to find something to suit your tastes. You also need not be afraid to try the easy-to-follow game recipes, such as the Pheasant with Sage & Blueberries or the Braised Rabbit with Red Peppers.

Saffron Roast Chicken with Crispy Onions

Serves 4–6

Ingredients

1.6 kg/3½ lb oven-ready chicken, preferably free range

75 g/3 oz/6 tbsp butter, softened

1 tsp lightly toasted saffron strands

grated zest of 1 lemon

2 tbsp freshly chopped flat-leaf parsley

2 tbsp extra virgin olive oil

450 g/1 lb/2½ cups peeled and thickly sliced onions

8–12 garlic cloves, peeled

1 tsp cumin seeds

½ tsp ground cinnamon

50 g/2 oz/⅓ cup pine nuts

50 g/2 oz/⅓ cup sultanas/golden raisins

salt and freshly ground black pepper

fresh flat-leaf parsley sprig, to garnish

Preheat the oven to 200°C/400°F/Gas Mark 6. Using your fingertips, gently loosen the skin from the chicken breast by sliding your hand between the skin and flesh. Cream together 50 g/2 oz/4 tbsp of the butter with the saffron strands, the lemon zest and half the parsley until smooth. Push the butter under the skin. Spread over the breast and the top of the thighs with your fingers. Pull the neck skin to tighten the skin over the breast and tuck under the bird, then secure with a skewer or cocktail stick/toothpick.

Heat the olive oil and the remaining butter in a large, heavy-based frying pan and cook the onions and garlic cloves for 5 minutes, or until the onions are soft. Stir in the cumin seeds, cinnamon, pine nuts and sultanas/golden raisins and cook for 2 minutes. Season to taste with salt and pepper and place in a roasting tin/pan.

Place the chicken, breast-side down, on the base of the onions and roast in the preheated oven for 45 minutes. Reduce the oven temperature to 170°C/325°F/Gas Mark 3. Turn the chicken breast-side up and stir the onions. Continue roasting until the chicken is a deep golden yellow and the onions are crisp.

Allow to rest for 10 minutes, then sprinkle with the remaining parsley. Garnish with a parsley sprig and serve immediately with the onions and garlic.

Health Rating: 2 points

Pheasant with Portabello Mushrooms & Red Wine Gravy

Serves 4

Ingredients

25 g/1 oz/2 tbsp butter

1 tbsp olive oil

2 small pheasants (preferably hens)/game hens, rinsed, well dried and halved

8 shallots, peeled

300 g/11 oz/2¾ cups thickly sliced portabello/large mushrooms

2–3 fresh thyme or rosemary sprigs, leaves stripped

300 ml/½ pint/1¼ cups Valpolicella, or fruity red wine

300 ml/½ pint/1¼ cups chicken stock, heated

1 tbsp cornflour/cornstarch

2 tbsp balsamic vinegar

2 tbsp redcurrant jelly, or to taste

2 tbsp freshly chopped flat-leaf parsley

salt and freshly ground black pepper

fresh thyme sprigs, to garnish

Preheat the oven to 180°C/350°F/Gas Mark 4. Heat the butter and oil in a large saucepan or frying pan. Add the pheasant/hen halves and shallots, working in batches if necessary, and cook for 10 minutes, or until golden on all sides, shaking the pan to glaze the shallots. Transfer to a casserole dish large enough to hold the pieces in a single layer.

Add the mushrooms and thyme to the pan. Cook for 2–3 minutes until beginning to colour. Transfer to the dish with the pheasant halves.

Add the wine to the saucepan. Cook, stirring up any browned bits from the pan, and allow to reduce by half. Pour in the stock, bring to the boil, then pour over the pheasant halves. Cover and braise in the preheated oven for 50 minutes, or until tender.

Remove the pheasant halves and vegetables to a wide, shallow serving dish. Set the casserole dish over a medium–high heat.

Skim off any surface fat and bring to the boil. Blend the cornflour/cornstarch with the vinegar. Stir into the sauce with the redcurrant jelly. Boil until the sauce is reduced and thickened slightly. Stir in the parsley. Season to taste with salt and pepper. Pour over the pheasant halves, garnish with fresh thyme sprigs and serve immediately.

Health Rating: 3 points

Pheasant with Sage & Blueberries

Serves 4

Ingredients

3 tbsp olive oil

3 shallots, peeled and coarsely chopped

2 fresh sage sprigs, coarsely chopped

1 bay leaf

1 lemon, halved

salt and freshly ground black pepper

2 pheasants or guinea fowl/game hens, rinsed and dried

125 g/4 oz/1 cup blueberries

4 slices Parma ham/prosciutto or bacon

125 ml/4 fl oz/½ cup vermouth or dry white wine

200 ml/⅓ pint/¾ cup chicken stock

3 tbsp double/heavy cream or butter (optional)

1 tbsp brandy

roast potatoes and gravy, to serve

Preheat the oven to 180°C/350°F/Gas Mark 4, 10 minutes before cooking. Place the oil, shallots, sage and bay leaf in a bowl with the juice from the lemon halves. Season with salt and pepper. Tuck each of the squeezed lemon halves into the birds with 75 g/3 oz/¾ cup of the blueberries. Rub the birds with the marinade. Leave for 2–3 hours, basting occasionally.

Remove the birds from the marinade and cover each with two slices of Parma ham/prosciutto. Tie the legs of each bird with string and place in a roasting tin/pan. Pour over the marinade and add the vermouth or wine. Roast in the preheated oven for 1 hour, or until tender and golden and the juices run clear when a thigh is pierced with a sharp knife or skewer.

Transfer to a warmed serving plate, cover with kitchen foil and discard the string. Skim off any surface fat from the tin and set over a medium–high heat.

Add the stock to the tin and bring to the boil, scraping any browned bits from the bottom and mixing in. Boil until slightly reduced. Whisk in the cream or butter, if using, and simmer until thickened, whisking constantly. Stir in the brandy and strain into a gravy jug. Add the remaining blueberries and keep warm.

Using a sharp carving knife, cut each of the birds in half and arrange on the plate with the crispy Parma ham. Serve immediately with roast potatoes and gravy.

Health Rating: 2 points

Spatchcocked Poussins with Garlic Sage Butter

Serves 4

Ingredients

For the herb butter:
6 large garlic cloves
150 g/5 oz/²/₃ cup (1¼ sticks) butter, softened
2 tbsp freshly snipped chives; 2 tbsp freshly chopped sage
grated zest and juice of 1 small lemon
salt and freshly ground black pepper

For the poussins:
4 spatchcocked poussins/game hens
2 tbsp extra virgin olive oil

To garnish:
chives
fresh sage leaves

To serve:
grilled polenta (*see page 230*)
grilled tomatoes

Preheat the grill/broiler or light an outdoor charcoal grill and line the grill rack with kitchen foil just before cooking. Put the garlic cloves in a small saucepan and cover with cold water. Bring to the boil, then simmer for 5 minutes, or until softened. Drain and cool slightly. Cut off the root end of each clove and squeeze the softened garlic into a bowl. Pound the garlic until smooth, then beat in the butter, chives, sage and lemon zest and juice. Season to taste with salt and pepper.

Using your fingertips, gently loosen the skin from each poussin/hen breast by sliding your hand between the skin and the flesh. Push one quarter of the herb butter under the skin, spreading evenly over the breast and the top of the thighs. Pull the neck skin gently to tighten the skin over the breast and tuck under the bird. Repeat with the remaining birds and herb butter.

Thread two wooden skewers crossways through each bird, from one wing through the opposite leg, to keep the poussin flat.

Repeat with the remaining birds, brush with the olive oil and season with salt and pepper. Arrange the poussins on the rack and grill for 25 minutes, turning occasionally, until golden and crisp and the juices run clear when a thigh is pierced with a sharp knife or skewer. (Position the rack about 12.5 cm/5 inches from the heat source, or the skin will brown before the birds are cooked through.) Garnish with chives and sage leaves and serve immediately with grilled polenta and a few grilled tomatoes.

Health Rating: 2 points

Chicken Cacciatore

Serves 4

Ingredients

2–3 tbsp olive oil

125 g/4 oz pancetta or streaky/fatty bacon, diced

3 tbsp plain/all-purpose flour

salt and freshly ground black pepper

1.4–1.6 kg/3–3½ lb chicken, cut into 8 pieces

2 garlic cloves, peeled and chopped

125 ml/4 fl oz/½ cup red wine

400 g/14 oz/2 cups canned chopped tomatoes

150 ml/¼ pint/⅔ cup chicken stock

12 small onions, peeled

1 bay leaf; 1 tsp brown sugar; 1 tsp dried oregano

1 green pepper, deseeded and chopped

225 g/8 oz/3 cups thickly sliced chestnut/cremini or
    field mushrooms

2 tbsp freshly chopped parsley

freshly cooked tagliatelle, to serve

Heat 1 tablespoon of the olive oil in a large, deep frying pan and add the diced pancetta or bacon and stir–fry for 2–3 minutes until crisp and golden brown. Using a slotted spoon, transfer the pancetta or bacon to a plate and reserve.

Season the flour with salt and pepper, then use to coat the chicken. Heat the remaining oil in the pan and brown the chicken pieces on all sides for about 15 minutes. Remove from the pan and add to the pancetta.

Stir the garlic into the pan and cook for about 30 seconds. Add the wine and cook, stirring and scraping any browned bits from the base of the pan. Allow the wine to boil until it is reduced by half. Add the tomatoes, stock, onions, bay leaf, brown sugar and oregano and stir well. Season to taste. Return the chicken and pancetta to the pan and bring to the boil. Cover and simmer for 30 minutes, then stir in the pepper and mushrooms and simmer for a further 15–20 minutes until the chicken and vegetables are tender and the sauce is reduced and slightly thickened. Stir in the parsley and serve immediately with freshly cooked tagliatelle.

Health Rating: 3 points

Lemon Chicken with Potatoes, Rosemary & Olives

Serves 6

Ingredients

12 skinless and boneless chicken thighs
1 large lemon
125 ml/4 fl oz/½ cup extra virgin olive oil
6 garlic cloves, peeled and sliced
2 onions, peeled and thinly sliced
bunch fresh rosemary
1.1 kg/2½ lb potatoes, peeled and cut into 4 cm/1½ inch pieces
salt and freshly ground black pepper
18–24 black/ripe olives, pitted

To serve:
steamed carrots
steamed courgettes/zucchini

Preheat the oven to 200°C/400°F/Gas Mark 6, 15 minutes before cooking. Trim the chicken thighs and place in a shallow baking dish large enough to hold them in a single layer.

Remove the zest from the lemon with a zester or, if using a peeler, cut into thin julienne strips. Reserve half and add the remainder to the chicken. Squeeze the lemon juice over the chicken, toss to coat well and leave to stand for 10 minutes. Add the remaining lemon zest or julienne strips, olive oil, garlic, onions and half of the rosemary sprigs. Toss gently and leave for about 20 minutes.

Cover the potatoes with lightly salted water and bring to the boil. Cook for 2 minutes, then drain well and add to the chicken. Season to taste with salt and pepper. Roast the chicken in the preheated oven for 50 minutes, turning frequently and basting, or until the chicken is cooked. Just before the end of cooking time, discard the rosemary and add fresh rosemary sprigs. Add the olives and stir. Serve immediately with the steamed vegetables.

Health Rating: 3 points

Chicken with Porcini Mushrooms

Serves 4

Ingredients

2 tbsp olive oil

4 boneless chicken breasts, preferably free range

2 garlic cloves, peeled and crushed

150 ml/¼ pint/⅔ cup dry vermouth or dry white wine

salt and freshly ground black pepper

25 g/1 oz/2 tbsp butter

450 g/1 lb/4 cups thickly sliced porcini or wild mushrooms

1 tbsp freshly chopped oregano

fresh basil sprigs, to garnish (optional)

freshly cooked rice, to serve

Health Rating: 3 points

Heat the olive oil in a large, heavy-based frying pan, then add the chicken breasts, skin-side down, and cook for about 10 minutes until they are well browned. Remove the chicken breasts and reserve. Add the garlic, stir into the juices and cook for 1 minute.

Pour the vermouth or white wine into the pan and season to taste with salt and pepper. Return the chicken to the pan. Bring to the boil, reduce the heat to low and simmer for about 20 minutes until tender.

In another large frying pan, heat the butter and add the sliced porcini or wild mushrooms. Stir-fry for about 5 minutes until the mushrooms are golden and tender.

Add the porcini or wild mushrooms and any juices to the chicken. Season to taste, then add the chopped oregano. Stir together gently and cook for 1 minute longer. Transfer to a large serving plate and garnish with fresh basil sprigs if desired. Serve immediately with rice.

Turkey Escalopes Marsala with Wilted Watercress

Serves 4

Ingredients

4 turkey escalopes/cutlets, 150 g/5 oz/¹/₄ lb each

25 g/1 oz/¹/₄ cup plain/all-purpose flour

¹/₂ tsp dried thyme

salt and freshly ground black pepper

1–2 tbsp olive oil

125 g/4 oz/2¹/₄ cups watercress

40 g/1¹/₂ oz/3 tbsp butter

225 g/8 oz/2 cups wiped and quartered mushrooms

4 tbsp dry Marsala or Italian fortified wine

4 tbsp chicken stock or water

Place each turkey escalope/cutlet between two sheets of nonstick baking parchment. Using a meat mallet or rolling pin, pound until about 3 mm/¹/₈ inch thick.

Put the flour in a shallow dish, add the thyme, season to taste with salt and pepper and stir to blend. Coat each escalope lightly on both sides with the flour mixture, then reserve.

Heat the olive oil in a large frying pan. Add the watercress and stir-fry for about 2 minutes until just wilted and brightly coloured. Season to taste with salt and pepper. Using a slotted spoon, transfer the watercress to a plate and keep warm.

Add half the butter to the frying pan and, when melted, add the mushrooms. Stir-fry for 4 minutes, or until golden and tender. Remove from the pan and reserve.

Add the remaining butter to the pan and, working in batches if necessary, cook the flour-coated escalope for 2–3 minutes on each side until golden and cooked thoroughly, adding the remaining oil if needed.

Remove from the pan and keep warm. Add the Marsala or Italian fortified wine to the pan and stir, scraping up any browned bits from the bottom. Add the stock or water and bring to the boil over a high heat. Season lightly.

Return the escalope and mushrooms to the pan and reheat gently until piping hot. Divide the warm watercress between four serving plates. Arrange an escalope over each serving of wilted watercress and spoon over the mushrooms and Marsala sauce. Serve immediately.

Health Rating: 3 points

Lemon Chicken with Basil & Linguine

Serves 4

Ingredients

1 tbsp grated lemon zest

3 tbsp lemon juice

2 garlic cloves, peeled and crushed

2 tbsp basil-flavoured extra virgin olive oil

4 tbsp freshly chopped basil

salt and freshly ground black pepper

450 g/1 lb skinless chicken breast fillets/halves, cut into
   bite-size pieces

1 onion, peeled and finely chopped

3 celery stalks, trimmed and thinly sliced

175 g/6 oz/1½ cups wiped and halved mushrooms

2 tbsp plain/all-purpose flour

150 ml/¼ pint/⅔ cup white wine

150 ml/¼ pint/⅔ cup chicken stock

350–450 g/12 oz–1 lb/4–6 cups linguine

To garnish:
lemon zest
fresh basil leaves

Blend the lemon zest and juice, garlic, half the oil, half the basil and the salt and pepper in a large bowl. Add the chicken pieces and toss well to coat. Allow to stand for about 1 hour, stirring occasionally.

Heat the remaining oil in a large, nonstick frying pan. Add the sliced onion and cook for 3–4 minutes until slightly softened. Using a slotted spoon, drain the chicken pieces and add to the frying pan, reserving the marinade. Cook the chicken for 2–3 minutes until golden brown. Add the sliced celery and mushrooms. Cook for a further 2–3 minutes.

Sprinkle in the flour and stir until the chicken and vegetables are coated. Gradually stir the wine into the pan until a thick sauce forms, then stir in the stock and reserved marinade. Bring to the boil, stirring constantly. Cover and simmer for about 10 minutes, then stir in the remaining basil.

Meanwhile, bring a large saucepan of lightly salted water to the boil. Slowly add the linguine and simmer for 7–10 minutes, or until *al dente*. Drain well and turn into a large serving bowl, pour over the sauce and garnish with the lemon zest and fresh basil leaves. Serve immediately.

Health Rating: 3 points

Chicken Liver & Tomato Sauce with Tagliolini

Serves 4

Ingredients

50 ml/2 fl oz/¼ cup extra virgin olive oil

1 onion, peeled and finely chopped

2 garlic cloves, peeled and finely chopped

125 ml/4 fl oz/½ cup dry red wine

800 g/28 oz/4 cups canned Italian peeled plum
  tomatoes with juice

1 tbsp tomato purée/paste

1 tbsp freshly chopped sage or thyme leaves

salt and freshly ground black pepper

350 g/12 oz/4 cups fresh or dried tagliolini, papardelle
  or tagliatelle

25 g/1 oz/2 tbsp butter

225 g/8 oz/2 cups fresh chicken livers, trimmed and cut
  in half

plain/all-purpose flour, for dusting

fresh sage sprigs, to garnish (optional)

Heat half the olive oil in a large, deep, heavy-based frying pan and add the onion. Cook, stirring frequently, for 4–5 minutes until soft and translucent. Stir in the garlic and cook for a further minute.

Add the red wine and cook, stirring, until the wine is reduced by half, then add the tomatoes, tomato purée/paste and half the sage or thyme. Bring to the boil, stirring to break up the tomatoes. Simmer for 30 minutes, stirring occasionally, or until the sauce has reduced and thickened. Season to taste with salt and pepper.

Bring a large saucepan of lightly salted water to the boil. Add the pasta and cook for 7–10 minutes, or until al dente.

Meanwhile, in a large, heavy-based frying pan, melt the remaining oil and the butter and heat until very hot. Pat the chicken livers dry and dust lightly with a little flour. Add to the pan, a few at a time, and cook for 5 minutes, or until crisp and browned, turning carefully – the livers should still be pink inside.

Drain the pasta well and turn into a large, warmed serving bowl. Stir the livers carefully into the tomato sauce, then pour the sauce over the drained pasta and toss gently to coat. Garnish with a sprig of fresh sage and serve immediately.

Health Rating: 3 points

Chicken Thighs with Pine Nuts

Serves 4–8

Ingredients

8 skinless and boneless chicken thighs
1 tbsp olive oil, plus a little extra for oiling
1 medium onion, peeled and finely chopped
2–3 garlic cloves
3 tbsp pine nuts
75 g/3 oz/1 cup wiped and finely chopped button/white mushrooms
75 g/3 oz/1⅓ cups fresh breadcrumbs
1–2 small rosemary sprigs, leaves stripped and finely chopped
finely grated zest of 1 small orange
salt and freshly ground black pepper
1 medium/large egg, beaten
1 medium/large egg yolk
8 unsmoked rashers/slices back/Canadian-style bacon
few fresh rosemary sprigs
seasonal vegetables or salad and warm Italian bread, to serve

Preheat the oven to 190°C/375°F/Gas Mark 5, 10 minutes before cooking. Cut off and discard any fat from the chicken thighs, then wipe or lightly rinse and pat dry with paper towels. Reserve, lightly covered, in the refrigerator. For the stuffing, heat the oil in a frying pan, add the onion and garlic and fry for 2 minutes. Add the pine nuts and mushrooms and continue to fry for 3 minutes. Remove from the heat and stir in the remaining ingredients. Mix to a stiff consistency with the egg and the egg yolk.

Place the chicken thighs skinned-side down on a chopping board. Place a spoonful of stuffing on top, then fold the thighs over to completely encase the stuffing. Wrap a rasher/slice of bacon around each thigh and secure with a cocktail stick/toothpick. Roll any remaining stuffing into balls. Lightly oil a roasting tin/pan and place a few rosemary sprigs in the base. Place the thighs on top, then add a few more rosemary sprigs. Roast for 25–30 minutes until thoroughly cooked, adding the stuffing balls around the chicken for the last 15 minutes of cooking time. Serve with seasonal vegetables or salad and warm Italian bread.

Health Rating: 2 points

Turkey Tetrazzini

Serves 4

Ingredients

275 g/10 oz/3¼ cups green and white tagliatelle
50 g/2 oz/4 tbsp butter
4 slices streaky/fatty bacon, diced
1 onion, peeled and finely chopped
175 g/6 oz/1¼ cups mushrooms, thinly sliced
40 g/1¼ oz/⅔ cup plain/all-purpose flour
450 ml/¾ pint/1¾ cups chicken stock
150 ml/¼ pint/⅓ cup double/heavy cream
2 tbsp sherry
450 g/1 lb cooked turkey meat, cut into bite-size pieces
1 tbsp freshly chopped parsley
freshly grated nutmeg
salt and freshly ground black pepper
25 g/1 oz/¼ cup grated Parmesan cheese
freshly chopped parsley and grated Parmesan cheese, to garnish

Preheat the oven to 180°C/350°F/Gas Mark 4. Lightly oil a large, ovenproof dish. Bring a large saucepan of lightly salted water to the boil. Add the tagliatelle and cook for 7–9 minutes, or until *al dente*. Drain well and reserve.

In a heavy-based saucepan, heat the butter and add the bacon. Cook for 2–3 minutes until crisp and golden. Add the onion and mushrooms and cook for 3–4 minutes until the vegetables are tender.

Stir in the flour and cook for 2 minutes. Remove from the heat and slowly stir in the stock. Return to the heat and cook, stirring, until a smooth, thick sauce has formed. Add the tagliatelle, then pour in the cream and sherry. Add the turkey and parsley. Season to taste with the nutmeg and salt and pepper. Toss well to coat.

Turn the mixture into the prepared dish, spreading evenly. Sprinkle the top with the Parmesan cheese and bake in the preheated oven for 30–35 minutes until crisp, golden and bubbling. Garnish with chopped parsley and Parmesan cheese and serve straight from the dish.

Health Rating: 1 point

Duck Lasagne with Porcini & Basil

Serves 6

Ingredients

1.4–1.8 kg/3–4 lb duck, quartered

1 onion, unpeeled and quartered

2 carrots, peeled and cut into pieces

1 celery stalk, cut into pieces

1 leek, trimmed and cut into pieces

2 garlic cloves, unpeeled and smashed

1 tbsp black peppercorns

2 bay leaves

6–8 fresh thyme sprigs

50 g/2 oz/½ cup dried porcini mushrooms

120 ml/4 fl oz/½ cup dry sherry

75 g/3 oz/6 tbsp butter, diced

1 bunch fresh basil leaves, stripped from stems

24 pre-cooked lasagne sheets

75 g/3 oz/1 cup grated Parmesan cheese

parsley sprig, to garnish

mixed salad, to serve

Preheat the oven to 180°C/350°F/Gas Mark 4, 10 minutes before cooking. Put the duck with the vegetables, garlic, peppercorns, bay leaves and thyme into a large stock pot and cover with cold water. Bring to the boil, skimming off any fat, then reduce the heat and simmer for 1 hour. Transfer the duck to a bowl and cool slightly.

When cool enough to handle, remove the meat from the duck and dice. Add all the bones and trimmings to the simmering stock and continue to simmer for 1 hour. Strain the stock into a large bowl and leave until cold. Remove and discard the fat that has risen to the top of the stock.

Put the porcini in a colander/strainer and rinse under cold running water. Leave for 1 minute to dry off, then turn out on to a chopping board and chop finely. Place in a small bowl, then pour over the sherry and leave for about 1 hour, or until the porcini are plump and all the sherry is absorbed.

Heat 25 g/1 oz/2 tbsp of the butter in a frying pan. Shred the basil leaves and add to the hot butter, stirring until wilted. Add the soaked porcini and any liquid, mix well and reserve.

Oil a 30 x 23 cm/12 x 9 inch deep baking dish and pour a little stock into the base. Cover with 6–8 lasagne sheets, making sure that the sheets overlap slightly. Continue to layer the pasta with a little stock, duck meat, the mushroom–basil mixture and Parmesan. Add a little butter every other layer.

Cover with kitchen foil and bake in the preheated oven for 40–45 minutes, or until cooked. Leave to stand for 10 minutes before serving. Garnish with a sprig of parsley and serve with salad.

Health Rating: 2 points

Creamy Chicken Cannelloni

Serves 6

Ingredients

50 g/2 oz/4 tbsp butter

2 garlic cloves, peeled and finely crushed

225 g/8 oz/2 cups thinly sliced button/white mushrooms

2 tbsp freshly chopped basil

450 g/1 lb/10 cups blanched fresh spinach

salt and freshly ground black pepper

2 tbsp plain/all-purpose flour

300 ml/½ pint/1¼ cups chicken stock

150 ml/¼ pint/⅔ cup dry white wine

150 ml/¼ pint/⅔ cup double/heavy cream

350 g/12 oz/3¾ cups chopped skinless and boneless,
    cooked chicken

175 g/6 oz/¾ cup finely chopped Parma ham/prosciutto

½ tsp dried thyme

225 g/8 oz/16 precooked cannelloni tubes

175 g/6 oz/1½ cups grated Gruyère cheese

40 g/1½ oz/½ cup grated Parmesan cheese

fresh basil sprig, to garnish

Preheat the oven to 190°C/375°F/Gas Mark 5, 10 minutes before cooking. Lightly butter a 28 x 23 cm/11 x 9 inch, ovenproof baking dish. Heat half the butter in a large, heavy-based frying pan, then add the garlic and mushrooms and cook gently for 5 minutes. Stir in the basil and the spinach and cook, covered, until the spinach is wilted and just tender, stirring frequently. Season to taste with salt and pepper, then spoon into the dish and reserve.

Melt the remaining butter in a small saucepan, then stir in the flour and cook for about 2 minutes, stirring constantly. Remove from the heat, stir in the stock, then the wine and the cream. Return to the heat, bring to the boil and simmer until the sauce is thick and smooth, then season to taste.

Measure 125 ml/4 fl oz/½ cup of the cream sauce into a bowl. Add the chopped chicken, Parma ham/prosciutto and the dried thyme. Season to taste, then spoon the chicken mixture into the cannelloni tubes, arranging them in two long

rows on top of the spinach layer. Add half the Gruyère cheese to the cream sauce and heat, stirring, until the cheese melts. Pour over the sauce and top with the remaining Gruyère and the Parmesan cheese. Bake in the oven for 35 minutes, or until golden and bubbling. Garnish with a sprig of fresh basil and serve immediately.

Health Rating: 2 point

Poached Chicken with Salsa Verde Herb Sauce

Serves 6

Ingredients

6 boneless chicken breasts, each about 175 g/6 oz

600 ml/1 pint/2½ cups chicken stock, preferably home-made

2 garlic cloves, peeled and chopped

4 tbsp freshly chopped parsley

3 tbsp freshly chopped mint

2 tsp capers

2 tbsp chopped gherkins/pickles (optional)

2–3 anchovy fillets in olive oil, drained and finely chopped (optional)

1 handful wild rocket/arugula leaves, chopped (optional)

2 tbsp lemon juice or red wine vinegar

125 ml/4 fl oz/½ cup extra virgin olive oil

salt and freshly ground black pepper

mint sprigs, to garnish

freshly cooked vegetables, to serve

Place the chicken breasts with the stock in a large frying pan and bring to the boil. Reduce the heat and simmer for 10–15 minutes until cooked. Leave to cool in the stock.

To make the salsa verde, switch on the motor on a food processor, then drop in the garlic cloves and chop finely. Add the parsley and mint and, using the pulse button, pulse 2–3 times. Add the capers and, if using, add the gherkins/pickles, anchovies and rocket/arugula. Pulse 2–3 times until the sauce is evenly textured. With the machine still running, pour in the lemon juice or red wine vinegar, then add the olive oil in a slow, steady stream until the sauce is smooth. Season to taste with salt and pepper, then transfer to a large serving bowl and reserve.

Carve each chicken breast into thick slices and arrange on serving plates, fanning out the slices slightly. Spoon over a little of the salsa verde onto each chicken breast, garnish with mint sprigs and serve immediately with freshly cooked vegetables.

Health Rating: 4 points

Chicken Parcels with Courgettes & Pasta

Serves 4

Ingredients

2 tbsp olive oil

125 g/4 oz/1 cup farfalle pasta

1 onion, peeled and thinly sliced

1 garlic clove, peeled and finely chopped

2 medium courgettes/zucchini, trimmed and thinly sliced

salt and freshly ground black pepper

2 tbsp freshly chopped oregano

4 plum tomatoes, deseeded and roughly chopped

4 x 175 g/6 oz skinless and boneless chicken breasts

150 ml/¼ pint/⅔ cup Italian white wine

Preheat the oven to 200°C/400°F/Gas Mark 6, 15 minutes before cooking. Lightly brush four large sheets of nonstick baking parchment with half the oil. Bring a saucepan of lightly salted water to the boil and cook the pasta for 10 minutes, or until *al dente*. Drain and reserve.

Heat the remaining oil in a frying pan and cook the onion for 2–3 minutes. Add the garlic and cook for 1 minute. Add the courgettes/zucchini and cook for 1 minute, then remove from the heat. Season to taste with salt and pepper and add half the oregano.

Divide the cooked pasta equally between the four sheets of baking parchment, positioning the pasta in the centre. Top the pasta with equal amounts of the vegetable mixture, and sprinkle a quarter of the chopped tomatoes over each.

Score the surface of each chicken breast about 1 cm/½ inch deep. Place a chicken breast on top of the pasta and sprinkle each with the remaining oregano and the white wine. Fold the edges of the paper along the top, then along each side, creating a sealed envelope.

Bake in the preheated oven for 30–35 minutes until cooked. Serve immediately.

Health Rating: 3 points

Chicken Under a Brick

Serves 4–6

Ingredients

1.8 kg/4 lb free range, corn-fed, oven-ready chicken
50 ml/2 fl oz olive oil
sea salt and freshly ground black pepper
tossed bitter salad leaves, to serve

To garnish:
fresh basil sprigs
chives

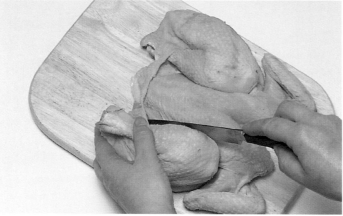

Rinse the chicken and dry well, inside and out. Using poultry shears or kitchen scissors, cut along each side of the backbone of the chicken and discard or use for stock. Place the chicken skin-side up on a work surface and, using the palm of your hand, press down firmly to break the breast bone and flatten the bird.

Turn the chicken breast-side up and use a sharp knife to slit the skin between the breast and thigh on each side. Fold the legs in and push the drumstick bones through the slits. Tuck the wings under; the chicken should be as flat as possible.

Heat the olive oil in a large, heavy-based frying pan until very hot but not smoking. Place the chicken in the pan, skin-side down, and place a flat lid or plate directly on top of the chicken. Top with a brick (hence the name) or 2 kg/5 lb weight. Cook for 12–15 minutes until golden brown.

Remove the weights and lid and, using a pair of tongs, turn the chicken carefully, then season to taste with salt and pepper. Cover and weight the lid again, then cook for 12–15 minutes longer, until the chicken is tender and the juices run clear when a thigh is pierced with a sharp knife or skewer.

Transfer the chicken to a serving plate and cover loosely with kitchen foil to keep warm. Allow to rest for at least 10 minutes before carving. Garnish with basil sprigs and chives and serve with salad leaves.

Health Rating: 3 points

Chicken & Asparagus with Tagliatelle

Serves 4

Ingredients

275 g/10 oz/2 cups fresh asparagus

50 g/2 oz/4 tbsp butter

4 spring onions/scallions, trimmed and roughly chopped

350 g/12 oz skinless and boneless chicken breast fillets/halves, thinly sliced

2 tbsp white vermouth

300 ml/½ pint/1¼ cups double/heavy cream

2 tbsp freshly chopped chives

400 g/14 oz/4½ cups fresh tagliatelle

50 g/2 oz/½ cup Parmesan or pecorino cheese, grated

snipped chives, to garnish

extra Parmesan cheese, to serve (optional)

Using a swivel-bladed vegetable peeler, lightly peel the asparagus stalks and then cook in lightly salted boiling water for 2–3 minutes until just tender. Drain and refresh in cold water, then cut into 4 cm/1½ inch pieces and reserve.

Melt the butter in a large frying pan, then add the spring onions/scallions and the chicken and fry for 4 minutes. Add the vermouth and allow to reduce until the liquid has evaporated. Pour in the cream and half the chives. Cook gently for 5–7 minutes until the sauce has thickened and slightly reduced and the chicken is tender.

Bring a large saucepan of lightly salted water to the boil and cook the tagliatelle for 4–5 minutes, or until *al dente*. Drain and immediately add to the chicken and cream sauce.

Using a pair of spaghetti tongs or kitchen forks, lightly toss the sauce and pasta until it is mixed thoroughly. Add the remaining chives and the Parmesan or pecorino cheese and toss gently. Garnish with snipped chives and serve immediately, with extra Parmesan cheese if wanted.

Health Rating: 3 points

Marinated Pheasant Breasts with Grilled Polenta

Serves 4

Ingredients

3 tbsp extra virgin olive oil

1 tbsp freshly chopped rosemary or sage leaves

$1/2$ tsp ground cinnamon

grated zest of 1 orange

salt and freshly ground black pepper

8 pheasant/game hen or wood pigeon breasts

600 ml/1 pint/$2^1/2$ cups water

125 g/4 oz/1 cup quick-cook polenta

25 g/1 oz/2 tbsp butter, diced

40 g/$1^1/2$ oz/$^1/2$ cup grated Parmesan cheese

1–2 tbsp freshly chopped parsley

assorted salad leaves, to serve

Preheat the grill/broiler just before cooking. Blend 2 tablespoons of the olive oil with the rosemary or sage, the cinnamon and orange zest and season to taste with salt and pepper.

Place the bird breasts in a large, shallow dish, pour over the flavoured oil and marinate until needed, turning occasionally.

Bring the water and 1 teaspoon salt to the boil in a large, heavy–based saucepan. Slowly whisk in the polenta in a thin, steady stream. Reduce the heat and simmer for 5–10 minutes until very thick, stirring constantly. Stir the butter, cheese, parsley and a little black pepper into the polenta.

Turn the polenta out onto a lightly oiled, nonstick baking sheet and spread in an even layer about 2 cm/$^3/4$ inch thick. Leave to cool, then chill in the refrigerator for about 1 hour until the polenta is chilled.

Turn the cold polenta onto a work surface/countertop. Cut into 10 cm/4 inch squares. Brush with olive oil and arrange on a grill rack. Grill for 2–3 minutes on each side until crisp and golden, then cut each square into triangles and keep warm.

Transfer the marinated pheasant breasts to the grill rack and grill for 5 minutes, or until crisp and beginning to colour, turning once. Serve the pheasants immediately with the polenta triangles and salad leaves.

Health Rating: 3 points

Chicken Tagliatelle

Serves 4

Ingredients

350 g/12 oz tagliatelle

125 g/4 oz/1 cup frozen peas

4 skinless and boneless chicken breast fillets/halves

2 tbsp olive oil

1/4 cucumber, cut into strips

150 ml/¼ pint/²⁄₃ cup dry vermouth

150 ml/¼ pint/²⁄₃ cup double/heavy cream

125 g/4 oz/1 cup Stilton cheese, crumbled

3 tbsp freshly snipped chives, plus extra to garnish

salt and freshly ground black pepper

fresh herbs, to garnish

Bring a large pan of lightly salted water to a rolling boil. Add the pasta and cook according to the packet instructions, or until *al dente*. Add the peas to the pan 5 minutes before the end of cooking time and cook until tender. Drain the pasta and peas, return to the pan and keep warm.

Trim the chicken if necessary, then cut into bite-size pieces. Heat the olive oil in a large frying pan, add the chicken and cook for 8 minutes, or until golden, stirring occasionally.

Add the cucumber and cook for 2 minutes, or until slightly softened, stirring occasionally. Stir in the vermouth, bring to the boil, then lower the heat and simmer for 3 minutes, or until reduced slightly. Add the cream to the pan, bring to the boil, stirring constantly, then stir in the Stilton cheese and snipped chives. Season to taste with salt and pepper. Heat through thoroughly, stirring occasionally, until the cheese is just beginning to melt.

Toss the chicken mixture into the pasta. Tip into a warmed serving dish or onto individual plates. Garnish and serve immediately.

Health Rating: 3 points

Herb-baked Chicken with Tagliatelle

Serves 4

Ingredients

75 g/3 oz/1½ cups fresh white breadcrumbs

3 tbsp olive oil

1 tsp dried oregano

2 tbsp sun-dried tomato paste

salt and freshly ground black pepper

4 skinless and boneless chicken breast fillets/halves, each
     about 150 g/5 oz

800 g/28 oz/4 cups canned plum tomatoes

4 tbsp freshly chopped basil

2 tbsp dry white wine

350 g/12 oz tagliatelle

fresh basil sprigs, to garnish

Preheat the oven to 200°C/400°F/Gas Mark 6, 15 minutes before cooking. Mix together the breadcrumbs, 1 tablespoon of the olive oil, the oregano and sun-dried tomato paste. Season to taste with salt and pepper. Place the chicken breasts well apart in a roasting tin and coat with the breadcrumb mixture.

Mix the plum tomatoes with the chopped basil and white wine. Season to taste, then spoon evenly round the chicken.

Drizzle the remaining olive oil over the chicken breasts and cook in the preheated oven for 20–30 minutes until the chicken is golden and the juices run clear when a skewer is inserted into the flesh.

Meanwhile, bring a large pan of lightly salted water to a rolling boil. Add the pasta and cook according to the packet instructions, or until *al dente*.

Drain the pasta thoroughly and transfer to warmed serving plates. Arrange the chicken breasts on top of the pasta and spoon over the sauce. Garnish with sprigs of basil and serve immediately.

Health Rating: 3 points

Creamy Chicken & Sausage Penne

Serves 4

Ingredients

2 tbsp olive oil

225 g/8 oz shallots, peeled

8 chicken thighs

175 g/6 oz smoked sausage, thickly sliced

125 g/4 oz/1¼ cups wiped and halved
   chestnut/cremini mushrooms

2 garlic cloves, peeled and chopped

1 tbsp paprika

1 small bunch fresh thyme, chopped, plus leaves to garnish

150 ml/¼ pint/⅔ cup water

300 ml/½ pint/1¼ cups chicken stock

freshly ground black pepper

350 g/12 oz/3 cups penne

250 g tub/1 cup mascarpone cheese

Heat the olive oil in a large frying pan, add the shallots and cook for 3 minutes, or until golden. Remove and drain on absorbent paper towels. Add the chicken thighs to the pan and cook for 5 minutes, turning frequently, until browned. Drain on paper towels.

Add the smoked sausage and mushrooms to the pan and cook for 3 minutes, or until browned. Drain separately on paper towels. Return the shallots, chicken and sausage to the pan, then add the garlic, paprika and thyme and cook for 1 minute, stirring. Pour in the water and stock and season to taste with black pepper. Bring to the boil, lower the heat and simmer, covered, for 15 minutes. Add the mushrooms to the pan and simmer, covered, for 15 minutes, or until the chicken is tender.

Meanwhile, bring a large pan of lightly salted water to a rolling boil. Add the penne and cook according to the packet instructions, or until *al dente*. Drain thoroughly. Stir the mascarpone cheese into the chicken sauce and heat through, stirring gently. Spoon the pasta onto a warmed serving dish, top with the sauce, garnish and serve immediately.

Health Rating: 3 points

Stuffed Turkey Breast Fillet

Serves 4–6

Ingredients

1 fresh whole turkey breast fillet, about 700 g/1½ lb in weight
125 g/4 oz Parma ham/prosciutto

For the stuffing:
15 g/½ oz/generous ⅛ cup sun-dried tomatoes in oil
2 tbsp olive oil
1 medium onion, peeled and chopped
2 garlic cloves, peeled and crushed
50 g/2 oz/scant 1 cup fresh breadcrumbs
50 g/2 oz/scant ¼ cup ricotta cheese
50 g/2 oz/scant ½ cup dried cranberries
1 tbsp freshly chopped oregano
1–2 tsp freshly chopped fresh rosemary (strip the spiky leaves off the stalks before chopping)
salt and freshly ground black pepper
freshly cooked vegetables, to serve

Preheat the oven to 190°C/375°F/Gas Mark 5, 10 minutes before roasting the turkey. Drain the sun-dried tomatoes, chop finely and reserve. Heat the oil in a saucepan, add the onion and garlic and fry gently for 5 minutes, or until softened. Remove from the heat and stir in the remaining stuffing ingredients, including the sun-dried tomatoes. Season with salt and pepper, then mix together, adding a little of the sun-dried tomato oil if liked.

Make a slit down the length of the turkey fillet and open to form a pocket. Fill with the prepared stuffing, then push together to encase the stuffing. Wrap the turkey fillet with the Parma ham/prosciutto. Roll any remaining stuffing into balls.

Place the turkey in a roasting tin/pan and roast for 1 hour 10 minutes, or until completely cooked through and the juices run clear when the turkey is pierced in the thickest part with a skewer. Put the stuffing balls around the joint for the last 15 minutes of cooking time. Serve with the stuffing balls and cooked vegetables.

Health Rating: 3 points

Creamy Turkey & Tomato Pasta

Serves 4

Ingredients

4 tbsp olive oil
450 g/1 lb turkey breasts, cut into bite-size pieces
550 g/1 lb 3 oz cherry tomatoes on the vine
2 garlic cloves, peeled and chopped
4 tbsp balsamic vinegar
salt and freshly ground black pepper
350 g/12 oz tagliatelle
4 tbsp freshly chopped basil
200 ml tub/¾ cup crème fraîche
shaved Parmesan cheese, to garnish

Preheat the oven to 200°C/400°F/Gas Mark 6. Heat 2 tablespoons of the olive oil in a large frying pan. Add the turkey and cook for 5 minutes, or until sealed, turning occasionally. Transfer to a roasting tin/pan and add the remaining olive oil, the vine tomatoes, garlic and balsamic vinegar. Stir well and season to taste with salt and pepper. Cook in the preheated oven for 30 minutes, or until the turkey is tender, turning the tomatoes and turkey once.

Meanwhile, bring a large pan of lightly salted water to a rolling boil. Add the pasta and cook according to the packet instructions, or until al dente. Drain, return to the pan and keep warm. Stir the basil and seasoning into the crème fraîche.

Remove the roasting tin from the oven and discard the vines. Stir the crème fraîche/sour cream and basil mix into the turkey and tomato mixture and return to the oven for 1–2 minutes until thoroughly heated through. Stir the turkey and tomato mixture into the pasta and toss lightly together. Tip into a warmed serving dish. Garnish with Parmesan cheese shavings and serve immediately.

Health Rating: 2 points

Prosciutto–wrapped Chicken with Ribbon Pasta

Serves 4

Ingredients

4 skinless and boneless chicken breast fillets/halves

salt and freshly ground black pepper

12 slices Parma ham/prosciutto

2 tbsp olive oil

350 g/12 oz ribbon pasta

1 garlic clove, peeled and chopped

1 bunch spring onions/scallions, trimmed and diagonally sliced

400 g/14 oz/2 cups canned chopped tomatoes

juice of 1 lemon

150 ml/¼ pint/⅔ cup crème fraîche

3 tbsp freshly chopped parsley

pinch sugar

freshly grated Parmesan cheese, to garnish

Cut each chicken breast into three pieces. Season well with salt and pepper. Enclose each chicken piece completely with a slice of Parma ham/prosciutto, securing if necessary with either fine twine or cocktail sticks/toothpicks. Heat the oil in a large frying pan and cook the chicken, turning occasionally, for 12–15 minutes until thoroughly cooked. Remove from the pan with a slotted spoon and reserve.

Bring a pan of lightly salted water to a rolling boil. Add the pasta and cook according to the packet instructions, or until *al dente*.

Add the garlic and spring onions/scallions to the frying pan and cook, stirring occasionally, for 2 minutes, or until softened. Stir in the tomatoes, lemon juice and crème fraîche. Bring to the boil, lower the heat and simmer, covered, for 3 minutes. Stir in the parsley and sugar, season to taste, then return the chicken to the pan and heat for 2–3 minutes until piping hot.

Drain the pasta thoroughly and mix in the chopped parsley, then spoon onto a serving dish or individual plates. Arrange the chicken and sauce over the pasta. Garnish and serve immediately.

Health Rating: 2 points

Baked Aubergines with Tomato & Mozzarella

Serves 4

Ingredients

3 aubergines/eggplants, trimmed and sliced

salt and freshly ground black pepper

4–6 tbsp olive oil

450 g/1 lb fresh minced/ground turkey

1 onion, peeled and chopped

2 garlic cloves, peeled and chopped

800 g/28 oz/4 cups canned chopped tomatoes

1 tbsp fresh mixed herbs

200 ml/7 fl oz/³/₄ cup red wine

350 g/12 oz/3 cups macaroni

5 tbsp freshly chopped basil

125 g/4 oz/1 cup drained and chopped mozzarella cheese

50 g/2 oz freshly grated Parmesan cheese

Preheat the oven to 200°C/400°F/Gas Mark 6, 15 minutes before cooking. Place the aubergine/eggplant slices in a colander/strainer and sprinkle with salt. Leave for 1 hour, or until the juices run clear. Rinse and dry on absorbent paper towels.

Heat 3–5 tablespoons of the olive oil in a large frying pan and cook the aubergines in batches for 2 minutes on each side, or until softened. Remove and drain on absorbent paper towels.

Heat 1 tablespoon olive oil in a saucepan, add the minced/ground turkey and cook for 5 minutes, or until browned and sealed. Add the onion to the pan and cook for 5 minutes, or until softened.

Add the chopped garlic, the tomatoes and mixed herbs. Pour in the wine and season to taste with salt and pepper. Bring to the boil, lower the heat and simmer for 15 minutes, or until thickened.

Meanwhile, bring a large pan of lightly salted water to a rolling boil. Add the macaroni and cook according to the packet instructions, or until *al dente*. Drain thoroughly.

Spoon half the tomato mixture into a lightly oiled, ovenproof dish. Top with half the aubergine, pasta and chopped

basil, then season lightly. Repeat the layers, finishing with a layer of aubergine. Sprinkle with the mozzarella and Parmesan cheeses, then bake in the preheated oven for 30 minutes, or until golden and bubbling. Serve immediately.

Health Rating: 2 points

Mini Chicken Balls with Tagliatelle

Serves 4

Ingredients

450 g/1 lb fresh minced/ground chicken

50 g/2 oz/½ cup sun-dried tomatoes, drained and
   finely chopped

salt and freshly ground black pepper

25 g/1 oz/2 tbsp butter

350 g/12 oz leeks, trimmed and diagonally sliced

125 g/4 oz/1 cup frozen broad/fava beans

300 ml/½ pint/1¼ cups single/light cream

50 g/2 oz/½ cup freshly grated Parmesan cheese

350 g/12 oz tagliatelle

4 medium/large eggs

fresh herbs, to garnish

Mix the chicken and tomatoes together and season to taste with salt and pepper. Divide the mixture into 32 pieces and roll into balls. Transfer to a baking sheet, cover and leave in the refrigerator for 1 hour.

Melt the butter in a large frying pan, add the chicken balls and cook for 5 minutes, or until golden, turning occasionally. Remove, drain on absorbent paper towels and keep warm. Add the leeks and broad/fava beans to the frying pan and cook, stirring, for 10 minutes, or until cooked and tender. Return the chicken balls to the pan, then stir in the cream and Parmesan cheese and heat through.

Meanwhile, bring a large pan of lightly salted water to a rolling boil. Add the pasta and cook according to the packet instructions, or until *al dente*.

Bring a separate frying pan full of water to the boil, crack in the eggs and simmer for 2–4 minutes until poached to personal preference.

Meanwhile, drain the pasta thoroughly and return to the pan. Pour the chicken balls and vegetable sauce over the pasta, toss lightly and heat through for 1–2 minutes. Arrange on warmed individual plates and top with the poached eggs. Garnish with fresh herbs and serve immediately.

Health Rating: 3 points

Chicken Marengo

Serves 4

Ingredients

2 tbsp plain/all-purpose flour
salt and freshly ground black pepper
4 skinless and boneless chicken breasts, cut into bite-size pieces
4 tbsp olive oil
1 Spanish onion, peeled and chopped
1 garlic clove, peeled and chopped
400 g/14 oz/2 cups canned chopped tomatoes
2 tbsp sun-dried tomato paste
3 tbsp freshly chopped basil
3 tbsp freshly chopped thyme
125 ml/4 fl oz/½ cup dry white wine or chicken stock
350 g/12 oz/2¼ cups rigatoni
3 tbsp freshly chopped flat-leaf parsley

Season the flour with salt and pepper and toss the chicken in the flour to coat. Heat 2 tablespoons of the olive oil in a large frying pan and cook the chicken for 7 minutes, or until browned all over, turning occasionally. Remove from the pan using a slotted spoon and keep warm.

Add the remaining oil to the pan, add the onion and cook, stirring occasionally, for 5 minutes, or until softened and starting to brown. Add the garlic, tomatoes, sun-dried tomato paste, basil and thyme.

Pour in the wine or chicken stock and season well. Bring to the boil. Stir in the chicken pieces and simmer for 15 minutes, or until the chicken is tender and the sauce has thickened.

Meanwhile, bring a large pan of lightly salted water to a rolling boil. Add the rigatoni and cook according to the packet instructions, or until *al dente*.

Drain the rigatoni thoroughly, return to the pan and stir in the chopped parsley. Tip the pasta into a large, warmed serving dish or spoon onto individual plates. Spoon over the chicken sauce and serve immediately.

Health Rating: 3 points

Turkey & Oven-roasted Vegetable Salad

Serves 4

Ingredients

6 tbsp olive oil

3 medium courgettes/zucchinis, trimmed and sliced

2 yellow peppers, deseeded and sliced

125 g/4 oz/½ cup pine nuts

275 g/10 oz/2½ cups macaroni

350 g/12 oz cooked turkey

280 g/10 oz jarred or canned chargrilled artichokes, drained
   and sliced

225 g/8 oz baby plum tomatoes, quartered

4 tbsp freshly chopped coriander/cilantro

1 garlic clove, peeled and chopped

3 tbsp balsamic vinegar

salt and freshly ground black pepper

Preheat the oven to 200°C/400°F/Gas Mark 6, 15 minutes
before cooking. Line a large roasting tin/pan with foil, pour in
half the olive oil and place in the oven for 3 minutes, or until
very hot. Remove from the oven, add the courgettes/zucchini
and peppers and stir until evenly coated. Bake for 30–35
minutes until slightly charred, turning occasionally.

Add the pine nuts to the tin. Return to the oven and bake for
10 minutes, or until the pine nuts are toasted. Remove from the
oven and allow the vegetables to cool completely.

Bring a large pan of lightly salted water to a rolling boil. Add the
macaroni and cook according to the packet instructions, or until
al dente. Drain and refresh under cold running water, then drain
thoroughly and place in a large salad bowl.

Cut the turkey into bite-size pieces and add to the
macaroni. Add the artichokes and tomatoes with the cooled
vegetables and pan juices to the bowl. Blend together the
coriander/cilantro, garlic, remaining oil, vinegar and
seasoning. Pour over the salad, toss lightly and serve.

Health Rating: 4 points

Chicken, Gorgonzola & Mushroom Macaroni

Serves 4

Ingredients

450 g/1 lb/4 cups macaroni

75 g/3 oz/6 tbsp butter

225 g/8 oz/2½ cups wiped and sliced
chestnut/cremini mushrooms

225 g/8 oz/2½ cups wiped and halved baby
button/white mushrooms

350 g/12 oz cooked chicken, skinned and chopped

2 tsp cornflour/cornstarch

300 ml/½ pint/1¼ cups semi-skimmed/low-fat milk

50 g/2 oz/½ cup chopped Gorgonzola cheese, plus extra to serve

2 tbsp freshly chopped sage

1 tbsp freshly chopped chives, plus extra chive leaves to garnish

salt and freshly ground black pepper

Bring a large pan of lightly salted water to a rolling boil. Add the macaroni and cook according to the packet instructions, or until *al dente*.

Meanwhile, melt the butter in a large frying pan, add both types of mushrooms and cook for 5 minutes, or until golden, stirring occasionally. Add the chicken to the pan and cook for 4 minutes, or until thoroughly heated through and slightly golden, stirring occasionally.

Blend the cornflour/cornstarch with a little of the milk in a jug/pitcher to form a smooth paste, then gradually blend in the remaining milk and pour into the frying pan. Bring to the boil slowly, stirring constantly. Add the cheese and cook for 1 minute, stirring frequently, until melted.

Stir the sage and chives into the frying pan. Season to taste with salt and pepper, then heat through. Drain the macaroni thoroughly and return to the pan. Pour the chicken and mushroom sauce over the macaroni and toss lightly to coat. Tip into a warmed serving dish and serve immediately with extra Gorgonzola

Health Rating: 2 points

Spaghetti with Turkey & Bacon Sauce

Serves 4

Ingredients

450 g/1 lb spaghetti

25 g /1 oz/2 tbsp butter

225 g/8 oz smoked streaky/fatty bacon, rind removed

350 g/12 oz fresh turkey strips

1 onion, peeled and chopped

1 garlic clove, peeled and chopped

3 medium/large eggs, beaten

300 ml/½ pint/1¼ cups double/heavy cream

salt and freshly ground black pepper

50 g/2 oz/½ cup freshly grated Parmesan cheese

2–3 tbsp freshly chopped coriander/cilantro, to garnish

Bring a large pan of lightly salted water to a rolling boil. Add the spaghetti and cook according to the packet instructions, or until *al dente*.

Meanwhile, melt the butter in a large frying pan. Using scissors, cut the streaky/fatty bacon into small pieces. Add the bacon to the pan with the turkey strips. Cook for 8 minutes, or until browned, stirring occasionally to prevent sticking. Add the onion and garlic and cook for 5 minutes, or until softened, stirring occasionally.

Place the eggs and cream in a bowl. Season to taste with salt and pepper. Beat together, pour into the frying pan and cook, stirring, for 2 minutes, or until the mixture begins to thicken but does not scramble.

Drain the spaghetti thoroughly and return to the pan. Pour over the sauce, add the grated Parmesan cheese and toss lightly. Heat through for 2 minutes, or until piping hot. Tip into a warmed serving dish and sprinkle with freshly chopped coriander/cilantro. Serve immediately.

Health Rating: 1 point

Cheesy Baked Chicken Macaroni

Serves 4

Ingredients

1 tbsp olive oil

350 g/12 oz skinless and boneless chicken breast
    fillets/halves, diced

75 g/3 oz/$^1/_3$ cup pancetta, diced

1 onion, peeled and chopped

1 garlic clove, peeled and chopped

350 g packet or jar/1$^1/_2$ cups fresh tomato sauce

400 g/14 oz/2 cups canned chopped tomatoes

2 tbsp freshly chopped basil, plus leaves to garnish

salt and freshly ground black pepper

350 g/12 oz/3 cups macaroni

150 g/5 oz/1$^1/_4$ cups drained and chopped mozzarella cheese

50 g/2 oz/$^1/_2$ cup grated Gruyère cheese

50 g/2 oz/$^1/_2$ cup freshly grated Parmesan cheese

Preheat the grill/broiler just before cooking. Heat the oil in large frying pan and cook the chicken for 8 minutes, or until browned, stirring occasionally. Drain on absorbent paper towels and reserve. Add the pancetta slices to the pan and fry on both sides until crispy. Remove from the pan and reserve.

Add the onion and garlic to the frying pan and cook for 5 minutes, or until softened. Stir in the tomato sauce, chopped tomatoes and basil and season to taste with salt and pepper. Bring to the boil, lower the heat and simmer for 5 minutes.

Meanwhile, bring a large pan of lightly salted water to a rolling boil. Add the macaroni and cook according to the packet instructions, or until *al dente*. Drain the macaroni thoroughly, return to the pan and stir in the sauce, chicken and mozzarella cheese. Spoon into a shallow, ovenproof dish.

Sprinkle the pancetta over the macaroni. Sprinkle over the Gruyère and Parmesan cheeses. Place under the preheated grill and cook for 5–10 minutes until golden brown, turning the dish occasionally. Garnish and serve immediately.

Health Rating: 2 points

Pesto Chicken Tagliatelle

Serves 4

Ingredients

2 tbsp olive oil

350 g/12 oz skinless and boneless chicken breast fillets/halves,
cut into chunks

75 g/3 oz/6 tbsp butter

2 leeks, trimmed and thinly sliced

125 g/4½ oz/1¼ cups trimmed and halved oyster mushrooms

200 g/7 oz/2¼ cups small open chestnut/cremini mushrooms,
wiped and halved

450 g/1 lb fresh tagliatelle

4–6 tbsp red pesto

200 ml/7 fl oz/¾ cup crème fraîche

50 g/2 oz/½ cup freshly grated Parmesan cheese

salt and freshly ground black pepper

Heat the oil in a large frying pan, add the chicken and cook for
8 minutes, or until golden brown, stirring occasionally. Using a
slotted spoon, remove the chicken from the pan, drain on
absorbent paper towels and reserve.

Melt the butter in the pan. Add the leeks and cook for 3–5
minutes until slightly softened, stirring occasionally.

Add the oyster and chestnut/cremini mushrooms and cook for
5 minutes, or until browned, stirring occasionally.

Bring a large pan of lightly salted water to the boil, add the
tagliatelle, return to the boil and cook for 4 minutes, or until
al dente.

Add the chicken, pesto and crème fraîche/sour cream to the
mushroom mixture. Stir, then thoroughly heat through. Stir in the
grated Parmesan cheese and season to taste with salt and pepper.

Drain the tagliatelle thoroughly and pile onto warmed plates.
Spoon over the sauce and serve immediately.

Health Rating: 3 points

Chicken & Prawn-stacked Ravioli

Serves 4

Ingredients

1 tbsp olive oil

1 onion, peeled and chopped

1 garlic clove, peeled and chopped

450 g/1 lb cooked chicken, boned, skinned and cut into
   large pieces

1 beef tomato, deseeded and chopped

150 ml/¼ pint/⅔ cup dry white wine

150 ml/¼ pint/⅔ cup double/heavy cream

250 g/9 oz cooked prawns/shrimp, peeled and thawed if frozen

2 tbsp freshly chopped tarragon, plus sprigs to garnish

salt and freshly ground black pepper

8 sheets fresh lasagne

Heat the olive oil in a large frying pan, add the onion and garlic and cook for 5 minutes, or until softened, stirring occasionally. Add the chicken pieces and fry for 4 minutes, or until heated through, turning occasionally.

Stir in the chopped tomato, wine and cream and bring to the boil. Lower the heat and simmer for about 5 minutes until reduced and thickened. Stir in the prawns/shrimp and tarragon. Season to taste with salt and pepper. Heat the sauce through gently.

Meanwhile, bring a large pan of lightly salted water to the boil and add 2 lasagne sheets. Return to the boil and cook for 2 minutes, stirring gently to avoid sticking. Remove from the pan using a slotted spoon and keep warm. Repeat with the remaining sheets.

Cut each lasagne sheet in half. Place two pieces on each of the plates and divide half of the chicken mixture among them. Top each serving with a second lasagne sheet and divide the remainder of the chicken mixture among them. Top with a final layer of lasagne. Garnish with tarragon and serve immediately.

Health Rating: 2 points

Penne with Pan-fried Chicken & Capers

Serves 4

Ingredients

4 skinless and boneless chicken breast fillets/halves

2 tbsp plain/all-purpose flour

salt and freshly ground black pepper

350 g/12 oz/3 cups penne

2 tbsp olive oil

25 g/1 oz/2 tbsp butter

1 red onion, peeled and sliced

1 garlic clove, peeled and chopped

4–6 tbsp pesto

250 g carton/1 cup mascarpone cheese

1 tsp wholegrain mustard

1 tbsp lemon juice

2 tbsp freshly chopped basil

3 tbsp capers in brine, rinsed and drained

freshly grated pecorino cheese

Trim the chicken and cut into bite-size pieces. Season the flour with salt and pepper, then toss the chicken in the seasoned flour and reserve.

Bring a large saucepan of lightly salted water to a rolling boil. Add the penne and cook according to the packet instructions, or until *al dente*.

Meanwhile, heat the olive oil in a large frying pan. Add the chicken to the pan and cook for 8 minutes, or until golden on all sides, stirring frequently. Transfer the chicken to a plate and reserve.

Add the onion and garlic to the oil remaining in the frying pan and cook for 5 minutes, or until softened, stirring frequently.

Return the chicken to the frying pan. Stir in the pesto and mascarpone cheese and heat through, stirring gently, until smooth.

Stir in the wholegrain mustard, lemon juice, basil and capers. Season to taste, then continue to heat through until piping hot.

Drain the penne thoroughly and return to the saucepan. Pour over the sauce and toss well to coat. Arrange the pasta on individual warmed plates. Scatter with the cheese and serve immediately.

Health Rating: 2 points

Chicken & Summer Vegetable Risotto

Serves 4

Ingredients

1 litre/1³⁄₄ pints/4 cups chicken or vegetable stock

225 g/8 oz/1¹⁄₄ cups baby asparagus spears

125 g/4 oz/³⁄₄ cup French/green beans

15 g/¹⁄₂ oz/1 tbsp butter

1 small onion, peeled and finely chopped

150 ml/¹⁄₄ pint/²⁄₃ cup dry white wine

275 g/10 oz/1¹⁄₄ cups Arborio/risotto rice

pinch saffron strands

juice of ¹⁄₂ lemon

75 g/3 oz/³⁄₄ cup thawed frozen peas

225 g/8 oz/2¹⁄₂ cups skinned and diced cooked chicken

salt and freshly ground black pepper

25 g/1 oz/¹⁄₄ cup grated Parmesan cheese

Bring the stock to the boil in a large saucepan. Trim the asparagus and cut into 4 cm/1¹⁄₂ inch lengths. Blanch the asparagus in the stock for 1–2 minutes until tender, then remove with a slotted spoon and reserve.

Halve the French/green beans and cook in the boiling stock for 4 minutes. Remove and reserve. Turn down the heat and keep the stock barely simmering.

Melt the butter in a heavy-based saucepan. Add the onion and cook gently for about 5 minutes. Pour the wine into the pan and boil rapidly until the liquid has almost reduced. Add the rice and cook, stirring, for 1 minute until the grains are coated and look translucent. Add the saffron and a ladleful of the stock. Simmer, stirring all the time, until the stock has been absorbed. Continue adding the stock, a ladleful at a time, until it has all been absorbed.

After 15 minutes, the risotto should be creamy with a slight bite to it. If not, add a little more stock and cook for a few more minutes, or until it is of the correct texture and consistency. Add the lemon juice, peas, reserved vegetables and chicken. Season to taste with salt and pepper and cook

for 3–4 minutes until the chicken is thoroughly heated and piping hot. Spoon the risotto onto warmed serving plates. Scatter each portion with a few shavings of Parmesan cheese and serve immediately.

Health Rating: 4 points

Smoked Turkey Tagliatelle

Serves 4

Ingredients

2 tsp olive oil

1 bunch spring onions/scallions, trimmed and diagonally sliced

1 garlic clove, peeled and crushed

1 small courgette/zucchini, trimmed, halved and sliced

4 tbsp dry white wine

400 g/14 oz/2 cups canned chopped tomatoes

2 tbsp freshly shredded basil

salt and freshly ground black pepper

225 g/8 oz/2 cups spinach and egg tagliatelle

225 g/8 oz/¼ lb smoked turkey breast, cut into strips

small fresh basil leaves, to garnish

Health Rating: 4 points

Heat the oil in a saucepan. Add the spring onions/scallions and garlic and cook gently for 2–3 minutes until beginning to soften. Stir in the sliced courgette/zucchini and cook for 1 minute.

Add the wine and let it bubble for 1–2 minutes. Stir in the chopped tomatoes, bring to the boil and simmer, uncovered, over a low heat for 15 minutes, or until the courgette is tender and the sauce slightly reduced. Stir the shredded basil into the sauce and season to taste with salt and pepper.

Meanwhile, bring a large pan of salted water to the boil. Add the tagliatelle and cook for 10 minutes until *al dente*, or according to the packet instructions. Drain thoroughly.

Return the tagliatelle to the pan, add half the tomato sauce and toss together to coat the pasta thoroughly in the sauce. Cover with a lid and reserve.

Add the strips of turkey to the remaining sauce and heat gently for 2–3 minutes until piping hot.

Divide the tagliatelle among four serving plates. Spoon over the sauce, garnish with basil leaves and serve immediately.

Turkey & Mixed Mushroom Lasagne

Serves 4

Ingredients

1 tbsp olive oil

225 g/8 oz/2 cups wiped and sliced mixed mushrooms e.g.
button/white, chestnut/cremini and portabello

15 g/¹/₂ oz/1 tbsp butter

25 g/1 oz/¹/₄ cup plain/all-purpose flour

300 ml/¹/₂ pint/1¹/₄ cups skimmed milk

1 bay leaf

225 g/8 oz/2¹/₂ cups cubed cooked turkey

¹/₄ tsp freshly grated nutmeg

salt and freshly ground black pepper

400 g/14 oz/2 cups drained and chopped canned
plum tomatoes

1 tsp dried mixed herbs

9 lasagne sheets (about 150 g/5 oz)

For the topping:

200 ml/7 fl oz/³/₄ cup Greek yogurt

1 medium/large egg, lightly beaten

1 tbsp finely grated Parmesan cheese

mixed salad leaves, to serve

Preheat the oven to 180°C/350°F/Gas Mark 4. Heat the oil and cook the mushrooms until tender and all the juices have evaporated. Remove and reserve.

Put the butter, flour, milk and bay leaf in the pan. Slowly bring to the boil, stirring, until thickened. Simmer for 2–3 minutes. Remove the bay leaf and stir in the mushrooms, turkey, nutmeg, salt and pepper.

Mix together the tomatoes and mixed herbs and season with salt and pepper. Spoon half into the base of a 1.7 litre/3 pint, ovenproof dish.

Top with 3 lasagne sheets, then with half the turkey mixture. Repeat the layers, then arrange the remaining 3 pasta sheets on top.

Mix together the yogurt and egg. Spoon over the lasagne, spreading the mixture into the corners. Sprinkle with the Parmesan and bake in the preheated oven for 45 minutes. Serve with the mixed salad.

Health Rating: 2 points

Chicken & White Wine Risotto

Serves 4–6

Ingredients

2 tbsp oil
125 g/4 oz/¹/₂ cup (1 stick) unsalted butter
2 shallots, peeled and finely chopped
300 g/11 oz/1¹/₂ cups Arborio/risotto rice
600 ml/1 pint/2¹/₂ cups dry white wine
750 ml/1¹/₄ pints/3¹/₄ cups chicken stock, heated
350 g/12 oz skinless chicken breast fillets, thinly sliced
50 g/2 oz/¹/₂ cup grated Parmesan cheese
2 tbsp freshly chopped dill or parsley
salt and freshly ground black pepper

Heat the oil and half the butter in a large, heavy–based saucepan over a medium–high heat. Add the shallots and cook for 2 minutes, or until softened, stirring frequently. Add the rice and cook for 2–3 minutes, stirring frequently, until the rice is translucent and well coated.

Pour in half the wine; it will bubble and steam rapidly. Cook, stirring constantly, until the liquid is absorbed. Add a ladleful of the hot stock and cook until the liquid is absorbed. Carefully stir in the chicken.

Continue adding the stock, about half a ladleful at a time, allowing each addition to be absorbed before adding the next; never allow the rice to cook dry. This process should take about 20 minutes. The risotto should have a creamy consistency and the rice should be tender but firm to the bite.

Stir in the remaining wine and cook for 2–3 minutes. Remove from the heat and stir in the remaining butter with the Parmesan cheese and half the chopped herbs. Season to taste with salt and pepper. Spoon into warmed, shallow bowls and sprinkle each with the remaining chopped herbs. Serve immediately.

Health Rating: 2 points

Chicken & Seafood Risotto

Serves 6–8

Ingredients

125 ml/4 fl oz/½ cup olive oil

1.4 kg/3 lb chicken, cut into 8 pieces

350 g/12 oz/¾ cup sliced spicy chorizo sausage

125 g/4 oz/⅔ cup diced cured ham

1 onion, peeled and chopped

2 red or yellow peppers, deseeded and cut into
2.5 cm/1 inch pieces

4 garlic cloves, peeled and finely chopped

750 g/1 lb 10 oz/4⅓ cups short-grain Spanish rice or
Arborio/risotto rice

2 bay leaves

1 tsp dried thyme

1 tsp lightly crushed saffron strands

200 ml/7 fl oz/¾ cup dry white wine

1.6 litres/2¾ pints6⅔ cups chicken stock

salt and freshly ground black pepper

125 g/4 oz/⅔ cup fresh shelled peas

450 g/1 lb uncooked prawns/shrimp

36 well-scrubbed clams and/or mussels

2 tbsp freshly chopped parsley

To garnish:
lemon wedges
fresh parsley sprigs

Heat half the oil in a 45.5 cm/18 inch paella pan or deep, wide frying pan. Add the chicken pieces and fry for 15 minutes, turning frequently, until golden. Remove from the pan and reserve. Add the chorizo and ham to the pan and cook for 6 minutes until crisp, stirring occasionally. Remove and add to the chicken.

Add the onion to the pan and cook for 3 minutes, or until beginning to soften. Add the peppers and garlic and cook for 2 minutes; add to the reserved chicken, chorizo and ham.

Add the remaining oil to the pan and stir in the rice until well coated. Stir in the bay leaves, thyme and saffron, then pour in the wine and bubble until evaporated, stirring and scraping up any bits on the bottom of the pan. Stir in the stock and bring to the boil, stirring occasionally.

Return the chicken, chorizo, ham and vegetables to the pan, burying them gently in the rice. Season to taste with salt and pepper. Reduce the heat and simmer for 10 minutes, stirring occasionally.

Add the peas and seafood, pushing them gently into the rice. Cover and cook over a low heat for 5 minutes, or until the rice and prawns/shrimp are tender and the clams and mussels open (discard any that do not open). Stand for 5 minutes. Sprinkle with the parsley, garnish and serve.

Health Rating: 2 points

Vegetables, Cheese & Salads

Vegetables add vital nutrients to your diet, but that does not mean that eating your daily dose needs to be a chore. This section is filled with recipes such as Spaghetti with Pesto, Melanzane Parmigiana and Spring Vegetable & Herb Risotto that can be served as a whole meal or as an accompaniment, and that will all provide a delicious and healthy addition to your daily meals.

Fusilli with Ricotta, Mozzarella & Basil

Serves 4

Ingredients

125 g/4 oz/generous ¾ cup broad/fava beans

125 g/4 oz broccoli, cut into tiny florets

2 tbsp olive oil

1 medium onion, peeled and sliced

2–3 smoked garlic cloves, peeled and chopped (if not available, use ordinary garlic)

1 yellow pepper, deseeded and chopped

225 g/8 oz dried fusilli pasta

600 ml/1 pint/2½ cups prepared white sauce (see page 141)

100 g/3½ oz/scant ½ cup ricotta cheese

salt and freshly ground black pepper

125 g/4 oz/1 cup mozzarella cheese

2 tbsp freshly chopped basil, to garnish

salad, to serve

Preheat the oven to 190°C/375°F/Gas Mark 5, 10 minutes before cooking. Cook the broad/fava beans and broccoli in a pan of boiling water for 3 minutes. Drain, then refresh in cold water to stop the cooking process. Reserve.

Heat the oil in a frying pan, add the onion, garlic and pepper and fry for 5–8 minutes until softened. Stir in the broad beans and broccoli and keep warm.

Bring a large saucepan of water to a rolling boil. Add the pasta and cook for 8–10 minutes until *al dente*. Drain and return to the saucepan. Add the vegetables together with the prepared white sauce, the ricotta and seasoning to taste. Stir lightly together, then spoon into a large, ovenproof dish.

Cut the mozzarella cheese into small pieces and dot over the top. Bake in the preheated oven for 25–30 minutes until the cheese has melted and the top is golden brown. Garnish with basil and serve with salad.

Health Rating: 3 points

Risi e Bisi

Serves 4

Ingredients

700 g/1½ lb/5 cups fresh or thawed peas

25 g/1 oz/2 tbsp unsalted butter

1 tsp olive oil

3 rashers/slices pancetta or unsmoked back/Canadian-style bacon, chopped

1 small onion, peeled and finely chopped

1 garlic clove, peeled and finely chopped

1.25 litres/2¼ pints/5¼ cups vegetable stock

pinch caster/superfine sugar

1 tsp lemon juice; 1 bay leaf

200 g/7 oz/1 cup Arborio/risotto rice

3 tbsp freshly chopped parsley

50 g/2 oz/½ cup finely grated Parmesan cheese

salt and freshly ground black pepper

To garnish:

fresh parsley sprig

julienne strips of orange zest

Shell the peas, if using fresh ones. Melt the butter and olive oil together in a large, heavy-based saucepan. Add the chopped pancetta or bacon, the chopped onion and the garlic and fry gently for about 10 minutes until the onion is softened and is just beginning to colour. Pour in the vegetable stock, then add the caster/superfine sugar, lemon juice and bay leaf. Add the fresh peas, if using. Bring the mixture to a fast boil. Add the rice, stir and simmer, uncovered, for about 20 minutes until the rice is tender. Occasionally stir the mixture gently while it cooks. If using frozen peas, stir them into the rice about 2 minutes before the end of the cooking time.

When the rice is cooked, remove the bay leaf and discard. Stir in 2½ tablespoons of the chopped parsley and the grated Parmesan cheese. Season to taste with salt and pepper. Transfer the rice to a large serving dish. Garnish with the remaining chopped parsley, a fresh parsley sprig and julienne strips of orange zest. Serve immediately while piping hot.

Health Rating: 3 points

Rice & Vegetable Timbale

Serves 6

Ingredients

25 g/1 oz/¼ cup dried white breadcrumbs

3 tbsp olive oil

2 courgettes/zucchini, sliced

1 small aubergine/eggplant, cut into 1 cm/½ inch dice

175 g/6 oz/1½ cups sliced mushrooms

1 garlic clove, peeled and crushed

1 tsp balsamic vinegar

1 onion, peeled and finely chopped

25 g/1 oz/2 tbsp unsalted butter

400 g/14 oz Arborio/risotto rice

about 1.25 litres/2¼ pints/5¼ cups vegetable stock, boiling

2 medium/large eggs, lightly beaten

25 g/1 oz/¼ cup finely grated Parmesan cheese

2 tbsp freshly chopped basil

salt and freshly ground black pepper

To garnish:

fresh basil sprig

1 radish, thinly sliced

Preheat the oven to 190°C/375°F/Gas Mark 5, 10 minutes before cooking. Sprinkle the breadcrumbs over the base and sides of a thickly buttered 20.5 cm/8 inch, round, loose–bottomed tin/pan.

Heat the olive oil in a large frying pan and gently fry the courgettes/zucchini, aubergine/eggplant, mushrooms and garlic for 5 minutes, or until beginning to soften. Stir in the vinegar. Tip the vegetables into a large sieve placed over a bowl to catch the juices.

Fry the onion gently in the butter for 10 minutes, or until soft. Add the rice and stir for a minute to coat. Add a ladleful of stock and any juices from the vegetables and simmer, stirring, until the rice has absorbed all of the liquid. Continue adding the stock in this way until the rice is just tender. This should take about 20 minutes. Remove from the heat and leave to cool for 5 minutes. Stir in the eggs, cheese and basil. Season to taste with salt and pepper.

Spoon a quarter of the rice into the tin. Top with one third of the vegetable mixture. Continue layering up in this way, finishing with a layer of rice. Level the top of the layer of rice, gently pressing down the mixture. Cover with a piece of foil. Put on a baking sheet and bake in the oven for 50 minutes, or until firm. Leave the timbale to stand in the tin for 10 minutes, still covered with foil, then turn out onto a warmed serving platter. Garnish with a sprig of fresh basil and slices of radish and serve immediately.

Health Rating: 3 points

Vegetables Braised in Olive Oil & Lemon

Serves 4

Ingredients

pared zest and juice of ½ lemon
4 tbsp olive oil
1 bay leaf
1 large thyme sprig
150 ml/¼ pint/⅔ cup water
4 spring onions/scallions, trimmed and chopped
175 g/6 oz/1½ cups button/white mushrooms
175 g/6 oz/2 cups broccoli florets
175 g/6 oz/2 cups cauliflower florets
1 courgette/zucchini, diagonally sliced
2 tbsp freshly snipped chives
salt and freshly ground black pepper
lemon zest, to garnish

Put the pared lemon zest and juice into a large saucepan. Add the olive oil, bay leaf, thyme and the water. Bring to the boil. Add the spring onions/scallions and mushrooms. Top with the broccoli and cauliflower florets, adding them so that the stalks are submerged in the water and the tops are just above it. Cover and simmer for 3 minutes.

Scatter the courgettes/zucchini on top, so that they are steamed rather than boiled. Cook, covered, for a further 3–4 minutes until all the vegetables are tender.

Using a slotted spoon, transfer the vegetables from the liquid into a warmed serving dish.

Increase the heat and boil rapidly for 3–4 minutes until the liquid is reduced to about 8 tablespoons. Remove the lemon zest, bay leaf and thyme sprig and discard.

Stir the chives into the reduced liquid, season to taste with salt and pepper and pour over the vegetables. Sprinkle with lemon zest and serve immediately.

Health Rating: 5 points

Baked Artichoke Hearts with Parmesan Cheese

Serves 4

Ingredients

4 fresh artichokes
juice of 1 lemon
1 onion, peeled and sliced
1 red chilli, deseeded and chopped
1 red pepper, deseeded and sliced
1 beefsteak tomato, sliced
salt and freshly ground black pepper
200 ml/7 fl oz/³/₄ cup vegetable or chicken stock
25 g/1 oz/scant ¼ cup freshly grated Parmesan cheese
warm focaccia, to serve

Prepare the artichokes by cutting off and discarding the hard stem and tough outer leaves. If large, cut the artichokes in half and trim the tops of the leaves. Scoop out the choke (the feathery centre) and discard. Place in a bowl with 1 teaspoon of the lemon juice.

Bring a saucepan of water to the boil (large enough to hold the artichokes in a single layer), add the remaining lemon juice and prepared artichokes. Cover with a lid and simmer for 25 minutes, or until tender. Drain and reserve.

Preheat the oven to 190°C/375°F/Gas Mark 5 and lightly oil an ovenproof dish large enough to easily hold all the artichokes. Starting with the artichokes, layer all the ingredients, lightly seasoning each layer, then pour over the stock.

Sprinkle with the grated Parmesan cheese and bake in the preheated oven for 25 minutes, or until the top is golden. Serve with warm focaccia.

Health Rating: 4 points

Melanzane Parmigiana

Serves 4

Ingredients

900 g/2 lb aubergines/eggplants
salt and freshly ground black pepper
5 tbsp/¹/₃ cup olive oil
1 red onion, peeled and chopped
½ tsp mild paprika
150 ml/¹/₄ pint/²/₃ cup dry red wine
150 ml/¹/₄ pint/²/₃ cup vegetable stock
400 g/14 oz/2 cups canned chopped tomatoes
1 tsp tomato purée/paste
1 tbsp freshly chopped oregano
175 g/6 oz/1½ cups thinly sliced mozzarella cheese
40 g/1½ oz/½ cup coarsely grated Parmesan cheese
fresh basil sprig, to garnish

Preheat the oven to 200°C/400°F/Gas Mark 6, 15 minutes before cooking. Cut the aubergines/eggplants lengthways into thin slices. Sprinkle with salt and leave to drain in a colander/strainer over a bowl for 30 minutes.

Heat 1 tablespoon of the olive oil in a saucepan and fry the onion for 10 minutes, or until softened. Add the paprika and cook for 1 minute. Stir in the wine, stock, tomatoes and tomato purée/paste. Simmer, uncovered, for 25 minutes, or until fairly thick. Stir in the oregano and season to taste. Remove from the heat.

Rinse the aubergine slices thoroughly under cold water. Pat dry on paper towels. Heat 2 tablespoons of the oil in a griddle pan/ridged grill pan and cook the aubergines in batches, for 3 minutes on each side, until golden. Drain well on paper towels.

Pour half of the tomato sauce into the base of an ovenproof dish. Cover with half the aubergine slices, then top with the mozzarella. Cover with the remaining aubergine slices and pour over the remaining tomato sauce. Sprinkle with the grated Parmesan. Bake in the preheated oven for 30 minutes, or until the aubergines are tender and the sauce is bubbling. Garnish with a sprig of fresh basil and cool for a few minutes before serving.

Health Rating: 3 points

Stuffed Tomatoes with Grilled Polenta

Serves 4

Ingredients

For the polenta/cornmeal:
300 ml/½ pint/1¼ cups vegetable stock
salt and freshly ground black pepper
50 g/2 oz/½ cup quick-cook polenta
15 g/½ oz/1 tbsp butter

For the stuffed tomatoes:
4 large tomatoes
1 tbsp olive oil
1 garlic clove, peeled and crushed
1 bunch spring onions/scallions, trimmed and finely chopped
2 tbsp freshly chopped parsley
2 tbsp freshly chopped basil
2 slices Parma ham/prosciutto, cut into thin slivers
50 g/2 oz/½ cup fresh white breadcrumbs
snipped chives, to garnish

Preheat the grill/broiler just before cooking. To make the polenta, pour the stock into a saucepan. Add a pinch of salt and bring to the boil. Pour in the polenta in a fine stream, stirring all the time. Simmer for about 15 minutes until very thick. Stir in the butter and add a little black pepper. Turn the polenta/cornmeal out onto a chopping board and spread to a thickness of just over 1 cm/½ inch. Cool, cover with plastic wrap and chill in the refrigerator for 30 minutes.

For the stuffed tomatoes, cut the tomatoes in half, scoop out the seeds and press through a fine sieve to extract the juices. Season the insides of the tomatoes with salt and pepper and reserve.

Heat the olive oil in a saucepan and gently fry the garlic and spring onions/scallions for 3 minutes. Add the tomatoes' juices and bubble for 3–4 minutes until most of the liquid has evaporated. Stir in the herbs, Parma ham/prosciutto and a little black pepper with half the breadcrumbs. Spoon into the hollowed-out tomatoes and reserve.

Cut the polenta into 5 cm/2 inch squares, then cut each in half diagonally to make triangles. Place on a piece of foil on the grill rack and grill for 4–5 minutes on each side until golden. Cover and keep warm. Place the tomatoes under a medium–hot grill for about 4 minutes – any exposed Parma ham will become crisp. Sprinkle with the remaining breadcrumbs and grill for 1–2 minutes, until the breadcrumbs are golden brown. Garnish with snipped chives and serve immediately with the grilled polenta.

Health Rating: 4 points

Fettuccine with Roasted Beetroot & Rocket

Serves 4

Ingredients

350 g/12 oz/³/₄ lb raw baby beetroot, unpeeled

1 garlic clove, peeled and crushed

¹/₂ tsp finely grated orange zest

1 tbsp orange juice

1 tsp lemon juice

2 tbsp walnut oil

salt and freshly ground black pepper

350 g/12 oz dried fettuccine

75 g/3 oz rocket/arugula leaves

125 g/4 oz Dolcelatte cheese, cubed

Preheat the oven to 150°C/300°F/Gas Mark 2, 10 minutes before cooking. Wrap the beetroot individually in foil and bake for 1–1¹/₂ hours until tender. (Test by opening one of the parcels and scraping the skin away from the stem end – it should come off very easily.)

Leave the beetroot until cool enough to handle, then peel and cut each beetroot into 6–8 wedges, depending on the size. Mix the garlic, orange zest and juice, lemon juice, walnut oil and salt and pepper together, then drizzle over the beetroot and toss to coat well.

Meanwhile, bring a large saucepan of lightly salted water to the boil. Cook the pasta for 10 minutes, or until *al dente*.

Drain the pasta thoroughly, then add the warm beetroot, rocket/arugula leaves and Dolcelatte cheese. Quickly and gently toss together, then divide between serving bowls and serve immediately before the rocket wilts.

Health Rating: 4 **points**

Red & Yellow Peppers with Bagna Cauda

Serves 4

Ingredients

10 plump garlic cloves, peeled
300 ml/¹/₂ pint/1¹/₄ cups milk
20 anchovy fillets, drained
125 g/4 oz/¹/₂ cup (1 stick) butter
4 tbsp double/heavy cream
2 large red peppers
2 large yellow peppers
2 large orange peppers
grissini breadsticks, to serve

Put the garlic cloves in a saucepan with the milk. Bring to the boil, then reduce the heat to a gentle simmer and cook for 30 minutes.

Break the anchovies up a little, then add to the milk and garlic. Continue to cook for 10–12 minutes until the anchovies and garlic are very soft. Take the pan off the heat and mash together to form a paste. Return to a gentle heat and slowly beat in the butter, a little at a time. When all the butter has been added, remove from the heat and rub through a sieve. Stir in the cream and reserve.

Preheat the oven to 190°C/375°F/Gas Mark 5. Line a baking tray with foil. Cut the peppers in half and discard the seeds. If necessary, slice a thin sliver off the pepper halves so they sit squarely on the tray. Fill the pepper halves with the bagna cauda (the anchovy and garlic mix) and cook in the preheated oven for 15–20 minutes until the peppers and sauce are hot. Serve with breadsticks.

Tip: Other vegetables such as courgettes/zucchini, tomatoes and aubergines/eggplants can also be used. Just remove their centres so the sauce can be placed in the hollows.

Health Rating: 4 points

Rigatoni with Oven-dried Cherry Tomatoes & Mascarpone

Serves 4

Ingredients

350 g/12 oz/3 cups red cherry tomatoes
1 tsp caster/superfine sugar
salt and freshly ground black pepper
2 tbsp olive oil
400 g/14 oz/5¹/₄ cups dried rigatoni
125 g/4 oz/1 cup frozen peas
2 tbsp mascarpone cheese
1 tbsp freshly chopped mint
1 tbsp freshly chopped parsley
fresh mint sprigs, to garnish

Preheat the oven to 140°C/275°F/Gas Mark 1. Halve the cherry tomatoes and place close together on a nonstick baking tray, cut-side up. Sprinkle lightly with the sugar, then with a little salt and pepper. Bake in the preheated oven for 1¹/₄ hours, or until dry but not beginning to colour. Leave to cool on the baking tray. Put in a bowl, drizzle over the olive oil and toss to coat.

Bring a large saucepan of lightly salted water to the boil and cook the pasta for about 10 minutes, or until *al dente*.

Add the frozen peas 2–3 minutes before the end of the cooking time. Drain thoroughly and return the pasta and the peas to the saucepan.

Add the mascarpone to the saucepan. When melted, add the tomatoes, mint, parsley and a little black pepper. Toss gently together, then transfer to a warmed serving dish or individual plates and garnish with fresh mint sprigs. Serve immediately.

Health Rating: 3 points

Pasta with Spicy Red Pepper Sauce

Serves 4

Ingredients

2 red peppers

2 tbsp olive oil

1 onion, peeled and chopped

2 garlic cloves, peeled and crushed

4 anchovy fillets (optional)

1 red chilli, deseeded and finely chopped

200 g/7 oz/$\frac{1}{2}$ cup canned chopped tomatoes

finely grated rind and juice of $\frac{1}{2}$ lemon

salt and freshly ground black pepper

2–3 tbsp vegetable stock (optional)

400 g/14 oz/5$\frac{1}{4}$ cups dried pasta, such as tagliatelle, linguine or shells

To garnish:

shaved Parmesan cheese

fresh basil leaves

Preheat the grill/broiler. Set the whole peppers on the grill rack about 10 cm/4 inches away from the heat. Turn frequently for 10 minutes, or until the skins are blackened and blistered.

Put the peppers in a plastic container and leave until cool enough to handle. Peel off the skin, then halve the peppers and scrape away the seeds. Chop the pepper flesh roughly and put in a food processor or blender.

Heat the olive oil in a large saucepan and gently fry the onion for 5 minutes. Stir in the garlic, anchovy fillets (if using) and chilli and cook for a further 5 minutes, stirring. Add to the food processor and blend until fairly smooth.

Return the mixture to the saucepan with the tomatoes and stir in the lemon zest and juice. Season to taste with salt and freshly ground black pepper. Add 2–3 tablespoons vegetable stock if the sauce is a little thick. Bring to the boil and bubble for 1–2 minutes.

Meanwhile, bring a large saucepan of lightly salted water to the boil and cook the pasta for 10 minutes, or until *al dente*. Drain thoroughly. Add the sauce and toss well to coat. Tip into a warmed serving dish or onto individual plates. Scatter with shavings of Parmesan cheese and a few basil leaves before serving.

Health Rating: 3 points

Mixed Salad with Anchovy Dressing & Ciabatta Croutons

Serves 4

Ingredients

1 small head endive
1 small head chicory
1 fennel bulb
400 g/14 oz canned artichokes, drained and rinsed
½ cucumber
125 g/4 oz/1 cup cherry tomatoes
75 g/3 oz/½ cup black/ripe olives

For the anchovy dressing:
50 g/2 oz canned anchovy fillets
1 tsp Dijon mustard
1 small garlic clove, peeled and crushed
4 tbsp olive oil
1 tbsp lemon juice
freshly ground black pepper

For the ciabatta croutons:
2 thick slices ciabatta bread
2 tbsp olive oil

Divide the endive and chicory into leaves and reserve some of the larger ones. Arrange the smaller leaves in a wide salad bowl. Cut the fennel bulb in half from the stalk to the root end, then cut across in fine slices. Quarter the artichokes, then quarter and slice the cucumber and halve the tomatoes. Add to the salad bowl with the olives.

To make the dressing, drain the anchovies and whizz in a blender with the mustard, garlic, olive oil, lemon juice, 2 tablespoons hot water and black pepper until smooth and thickened.

To make the croutons, cut the bread into 1 cm/½ inch cubes. Heat the oil in a frying pan, add the bread cubes and fry for 3 minutes, turning frequently, until golden. Remove and drain on absorbent paper towels.

Drizzle half the anchovy dressing over the prepared salad and toss to coat. Arrange the reserved endive and chicory leaves around the edge, then drizzle over the remaining dressing. Scatter over the croutons and serve immediately.

Health Rating: 4 points

Warm Fried Courgettes with Peppers

Serves 4

Ingredients

2 courgettes/zucchini, about 225 g/8 oz
2 large assorted coloured peppers
vegetable oil, for deep-frying
lemon wedges, to serve

For the batter:
75 g/3 oz/½ cup plain/all-purpose flour
pinch salt
about 6 tbsp water
1 medium/large egg white, stiffly whisked just before using

Trim the courgettes/zucchini, cut in half, then into 7.5 cm/3 inch lengths and reserve. Cut the peppers into quarters, deseed and reserve.

To make the batter, sift the flour and salt into a mixing bowl and make a well in the centre. Slowly beat in the water a little at a time, beating well after each addition. Add a little extra water if necessary to form a smooth batter and allow to stand for 30 minutes.

When the batter is ready to use, beat well, then stir in the stiffly whisked egg white.

Heat the oil in a deep fryer or deep saucepan to a temperature of 190°C/375°F, or until a cube of bread dropped into the oil browns in 30 seconds. Dip the courgettes into the flour, then into the batter, allowing any extra batter to drip back into the bowl. Place in the frying basket and lower into the hot oil, or carefully drop the vegetables into the hot oil, in batches, and deep-fry for 2–3 minutes until golden and crisp, then remove and drain on absorbent paper towels. Repeat until all the vegetables are fried. Keep warm in the oven while frying the others. Serve with lemon wedges to squeeze over.

Health Rating: 3 points

Hot Grilled Chicory & Pears

Serves 4

Ingredients

50 g/2 oz/½ cup roughly chopped unblanched almonds
4 small chicory heads
2 tbsp olive oil
1 tbsp walnut oil
2 firm, ripe dessert pears
2 tsp lemon juice
1 tsp freshly chopped oregano
salt and freshly ground black pepper
freshly chopped oregano, to garnish
warmed ciabatta bread, to serve

Preheat the grill/broiler. Spread the chopped almonds in a single layer on the grill pan. Cook under the hot grill for about 3 minutes, moving the almonds around occasionally, until lightly browned. Reserve.

Halve the chicory lengthways and cut out the cores. Mix together the olive and walnut oils. Brush about 2 tablespoons all over the chicory.

Put the chicory in a grill pan cut-side up and cook under the hot grill for 2–3 minutes until beginning to char. Turn and cook for a further 1–2 minutes, then turn again.

Peel, core and thickly slice the pears. Brush with 1 tablespoon of the oils, then place the pears on top of the chicory. Grill for a further 3–4 minutes until both the chicory and pears are soft.

Transfer the chicory and pears to four warmed serving plates. Whisk together the remaining oil, the lemon juice and oregano and season to taste with salt and pepper.

Drizzle the dressing over the chicory and pears and scatter with the toasted almonds. Garnish with fresh oregano and serve with warm ciabatta bread.

Health Rating: 4 points

Spinach Dumplings with Rich Tomato Sauce

Serves 4

Ingredients

For the sauce:

2 tbsp olive oil

1 onion, peeled and chopped

1 garlic clove, peeled and crushed

1 red chilli, deseeded and chopped

150 ml/¼ pint/⅔ cup dry white wine

400 g/14 oz/2 cups canned chopped tomatoes

pared strip lemon zest

salt and freshly ground black pepper

For the dumplings:

450 g/1 lb/10 cups fresh spinach

50 g/2 oz/¼ cup ricotta cheese

25 g/1 oz/¼ cup fresh white breadcrumbs

25 g/1 oz/¼ cup grated Parmesan cheese

1 medium egg yolk

¼ tsp freshly grated nutmeg

5 tbsp plain/all-purpose flour

2 tbsp olive oil, for frying

fresh basil leaves, to garnish

freshly cooked tagliatelle, to serve

To make the tomato sauce, heat the olive oil in a large saucepan and fry the onion gently for 5 minutes. Add the garlic and chilli and cook for a further 5 minutes, or until softened. Stir in the wine, chopped tomatoes and lemon zest.

Bring to the boil, cover and simmer for 20 minutes, then uncover and simmer for 15 minutes, or until the sauce has thickened. Remove the lemon rind and season to taste with salt and pepper.

To make the spinach dumplings, wash the spinach thoroughly and remove any tough stalks. Cover and cook in a large saucepan over a low heat with just the water clinging to the leaves. Drain, then squeeze out all the excess water. Finely chop and put in a large bowl.

Add the ricotta, breadcrumbs, Parmesan cheese and egg yolk to the spinach. Season with nutmeg and salt and pepper. Mix together and shape into 20 walnut–size balls. Toss the spinach balls in the flour. Heat the olive oil in a large, nonstick frying pan and fry the balls gently for 5–6 minutes, carefully turning occasionally. Garnish with fresh basil leaves and serve immediately with the tomato sauce and tagliatelle.

Health Rating: 3 points

Venetian–style Vegetables & Beans

Serves 4

Ingredients

250 g/9 oz/1½ cups dried pinto beans

3 fresh parsley sprigs

1 fresh rosemary sprig

2 tbsp olive oil

200 g/7 oz/½ cup canned chopped tomatoes

2 shallots, peeled

For the vegetable mixture:

1 large red onion, peeled

1 large white onion, peeled

1 carrot, peeled

2 celery stalks, trimmed

3 tbsp olive oil

3 bay leaves

1 tsp sugar

3 tbsp red wine vinegar

salt and freshly ground black pepper

Put the beans in a bowl, cover with plenty of cold water and leave to soak for at least 8 hours, or overnight.

Drain and rinse the beans. Put in a large saucepan with 1.25 litres/2¼ pints/5¼ cups cold water. Tie the parsley and rosemary in muslin and add to the beans with the olive oil.

Boil rapidly for 10 minutes, then lower the heat and simmer for 20 minutes with the saucepan half covered. Stir in the tomatoes and shallots and simmer for a further 10–15 minutes until the beans are cooked.

Meanwhile, slice the red and white onions into rings, then finely dice the carrot and celery. Heat the olive oil in a saucepan and cook the onions over a very low heat for about 10 minutes. Add the carrot, celery and bay leaves to the saucepan and cook for a further 10 minutes, stirring frequently, until the vegetables are tender. Sprinkle with sugar, stir and cook for 1 minute.

Stir in the vinegar. Cook for 1 minute, then remove the saucepan from the heat. Drain the beans through a fine sieve, discarding all the herbs, then add the beans to the onion mixture and season well with salt and pepper. Mix gently, tip the beans into a large serving bowl. Leave to cool, then serve at room temperature.

Health Rating: 5 points

Grilled Polenta with Garlic & Parmesan Cheese

Serves 4

Ingredients

900 ml/1½ pints/3¾ cups milk and water
150 g/5 oz/scant 1 cup polenta/cornmeal
2 garlic cloves, peeled and crushed
50 g/2 oz/4 tbsp butter
50 g/2 oz/scant ½ cup grated Parmesan cheese
75 g/3 oz Dolcelatte cheese, crumbled
freshly ground black pepper
olive oil, for brushing
fresh tomato sauce (see page 244)

Pour the milk and water into a large saucepan and bring to the boil. Slowly pour in the polenta/cornmeal stirring all the time, then stir in the crushed garlic. Continue to cook, stirring constantly, until the polenta is thick and starts to come away from the sides of the pan.

Remove from the heat and stir in the butter, cheeses and black pepper. Lightly oil a shallow baking tin/pan and pour in the cooked polenta. Leave until cold.

When ready to serve, preheat the grill/broiler and line the grill rack with foil. Cut the polenta into squares or oblongs. Place on the foil-lined rack and brush the tops with oil. Grill for 3–5 minutes until golden and crispy, then serve with the tomato sauce.

Health Rating: 2 points

Vegetable Frittata

Serves 2

Ingredients

6 eggs
2 tbsp freshly chopped parsley; 1 tbsp freshly chopped tarragon
25 g/1 oz/¼ cup finely grated pecorino or Parmesan cheese
freshly ground black pepper
175 g/6 oz/1¼ cups tiny new potatoes
2 small carrots, peeled and sliced
125 g/4 oz/1¼ cups broccoli florets
1 courgette/zucchini, about 125 g/4 oz/¾ cup, sliced
2 tbsp olive oil
4 spring onions/scallions, trimmed and thinly sliced
mixed green salad and crusty Italian bread, to serve

Preheat the grill/broiler just before cooking. Lightly beat the eggs with the parsley, tarragon and half the cheese. Season to taste with black pepper and reserve. (Salt is not needed, as the pecorino is very salty.)

Bring a large saucepan of lightly salted water to the boil. Add the new potatoes and cook for 8 minutes. Add the carrots and cook for 4 minutes, then add the broccoli florets and the courgette/zucchini and cook for a further 3–4 minutes until all the vegetables are barely tender. Drain well.

Heat the oil in a 20.5 cm/8 inch, heavy-based frying pan. Add the spring onions/scallions and cook for 3–4 minutes until softened. Add all the vegetables and cook for a few seconds, then pour in the beaten egg mixture. Stir gently for about a minute. Cook for a further 1–2 minutes until the bottom of the frittata is set and golden brown.

Place the pan under the hot grill for 1 minute, or until almost set and just beginning to brown. Sprinkle with the remaining cheese and grill for a further 1 minute, or until it is lightly browned. Loosen the edges and slide out of the pan. Cut into wedges and serve hot or warm with a mixed green salad and crusty Italian bread.

Health Rating: 3 points

Red Pepper & Basil Tart

Serves 4–6

Ingredients

For the olive pastry/dough:
225 g/8 oz/2 cups plain/all-purpose flour
pinch salt
1 medium/large egg, lightly beaten, plus 1 egg yolk
3 tbsp olive oil
50 g/2 oz/⅓ cup pitted black/ripe olives, finely chopped

For the filling:
2 large red peppers, deseeded and quartered
175 g/6 oz/¾ cup mascarpone cheese
4 tbsp milk
2 medium/large eggs
3 tbsp freshly chopped basil
salt and freshly ground black pepper
fresh basil sprig, to garnish
mixed salad, to serve

Preheat the oven to 200°C/400°F/Gas Mark 6, 15 minutes before cooking. Sift the flour and salt into a bowl and make a well in the centre. Stir together the egg, oil and 1 tablespoon tepid water. Add to the dry ingredients, drop in the olives and mix to a dough. Knead on a lightly floured surface for a few seconds until smooth, then wrap in plastic wrap and chill for 30 minutes.

Roll out the pastry/dough and use to line a 23 cm/9 inch, loose-bottomed, fluted flan tin/quiche pan. Lightly prick the base with a fork. Cover and chill in the refrigerator for 20 minutes.

Cook the peppers under a hot grill/broiler for 10 minutes, or until the skins are blackened and blistered. Put the peppers in a plastic bag, cool for 10 minutes, then remove the skins and slice. Line the pastry case/tart shell with foil or baking parchment weighed down with baking beans/pie weights.

Bake in the preheated oven for 10 minutes. Remove the foil or paper and baking beans. Bake for a further 5 minutes. Reduce the oven temperature to 180°C/350°F/Gas Mark 4.

Beat the mascarpone cheese until smooth. Gradually add the milk and eggs. Stir in the peppers and basil and season to taste with salt and pepper. Spoon into the pastry case and bake for 25–30 minutes until lightly set. Garnish with a sprig of fresh basil and serve immediately with a mixed salad.

Health Rating: 2 point

Aubergine Cannelloni with Watercress Sauce

Serves 4

Ingredients

4 large aubergines/eggplants
5–6 tbsp olive oil
350 g/12 oz/1½ cups ricotta cheese
75 g/3 oz/⅔ cup grated Parmesan cheese
3 tbsp freshly chopped basil
salt and freshly ground black pepper

For the watercress sauce:

75 g/3 oz/¾ cup trimmed watercress
200 ml/⅓ pint/¾ cup vegetable stock
1 shallot, peeled and sliced
pared strip lemon zest
1 large thyme sprig
3 tbsp crème fraîche
1 tsp lemon juice

To garnish:

watercress sprigs
lemon zest

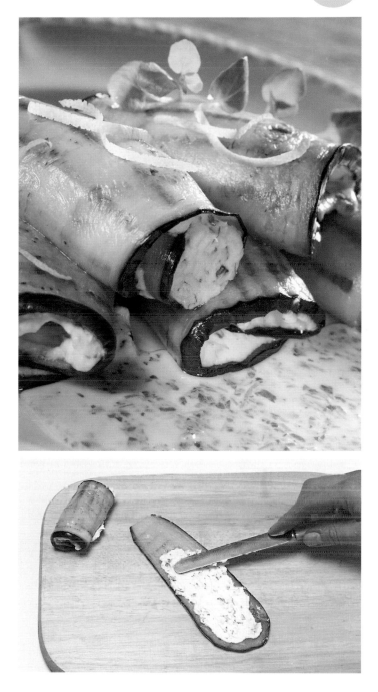

Preheat the oven to 190°C/375°F/Gas Mark 5, 10 minutes before cooking. Cut the aubergines/eggplants lengthways into thin slices, discarding the side pieces. Heat 2 tablespoons of the oil in a frying pan and cook the aubergine slices in a single layer in several batches, turning once, until golden on both sides.

Mix the cheeses, basil and seasoning together. Lay the aubergine slices on a clean surface and spread the cheese mixture evenly between them. Roll up the slices from one of the short ends to enclose the filling. Place seam-side down in a single layer in an ovenproof dish. Bake in the oven for 15 minutes, or until golden.

To make the watercress sauce, blanch the watercress leaves in boiling water for about 30 seconds. Drain well, then rinse in a sieve under cold running water and squeeze dry. Put the stock, shallot, lemon zest and thyme in a small saucepan. Boil rapidly until reduced by half, then remove from the heat and strain.

Put the watercress and strained stock in a food processor and blend until fairly smooth. Return to the saucepan, stir in the crème fraîche and lemon juice and season to taste with salt and pepper. Heat gently until the sauce is piping hot.

Serve a little of the sauce drizzled over the aubergines and the rest separately in a jug. Garnish the aubergine cannelloni with sprigs of watercress and lemon zest and serve immediately.

Health Rating: 4 points

Baked Semolina Gnocchi with Parmesan Cheese

Serves 4

Ingredients

50 g/2 oz/4 tbsp butter, plus extra for greasing

600 ml/1 pint/2½ cups milk

125 g/4 oz/generous ½ cup fine semolina

salt and freshly ground black pepper

2 medium/large eggs, beaten

75 g/3 oz/generous ½ cup freshly grated Parmesan cheese, plus extra for the top (optional)

¼ tsp freshly grated nutmeg

For the tomato sauce:

400 g/14 oz/2 cups canned chopped tomatoes

1 shallot, peeled and finely chopped

few drops Worcestershire sauce, or to taste

1 tbsp freshly chopped parsley

Preheat the oven to 200°C/400°F/Gas Mark 6, 15 minutes before baking. Lightly grease a 1.1 litre/2 pint/1 quart, ovenproof dish. Pour the milk into a saucepan and sprinkle in the semolina with seasoning to taste. Place over a gentle heat and bring to the boil, stirring. Continue to cook, stirring throughout, until really thick, then stir in half the butter, the eggs, grated Parmesan cheese and nutmeg.

Spoon into the prepared dish and level the top. Dot with the remaining butter and more cheese if liked and bake in the preheated oven for 25 minutes, or until golden brown.

Meanwhile, place all the tomato sauce ingredients in a saucepan, season with salt and pepper and heat until piping hot. Serve chunky or whizz in a blender or food processor until smooth. Serve the sauce with the gnocchi cut into wedges.

Health Rating: 3 points

Panzanella

Serves 4

Ingredients

1 tbsp red wine vinegar

250 g/9 oz/12 slices day-old Italian-style bread

4 tbsp olive oil

1 tsp lemon juice

1 small garlic clove, peeled and finely chopped

1 red onion, peeled and finely sliced

1 cucumber, peeled if preferred, halved, deseeded and cut into 1 cm/½ inch dice

2 tomatoes, deseeded and cut into 1 cm/½ inch dice

30 large pitted black/ripe olives

about 20 basil leaves, coarsely torn or left whole if small

sea salt and freshly ground black pepper

Add 1 teaspoon of the red wine vinegar to a measuring jug/pitcher of iced water. Put the slices of bread in a bowl and pour over sufficient water to cover the bread completely. Leave to soak for 3–4 minutes until just soft.

Remove the soaked bread from the water and squeeze it gently, first with your hands and then in a clean dish towel to remove any excess water. Put the bread on a plate, cover with plastic wrap and chill in the refrigerator for about 1 hour.

Meanwhile, whisk together the olive oil, the remaining red wine vinegar and the lemon juice in a large serving bowl. Add the garlic and onion and stir to coat well.

Add the cucumber and tomatoes to the garlic and onion with the olives. Tear the bread into bite-size chunks and add to the bowl with the fresh basil leaves. Toss together to mix and serve immediately with a grinding of sea salt and black pepper.

Health Rating: 5 points

Panzerotti

Serves 16

Ingredients

450 g/1 lb strong white/bread flour
pinch salt
1 tsp easy-blend/active dried yeast
2 tbsp olive oil
300 ml/½ pint/1¼ cups warm water
fresh rocket/arugula leaves, to serve

For the filling:

1 tbsp olive oil
1 small red onion, peeled and finely chopped
2 garlic cloves, peeled and crushed
½ yellow pepper, deseeded and chopped
1 small courgette/zucchini, about 75 g/3 oz, trimmed and chopped
50 g/2 oz/5 tbsp pitted and quartered black olives
125 g/4 oz/1 cup finely cubed mozzarella cheese
salt and freshly ground black pepper
5–6 tbsp tomato purée/paste
1 tsp dried mixed herbs
oil, for deep-frying

Sift the flour and salt into a bowl. Stir in the yeast. Make a well in the centre. Add the oil and the warm water and mix to a soft dough. Knead on a lightly floured surface until smooth and elastic. Put in an oiled bowl, cover and leave in a warm place to rise while making the filling.

To make the filling, heat the oil in a frying pan and cook the onion for 5 minutes. Add the garlic, yellow pepper and courgette/zucchini. Cook for about 5 minutes until the vegetables are tender. Tip into a bowl and leave to cool slightly. Stir in the olives and mozzarella cheese and season to taste with salt and pepper.

Briefly reknead the dough. Divide into 16 equal pieces. Roll out each to a circle about 10 cm/4 inches. Mix together the tomato purée/paste and dried herbs, then spread about 1 teaspoon on each circle, leaving a 2 cm/¾ inch border around the edge.

Divide the filling equally between the circles. It will seem a small amount, but if you overfill, they will leak during cooking. Brush the edges with water, then fold in half to enclose the filling. Press to seal, then crimp the edges.

Heat the oil in a deep fryer to 180°C/350°F. Deep-fry the panzerotti in batches for 3 minutes, or until golden. Drain on absorbent paper towels and keep warm in a low oven until ready to serve with fresh rocket/arugula leaves.

Health Rating: 3 points

Roast Butternut Squash Risotto

Serves 4

Ingredients

1 butternut squash

2 tbsp olive oil

1 garlic bulb, cloves separated but unpeeled

15 g/½ oz/1 tbsp unsalted butter

280 g/10 oz/1½ cups Arborio/risotto rice

large pinch saffron strands

150 ml/¼ pint/⅔ cup dry white wine

1 litre/1¾ pints/4 cups vegetable stock

1 tbsp freshly chopped parsley

1 tbsp freshly chopped oregano

50 g/2 oz/½ cup finely grated Parmesan cheese

salt and freshly ground black pepper

fresh oregano sprigs, to garnish

extra Parmesan cheese, to serve

Preheat the oven to 190°C/375°F/Gas Mark 5. Cut the butternut squash in half, thickly peel, then scoop out the seeds and discard. Cut the flesh into 2 cm/¾ inch cubes.

Pour the oil into a large roasting tin/pan and heat in the oven for 5 minutes. Add the butternut squash and garlic. Turn in the oil to coat, then roast for about 25–30 minutes until golden brown and very tender, turning the vegetables halfway through cooking time.

Melt the butter in a large saucepan. Add the rice and stir over a high heat for a few seconds. Add the saffron and the wine and bubble fiercely until almost totally reduced, stirring frequently. At the same time, heat the stock in a separate saucepan and keep at a steady simmer.

Reduce the heat under the rice to low. Add a ladleful of stock to the saucepan and simmer, stirring, until absorbed. Continue adding the stock in this way until the rice is tender. This will take about 20 minutes and it may not be necessary to add all the stock.

Turn off the heat, stir in the herbs, Parmesan cheese and seasoning. Cover and leave to stand for 2–3 minutes. Quickly

remove the skins from the roasted garlic. Add to the risotto with the butternut squash and mix gently. Garnish with oregano sprigs and serve immediately with Parmesan cheese.

Health Rating: 3 points

Cannelloni with Spinach & Ricotta Cheese

Serves 4

Ingredients

300 ml/¹/₂ pint/1¹/₄ cups milk; 3 shallots, peeled; small piece carrot;
   small piece celery; 1 fresh bay leaf; 4–5 black peppercorns; 25 g/
   1 oz/2 tbsp butter

25 g/1 oz/generous ¹/₈ cup plain/all-purpose flour

2–3 garlic cloves, peeled and crushed

2 tbsp pine nuts

300 g/11 oz fresh spinach

300 g/11 oz/1¹/₃ cups ricotta cheese

1 medium/large egg, beaten; salt and freshly ground pepper

20 precooked cannelloni tubes

450 ml/³/₄ pint/1³/₄ cups prepared tomato sauce (see page 244)

2 tbsp freshly grated Parmesan cheese

Preheat the oven to 190°C/375°F/Gas Mark 5, 10 minutes before cooking. For the Béchamel sauce, pour the milk into a saucepan and add 1 shallot, the carrot, celery, bay leaf and peppercorns. Bring slowly to the boil, then remove from the heat, cover with a lid and leave for at least 15 minutes. Strain before using. Melt the butter in a saucepan and stir in the flour. Cook for 2 minutes, remove from the heat and gradually stir in the flavoured milk. Return the pan to the heat and cook, stirring, for 3–5 minutes until the sauce is thick and smooth. Add salt to taste, then pour into a gratin dish/pan or medium-size ovenproof dish.

Heat olive oil in a saucepan, finely chop and add 2 shallots and the garlic and fry gently for 3 minutes. Add the pine nuts and fry for a further 1 minute, stirring frequently. Remove from the heat and leave to cool. Place the spinach in a bowl and cover with boiling water. Leave for 2 minutes, or until wilted, then drain thoroughly. Chop finely and place in a bowl with the shallot mixture and ricotta. Add the egg, season to taste, then mix together. Fill the pasta tubes with the spinach mixture and place on top of the white sauce in the dish. Cover with the tomato sauce and sprinkle with the grated Parmesan. Bake for 25 minutes, or until the top is golden and bubbling. Serve with Italian bread and green salad.

Health Rating: 3 points

Pasta Primavera

Serves 4

Ingredients

150 g/5 oz/1 cup French/green beans

150 g/5 oz/1 cup sugar snap peas

40 g/1¹/₂ oz/3 tbsp butter

1 tsp olive oil

225 g/8 oz/1 cup scrubbed baby carrots

2 courgettes/zucchini, trimmed and thinly sliced

175 g/6 oz/¹/₄ cup baby trimmed and thickly sliced leeks

200 ml/7 fl oz/³/₄ cup double/heavy cream

1 tsp finely grated lemon zest

350 g/12 oz/4 cups dried tagliatelle

25 g/1 oz/¹/₄ cup grated Parmesan cheese

1 tbsp freshly snipped chives

1 tbsp freshly chopped dill

salt and freshly ground black pepper

fresh dill sprigs, to garnish

Trim and halve the French/green beans. Bring a large saucepan of lightly salted water to the boil and cook the beans for 4–5 minutes, adding the sugar snap peas after 2 minutes so that both are tender at the same time. Drain the beans and sugar snap peas and briefly rinse under cold running water.

Heat the butter and oil in a large, nonstick frying pan. Add the baby carrots and cook for 2 minutes, then stir in the courgettes/zucchini and leeks and cook for 10 minutes, stirring, until the vegetables are almost tender. Stir the cream and lemon zest into the vegetables and bubble over a gentle heat until the sauce is slightly reduced and the vegetables are cooked.

Bring a large saucepan of lightly salted water to the boil and cook the tagliatelle for 10 minutes, or until al dente. Add the beans, sugar snaps, Parmesan and herbs to the sauce. Stir for 30 seconds, or until the cheese has melted and the vegetables are hot. Drain the tagliatelle, add the vegetables and sauce. Toss gently to mix. Season to taste with salt and pepper. Spoon into a warmed serving bowl, garnish with a few dill sprigs and serve immediately.

Health Rating: 4 points

Spaghetti with Pesto

Serves 4

Ingredients

200 g/7 oz/1¾ cups freshly grated Parmesan cheese, plus extra
   to serve
25 g/1 oz/⅓ cup fresh basil leaves, plus extra to garnish
6 tbsp pine nuts
3 large garlic cloves, peeled
200 ml/7 fl oz/¾ cup extra virgin olive oil, plus more if
   necessary
salt and freshly ground black pepper
400 g/14 oz spaghetti

To make the pesto, place the Parmesan cheese in a food processor with the basil leaves, pine nuts and garlic and process until well blended.

With the motor running, gradually pour in the extra virgin olive oil until a thick sauce forms. Add a little more oil if the sauce seems too thick.

Season to taste with salt and pepper. Transfer to a bowl, cover and store in the refrigerator until required.

Bring a large pan of lightly salted water to a rolling boil. Add the spaghetti and cook according to the packet instructions, or until *al dente*. Drain the spaghetti thoroughly and return to the pan.

Stir the pesto into the spaghetti and toss lightly. Heat through gently, then tip the pasta into a warmed serving dish or spoon onto individual plates. Garnish with basil leaves and serve immediately with extra Parmesan cheese.

Health Rating: 2 points

Pasta Shells with Broccoli & Capers

Serves 4

Ingredients

400 g/14 oz/3½ cups conchiglie (shells)

450 g/1 lb broccoli florets, cut into small pieces

5 tbsp olive oil

1 large onion, peeled and finely chopped

4 tbsp rinsed and drained capers in brine

½ tsp dried chilli flakes (optional)

75 g/3 oz/¾ cup freshly grated Parmesan cheese, plus extra
   to serve

25 g/1 oz/¼ cup grated pecorino cheese

salt and freshly ground black pepper

2 tbsp freshly chopped flat-leaf parsley, to garnish

Bring a large pan of lightly salted water to a rolling boil. Add the conchiglie, return to the boil and cook for 2 minutes. Add the broccoli to the pan. Return to the boil and continue cooking for 8–10 minutes until the conchiglie is *al dente*.

Meanwhile, heat the olive oil in a large frying pan, add the onion and cook for 5 minutes, or until softened, stirring frequently. Stir in the capers and chilli flakes, if using, and cook for a further 2 minutes.

Drain the pasta and broccoli and add to the frying pan. Toss the ingredients to mix thoroughly. Sprinkle over the cheeses, then stir until the cheeses have just melted. Season to taste with salt and pepper, then tip into a warmed serving dish. Garnish with chopped parsley and serve immediately with extra Parmesan cheese.

Health Rating: 3 points

Stuffed Peppers & Aubergine

Serves 4

Ingredients

4 assorted small peppers or 2 large peppers; 2 medium
   aubergines/eggplants; salt and freshly ground black pepper
fresh basil leaves, to garnish

For the stuffing:
25 g/1 oz capers
3 tbsp olive oil
1 medium onion, peeled and chopped
2–3 garlic cloves, peeled and crushed
2 tbsp pine nuts
15 g/½ oz/generous ⅛ cup sun-dried tomatoes in oil, chopped
50 g/2 oz Parma ham/prosciutto, chopped
50 g/2 oz canned anchovies, drained and mashed
40 g/1½ oz/scant ¼ cup sultanas/golden raisins
50 g/2 oz/scant 1 cup fresh white breadcrumbs
2 tbsp freshly chopped basil
1 large/extra-large egg, beaten

Preheat the oven to 180°C/350°F/Gas Mark 4, 10 minutes before cooking. Cut the peppers in half horizontally and discard the seeds. Place the pepper halves in a large bowl and cover with boiling water. Leave for 15 minutes, then drain and reserve. Cut the aubergines/eggplants horizontally in half and scoop out the centres. Sprinkle the cut surfaces with salt and leave for at least 30 minutes. Rinse well, pat dry with paper towels and reserve.

For the stuffing, soak the capers in cold water for 20 minutes, then drain and reserve. Heat 2 tablespoons olive oil in a saucepan, add the onion, garlic and pine nuts and fry gently for 4 minutes, stirring frequently. Add the remaining stuffing ingredients, season and mix together with the beaten egg. Use to fill the halved peppers and aubergines. Place the filled vegetables in a large roasting tin/pan and drizzle with 1 tablespoon olive oil. Cook in the oven for 30–35 minutes, garnish with fresh basil leaves and serve warm.

Health Rating: 4 points

Venetian Herb Orzo

Serves 4–6

Ingredients

200 g/7 oz/2½ cups baby spinach leaves
150 g/5 oz/1⅔ cups rocket/arugula leaves
50 g/2 oz/⅔ cup flat-leaf parsley
6 spring onions/scallions, trimmed
few fresh mint leaves
3 tbsp extra virgin olive oil, plus more if required
450 g/1 lb orzo
salt and freshly ground black pepper

Rinse the spinach leaves in several changes of cold water and reserve. Finely chop the rocket/arugula leaves with the parsley and mint. Thinly slice the green of the spring onions/scallions.

Bring a large saucepan of water to the boil, add the spinach leaves, herbs and spring onions and cook for about 10 seconds. Remove and rinse under cold running water. Drain well and, using your hands, squeeze out all the excess moisture.

Place the spinach, herbs and spring onions in a food processor. Blend for 1 minute, then, with the motor running, gradually pour in the olive oil until the sauce is well blended.

Meanwhile, bring a large pan of lightly salted water to a rolling boil. Add the pasta and cook according to the packet instructions, or until al dente. Drain thoroughly and place in a large, warmed bowl.

Add the spinach sauce to the orzo and stir lightly until the orzo is well coated. Stir in an extra tablespoon of olive oil if the mixture seems too thick. Season well with salt and pepper. Serve immediately on warmed plates or allow to cool to room temperature.

Health Rating: 3 points

Cheesy Pasta with Tomatoes & Cream

Serves 4–6

Ingredients

1 quantity fresh pasta dough (*see* page 268)

For the filling:
225 g/8 oz/1 cup fresh ricotta cheese
225 g/8 oz/2 cups grated smoked mozzarella (use normal if smoked is unavailable)
125 g/4 oz/1 cup freshly grated pecorino or Parmesan cheese
2 medium/large eggs, lightly beaten
2–3 tbsp finely chopped mint, basil or parsley
salt and freshly ground black pepper

For the sauce:
2 tbsp olive oil
1 small onion, peeled and finely chopped
2 garlic cloves, peeled and finely chopped
450g/1 lb ripe plum tomatoes, peeled, deseeded and finely chopped
50 ml/2 fl oz/¼ cup white vermouth
225 ml/8 fl oz/1 cup double/heavy cream

Place the ricotta cheese in a bowl and beat until smooth, then add the remaining cheeses with the eggs, herbs and seasoning to taste. Beat well until creamy and smooth.

Cut the prepared pasta dough into quarters. Working with one quarter at a time, and covering the remaining quarters with a clean, damp dish towel, roll out the pasta very thinly. Using a 10 cm/4 inch pastry cutter or small saucer, cut out as many rounds as possible. Place a small tablespoonful of the filling mixture slightly below the centre of each round. Lightly moisten the edge of the round with water and fold in half to form a filled half–moon shape. Using a dinner fork, press the edges together firmly. Transfer to a lightly floured baking sheet and continue filling the remaining pasta. Leave to dry for 15 minutes.

Heat the oil in a large saucepan, add the onion and cook for 3–4 minutes until beginning to soften. Add the garlic and

cook for 1–2 minutes, then add the tomatoes, vermouth and cream and bring to the boil. Simmer for 10–15 minutes until thickened and reduced.

Bring a large saucepan of salted water to the boil. Add the pasta and return to the boil. Cook, stirring frequently to prevent sticking, for 5 minutes, or until *al dente*. Drain and return to the pan. Pour over the sauce, garnish with basil leaves and serve immediately.

Health Rating: 2 points

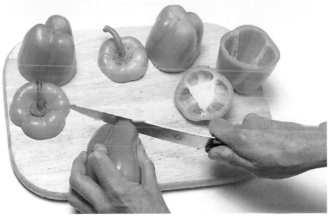

Pastini-stuffed Peppers

Serves 6

Ingredients

6 red, yellow or orange peppers, tops cut off and deseeded
salt and freshly ground black pepper
175 g/6 oz/1½ cups pastini/tiny pasta shapes
4 tbsp olive oil
1 onion, peeled and finely chopped
2 garlic cloves, peeled and finely chopped
3 ripe plum tomatoes, skinned, deseeded and chopped
50 ml/2 fl oz/¼ cup dry white wine
8 pitted black olives, chopped
4 tbsp freshly chopped mixed herbs, such as parsley, basil,
   oregano or marjoram
125 g/4 oz/1 cup diced mozzarella cheese
25 g/1 oz/¼ cup grated Parmesan cheese
fresh tomato sauce, preferably home-made, to serve

Preheat the oven to 190°C/375°F/Gas Mark 5, 10 minutes
before cooking. Bring a pan of water to the boil. Trim the
bottom of each pepper so it sits straight. Blanch the peppers
for 2–3 minutes, then drain on paper towels. Return the water
to the boil, add ½ teaspoon salt and the pastini/pasta shapes
and cook for 3–4 minutes, or until *al dente*. Drain thoroughly,
rinse under cold running water, drain again and reserve.

Heat 2 tablespoons of the olive oil in a large frying pan, add the
onion and cook for 3–4 minutes. Add the garlic and cook for 1
minute. Stir in the tomatoes and wine and cook for 5 minutes,
stirring frequently. Add the olives, herbs, mozzarella cheese and
half the Parmesan cheese. Season to taste with salt and pepper.
Remove from the heat and stir in the pastini.

Dry the insides of the peppers with paper towels, then season
lightly. Arrange the peppers in a lightly oiled, shallow baking dish
and fill with the pastini mixture. Sprinkle with the remaining
Parmesan cheese and drizzle over the remaining oil. Pour in
boiling water to come 1 cm/½ inch up the sides of the dish.
Cook in the preheated oven for 25 minutes, or until cooked.
Serve immediately with freshly made tomato sauce.

Health Rating: 3 points

Preserved Peppers in Oil

Serves 4

Ingredients

25 g/1 oz capers
2 red and 2 yellow peppers
1.5 litres/2½ pints/6⅓ cups vinegar, preferably white
    wine vinegar
600 ml/1 pint/2½ cups water
1 tbsp sea salt
2–3 chillies
2–3 fresh bay leaves
3–4 whole cloves
8 black peppercorns
600–900 ml/1–1½ pints/2½–3¾ cups olive oil

Soak the capers in water for 20 minutes, then drain and reserve. Cut the peppers into quarters and discard the seeds. Rinse and pat dry with absorbent paper towels.

Sterilise a large saucepan or preserving pan. Pour in boiling water and leave for 1–2 minutes, then discard the water. Sterilise two 450 g/1 lb/1¾ cup preserving jars. Wash well in soapy water, rinse and drain, then fill with boiling water. Leave for 2 minutes, then discard the water, drain and place in a warm oven to dry. Reserve.

Place the pepper quarters in the sterilised pan together with the vinegar, water and salt. Bring to the boil, then reduce the heat and boil gently for 5–8 minutes until softened. Ensure that the peppers are beneath the liquid at all times. Remove from the heat and drain, then leave until cool enough to handle.

Pack the peppers in the sterilised jars with the chillies, bay leaves, whole cloves, peppercorns and drained capers. Fill the jars with the oil, ensuring that the peppers are completely covered. Clip tightly and label. Leave for 2 months before using.

Health Rating: 5 points

Fusilli with Courgettes & Sun-dried Tomatoes

Serves 6

Ingredients

5 tbsp olive oil
1 large onion, peeled and thinly sliced
2 garlic cloves, peeled and finely chopped
700 g/1½ lb courgettes/zucchini, trimmed and sliced
400 g/14 oz/2 cups canned chopped plum tomatoes
12 sun-dried tomatoes, cut into thin strips
salt and freshly ground black pepper
450 g/1 lb/4 cups fusilli
25 g/1 oz/2 tbsp butter, diced
2 tbsp freshly chopped basil or flat-leaf parsley
grated Parmesan or pecorino cheese, to serve

Heat 2 tablespoons of the olive oil in a large frying pan, add the onion and cook for 5–7 minutes until softened. Add the chopped garlic and courgette/zucchini slices and cook for a further 5 minutes, stirring occasionally.

Stir the chopped tomatoes and the sun-dried tomatoes into the frying pan and season to taste with salt and pepper. Cook until the courgettes are just tender and the sauce is slightly thickened.

Bring a large pan of lightly salted water to a rolling boil. Add the fusilli and cook according to the packet instructions, or until *al dente*. Drain the fusilli thoroughly and return to the pan. Add the butter and remaining oil and toss to coat.

Stir the chopped basil or parsley into the courgette mixture and pour over the fusilli. Toss and tip into a warmed serving dish. Serve with grated Parmesan or pecorino cheese.

Health Rating: 4 points

Four–cheese Tagliatelle

Serves 4

Ingredients

300 ml/¹/₂ pint/1¹/₄ cups whipping cream
4 garlic cloves, peeled and lightly bruised
75 g/3 oz/³/₄ cup diced fontina cheese
75 g/3 oz/³/₄ cup grated Gruyère cheese
75 g/3 oz/³/₄ cup diced mozzarella cheese
50 g/2 oz/¹/₂ cup grated Parmesan cheese, plus extra to serve
salt and freshly ground black pepper
275 g/10 oz/3 cups fresh green tagliatelle
1–2 tbsp freshly snipped chives
fresh basil leaves, to garnish

Place the whipping cream with the garlic cloves in a medium pan and heat gently until small bubbles begin to form around the edge of the pan. Using a slotted spoon, remove and discard the garlic cloves.

Add all the cheeses to the pan and stir until melted. Season with a little salt and a lot of black pepper. Keep the sauce warm over a low heat, but do not allow to boil.

Meanwhile, bring a large pan of lightly salted water to the boil. Add the tagliatelle, return to the boil and cook for 2–3 minutes, or until *al dente*.

Drain the pasta thoroughly and return to the pan. Pour the sauce over the pasta, add the chives, then toss lightly until well coated. Tip into a warmed serving dish or spoon onto individual plates. Garnish with a few basil leaves and serve immediately with extra Parmesan cheese.

Health Rating: 1 point

Linguine with Walnut Pesto

Serves 4

Ingredients

125 g/4 oz/1 cup walnut halves

1–2 garlic cloves, peeled and roughly chopped

40 g/1½ oz/⅓ cup dried breadcrumbs

3 tbsp extra virgin olive oil

1 tbsp walnut oil

3–4 tbsp freshly chopped parsley

50 g/2 oz/4 tbsp softened butter

2 tbsp double/heavy cream

25 g/1 oz/¼ cup grated Parmesan cheese, plus extra
    to serve

salt and freshly ground black pepper

450 g/1 lb linguine

Bring a saucepan of water to the boil. Add the walnut halves and simmer for about 1 minute. Drain and turn onto a clean dish towel.

Using the towel, rub the nuts gently to loosen the skins, turn into a coarse sieve or colander and shake to separate the skins. Discard the skins and roughly chop the nuts.

With the food processor motor running, drop in the garlic cloves and chop finely. Remove the lid, then add the walnuts, breadcrumbs, olive and walnut oils and the parsley. Blend to a paste with a crumbly texture.

Scrape the nut mixture into a bowl, add the softened butter and, using a wooden spoon, cream them together. Gradually beat in the cream and the Parmesan cheese. Season the walnut pesto to taste with salt and pepper.

Bring a large pan of lightly salted water to a rolling boil. Add the linguine and cook according to the packet instructions, or until al dente.

Drain the linguine thoroughly, reserving 1–2 tablespoons of the cooking water. Return the linguine and reserved water to

the pan. Add the walnut pesto, 1 tablespoon at a time, tossing and stirring until well coated. Tip into a warmed serving dish or spoon onto individual plates. Serve immediately with the extra grated Parmesan cheese.

Health Rating: 2 points

Savoy Cabbage Salad

Serves 6–8

Ingredients

1 whole Savoy cabbage, about 350 g/12 oz

1 red onion, peeled and sliced

2 assorted peppers, deseeded and sliced

125 g/4 oz baby plum tomatoes, halved

salt and freshly ground black pepper

8 anchovy fillets, drained

25 g/1 oz caper berries

6 tbsp extra virgin olive oil

2 tbsp white wine vinegar

1 tbsp balsamic vinegar

Discard the outer leaves and hard central core from the cabbage and shred. Place in a colander/strainer and rinse well. Allow to drain, then place in a large bowl.

Add all the other vegetables with seasoning to taste and toss together until well mixed. Spoon into a serving dish and top with the anchovy fillets and caper berries.

Place the olive oil and the vinegars in a screw-top jar and shake vigorously until blended. Pour the dressing over the salad just before serving.

Health Rating: 5 points

Spaghetti alla Puttanesca

Serves 4

Ingredients

4 tbsp olive oil

50 g/2 oz canned anchovy fillets in olive oil, drained and roughly chopped

2 garlic cloves, peeled and finely chopped

½ tsp crushed dried chillies

400 g/14 oz/2 cups canned chopped plum tomatoes

125 g/4 oz/1 cup pitted black olives, cut in half

2 tbsp capers, rinsed and drained

1 tsp freshly chopped oregano

1 tbsp tomato purée/paste

salt and freshly ground black pepper

400 g/14 oz spaghetti

2 tbsp freshly chopped parsley

Heat the olive oil in a large frying pan, add the anchovies and cook, stirring with a wooden spoon and crushing the anchovies until they disintegrate. Add the garlic and dried chillies and cook for 1 minute, stirring frequently.

Add the tomatoes, olives, capers, oregano and tomato purée/paste and cook, stirring occasionally, for 15 minutes, or until the liquid has evaporated and the sauce is thickened. Season the tomato sauce to taste with salt and pepper.

Meanwhile, bring a large pan of lightly salted water to a rolling boil. Add the spaghetti and cook according to the packet instructions, or until *al dente*.

Drain the spaghetti thoroughly, reserving 1–2 tablespoons of the cooking water. Return the spaghetti with the reserved water to the pan. Pour the tomato sauce over the spaghetti, add the chopped parsley and toss to coat. Tip into a warmed serving dish or spoon onto individual plates and serve immediately.

Health Rating: 3 points

Tagliatelle Primavera

Serves 4

Ingredients

125 g/4 oz asparagus, lightly peeled and cut into
   6.5 cm/2½ inch lengths

2 carrots, peeled and cut into julienne strips

2 courgettes/zucchini, trimmed and cut into
   julienne strips

50 g/2 oz/⅓ cup small mangetout/snow peas

50 g/2 oz/4 tbsp butter

1 small onion, peeled and finely chopped

1 small red pepper, deseeded and finely chopped

50 ml/2 fl oz/¼ cup dry vermouth

225 ml/8 fl oz/1 cup double/heavy cream

1 small leek, trimmed and cut into julienne strips

75 g/3 oz/¾ cup fresh or thawed green peas

salt and freshly ground black pepper

400 g/14 oz fresh tagliatelle

2 tbsp freshly chopped flat-leaf parsley

25 g/1 oz/¼ cup grated Parmesan cheese

Bring a medium saucepan of salted water to the boil. Add the asparagus and blanch for 1–2 minutes until just beginning to soften. Using a slotted spoon, transfer to a colander/strainer and rinse under cold running water.

Repeat with the carrots and courgettes/zucchini. Add the mangetout/snow peas, return to the boil, drain, rinse immediately and drain again. Reserve the blanched vegetables.

Heat the butter in a large frying pan, add the onion and red pepper and cook for 5 minutes, or until they begin to soften and colour. Pour in the dry vermouth; it will bubble and steam and evaporate almost immediately. Stir in the cream and simmer over a medium–low heat until reduced by about half. Add the blanched vegetables with the leek, peas and seasoning and heat through for 2 minutes.

Meanwhile, bring a large saucepan of lightly salted water to the boil, add the tagliatelle and return to the boil. Cook for 2–3 minutes, or until *al dente*. Drain thoroughly and return to the pan.

Stir the chopped parsley into the cream and vegetable sauce, then pour over the pasta and toss to coat. Sprinkle with the grated Parmesan cheese and toss lightly. Tip into a warmed serving bowl or spoon onto individual plates and serve immediately.

Health Rating: 4 points

Aubergine & Ravioli Parmigiana

Serves 6

Ingredients

4 tbsp olive oil

1 large onion, peeled and finely chopped

2–3 garlic cloves, peeled and crushed

800 g/28 oz/4 cups canned chopped tomatoes

2 tsp brown sugar

1 dried bay leaf

1 tsp dried oregano

1 tsp dried basil

2 tbsp freshly shredded basil

salt and freshly ground black pepper

2–3 aubergines/eggplants, sliced crossways 1 cm/½ inch thick

2 eggs, beaten with 1 tbsp water

125 g/4 oz/1 cup dried breadcrumbs

75 g/3 oz/¾ cup freshly grated Parmesan cheese

400 g/14 oz mozzarella cheese, thinly sliced

250 g/9 oz cheese-filled ravioli, cooked and drained

Preheat the oven to 180°C/350°F/Gas Mark 4, about 15 minutes before cooking. Heat 2 tablespoons of the olive oil in a large, heavy-based pan, add the onion and cook for 6–7 minutes until softened.

Add the garlic, cook for 1 minute, then stir in the tomatoes, sugar, bay leaf, dried oregano and basil, then bring to the boil, stirring frequently. Simmer for 30–35 minutes until thickened and reduced, stirring occasionally.

Stir in the fresh basil and season to taste with salt and pepper. Remove the tomato sauce from the heat and reserve.

Heat the remaining olive oil in a large, heavy-based frying pan over a high heat. Dip the aubergine/eggplant slices in the egg mixture, then in the breadcrumbs. Cook in batches until golden on both sides. Drain on paper towels. Add more oil if necessary.

Spoon a little tomato sauce into the base of a lightly oiled, large baking dish. Cover with a layer of aubergine slices, a sprinkling of Parmesan, a layer of mozzarella, then more sauce. Repeat the layers, then cover the sauce with a layer of cooked ravioli. Continue to layer in this way, ending with a layer of mozzarella. Sprinkle the top with Parmesan cheese.

Drizzle with a little extra olive oil if liked, then bake in the preheated oven for 30 minutes, or until golden brown and bubbling. Serve immediately.

Health Rating: 2 points

Tomato & Fennel Salad

Serves 4–6

Ingredients

3–4 beefsteak tomatoes
1 fennel bulb
8 spring onions/scallions
salt and freshly ground black pepper
fresh basil leaves
3–4 tbsp extra virgin olive oil

Rinse the tomatoes and slice horizontally, then arrange on a flat serving platter.

Trim the fennel bulb and remove and reserve the feathery fronds. Coarsely grate the fennel and scatter across the tomatoes.

Trim the spring onions/scallions and slice diagonally. Sprinkle over the fennel and season with salt and pepper.

Scatter with fresh basil leaves and drizzle with the olive oil just before serving, garnished with the reserved feathery fennel leaves.

Health Rating: 5 points

Baked Macaroni Cheese

Serves 8

Ingredients

450 g/1 lb/4 cups macaroni
75 g/3 oz/6 tbsp butter
1 onion, peeled and finely chopped
3 tbsp plain/all-purpose flour
1 litre/1¾ pints/4 cups milk
1–2 dried bay leaves
½ tsp dried thyme
salt and freshly ground black pepper
cayenne pepper
freshly grated nutmeg
2 small leeks, trimmed, finely chopped, cooked and drained
1 tbsp Dijon mustard
200 g/7 oz/3½ cups mature Cheddar cheese, grated
2 tbsp dried breadcrumbs
2 tbsp freshly grated Parmesan cheese
basil sprig, to garnish

Preheat the oven to 190°C/375°F/Gas Mark 5, 10 minutes before cooking. Bring a large pan of lightly salted water to a rolling boil. Add the macaroni and cook according to the packet instructions, or until *al dente*. Drain thoroughly and reserve.

Melt 50 g/2 oz/4 tbsp of the butter in a large, heavy-based saucepan. Add the onion and cook, stirring frequently, for 5–7 minutes until softened. Sprinkle in the flour and cook, stirring constantly, for 2 minutes. Remove from the heat, stir in the milk, return to the heat and cook, stirring, until a smooth sauce has formed. Add the bay leaf and thyme and season to taste with salt, pepper, cayenne pepper and freshly grated nutmeg. Simmer for about 15 minutes, stirring frequently, until thickened and smooth.

Remove the sauce from the heat. Add the cooked leeks, mustard and Cheddar and stir until the cheese has melted. Stir in the macaroni, then tip into a lightly oiled baking dish. Sprinkle the breadcrumbs and Parmesan over the macaroni. Dot with the remaining butter, then bake in the oven for 1 hour, or until golden. Garnish with a basil sprig and serve immediately.

Health Rating: 1 point

Courgette Lasagne

Serves 4

Ingredients

2 tbsp olive oil

1 onion, peeled and finely chopped

225 g/8 oz/4 cups wiped and thinly sliced mushrooms

3–4 courgettes/zucchini, trimmed, thinly sliced

2 garlic cloves, peeled and finely chopped

½ tsp dried thyme

1–2 tbsp chopped basil or flat-leaf parsley

salt and freshly ground black pepper

1 quantity prepared white sauce (*see* page 141)

350 g/12 oz precooked lasagne sheets

225 g/8 oz/2 cups grated mozzarella cheese

50 g/2 oz/½ cup grated Parmesan cheese

400 g/14 oz/2 cups drained canned chopped tomatoes

Preheat the oven to 200°C/400°F/Gas Mark 6, 15 minutes before cooking. Heat the oil in a large frying pan, add the onion and cook for 3–5 minutes. Add the mushrooms, cook for 2 minutes, then add the courgettes/zucchini and cook for a further 3–4 minutes until tender. Stir in the garlic, thyme and basil or parsley and season to taste with salt and pepper. Remove from the heat and reserve.

Spoon a third of the white sauce onto the base of a lightly oiled, large baking dish. Arrange a layer of lasagne over the sauce. Spread half the courgette mixture over the pasta, then sprinkle with some of the mozzarella and some of the Parmesan cheese. Repeat with more white sauce and another layer of lasagne, then cover with half the drained tomatoes.

Cover the tomatoes with lasagne, the remaining courgette mixture and some mozzarella and Parmesan cheese. Repeat the layers, ending with a layer of lasagne sheets, white sauce and the remaining Parmesan cheese. Bake in the preheated oven for 35 minutes, or until golden. Serve immediately.

Health Rating: 3 points

Rigatoni with Gorgonzola & Walnuts

Serves 4

Ingredients

400 g/14 oz/3½ cups rigatoni

50 g/2 oz/4 tbsp butter

125 g/4 oz/1 cup crumbled Gorgonzola cheese

2 tbsp brandy (optional)

200 ml/7 fl oz/¾ cup whipping or double/heavy cream

75 g/3 oz/½ cup lightly toasted and roughly chopped
walnut pieces

1 tbsp freshly chopped basil

50 g/2 oz/½ cup freshly grated Parmesan cheese

salt and freshly ground black pepper

To serve:
cherry tomatoes
fresh green salad leaves

Bring a large pan of lightly salted water to a rolling boil. Add the rigatoni and cook according to the packet instructions, or until *al dente*. Drain the pasta thoroughly, reserve and keep warm.

Melt the butter in a large saucepan or wok over a medium heat. Add the Gorgonzola cheese and stir until just melted. Add the brandy, if using, and cook for 30 seconds, then pour in the cream and cook for 1–2 minutes, stirring, until the sauce is smooth.

Stir in the walnut pieces, basil and half the Parmesan cheese, then add the rigatoni. Season to taste with salt and pepper. Return to the heat, stirring frequently, until heated through. Divide the pasta among four warmed pasta bowls, sprinkle with the remaining Parmesan cheese and serve immediately with cherry tomatoes and fresh green salad leaves.

Health Rating: 2 points

Pumpkin-filled Pasta with Butter & Sage

Serves 6–8

Ingredients

For the pasta dough:

225 g/8 oz/1¾ cups strong plain bread flour, or type '00' pasta
   flour, plus extra for rolling

1 tsp salt

2 medium/large eggs

1 medium/large egg yolk

1 tbsp extra virgin olive oil

For the filling:

250 g/9 oz/1 cup freshly cooked pumpkin or sweet potato flesh,
   mashed and cooled

75–125 g/3–4 oz/about ⅓ cup dried breadcrumbs

125 g/4 oz/1 cup freshly grated Parmesan cheese

1 medium/large egg yolk

½ tsp soft brown sugar

2 tbsp freshly chopped parsley

freshly grated nutmeg

salt and freshly ground black pepper

125 g/4 oz/½ cup (1 stick) butter

2 tbsp freshly shredded sage leaves

50 g/2 oz/½ cup freshly grated Parmesan cheese, to serve

To make the dough, sift the flour and salt into a large bowl, make a well in the centre and add the eggs and yolk, oil and 1 teaspoon water. Gradually mix to form a soft but not sticky dough, adding a little more flour or water if necessary. Turn out onto a lightly floured surface and knead for 5 minutes, or until smooth and elastic. Wrap in plastic wrap and leave to rest at room temperature for about 30 minutes.

Mix together the ingredients for the filling in a bowl, seasoning to taste with freshly grated nutmeg, salt and pepper. If the mixture seems too wet, add a few more breadcrumbs to bind.

Cut the pasta dough into quarters. Work with one quarter at a time, covering the remaining quarters with a damp dish towel. Roll out a quarter very thinly into a strip 10 cm/4 inches wide.

Drop spoonfuls of the filling along the strip 6.5 cm/2½ inches apart, in two rows about 5 cm/2 inches apart. Moisten the outside edges and the spaces between the filling with water.

Roll out another strip of pasta and lay it over the filled strip. Press down gently along both edges and between the filled sections. Using a fluted pastry wheel, cut along both long sides, down the centre and between the fillings to form cushions. Transfer the cushions to a lightly floured baking sheet. Continue making cushions and allow to dry for 30 minutes.

Bring a large saucepan of lightly salted water to the boil. Add the pasta cushions and return to the boil. Cook, stirring frequently, for 4–5 minutes, or until *al dente*. Drain carefully.

Heat the butter in a pan, stir in the shredded sage leaves and cook for 30 seconds. Add the pasta cushions, stir gently, then spoon into serving bowls. Sprinkle with the grated Parmesan cheese and serve immediately.

Health Rating: 3 points

Tortellini, Cherry Tomato & Mozzarella Skewers

Serves 6

Ingredients

250 g/9 oz mixed green and plain cheese- or vegetable-filled
   fresh tortellini
150 ml/¹/₄ pint/²/₃ cup extra virgin olive oil
2 garlic cloves, peeled and crushed
pinch dried thyme or basil
salt and freshly ground black pepper
225 g/8 oz cherry tomatoes
450 g/1 lb mozzarella cheese, cut into 2.5 cm/1 inch cubes
basil leaves, to garnish
dressed salad leaves, to serve

Preheat the grill/broiler and line a grill pan with kitchen foil just before cooking. Bring a large pan of lightly salted water to a rolling boil. Add the tortellini and cook according to the packet instructions, or until *al dente*. Drain, rinse under cold running water, drain again and toss with 2 tablespoons of the olive oil and reserve.

Pour the remaining olive oil into a small bowl. Add the crushed garlic and thyme or basil, then blend well. Season to taste with salt and black pepper and reserve.

To assemble the skewers, thread the tortellini alternately with the cherry tomatoes and cubes of mozzarella. Arrange the skewers on the grill pan and brush generously on all sides with the olive oil mixture.

Cook the skewers under the preheated grill for about 5 minutes until they begin to turn golden, turning them halfway through cooking. Arrange two skewers on each plate and garnish with a few basil leaves. Serve immediately with dressed salad leaves.

Health Rating: 3 points

Linguine with Asparagus

Serves 4

Ingredients

350 g/12 oz linguine, fresh or dried

For the sauce:
225 g/8 oz fresh asparagus
4 tbsp olive oil
2 celery stalks, trimmed and sliced
2–4 garlic cloves, peeled and chopped
125 g/4 oz/generous ¾ cup broad/fava beans, thawed if frozen
125 g/4 oz Parma ham/prosciutto, cut into strips
125 g/4 oz baby plum tomatoes, halved
50 g/2 oz/generous ¼ cup pitted black/ripe olives
6–7 basil sprigs, shredded
freshly grated Parmesan cheese
extra virgin olive oil, for drizzling

Bring a large saucepan of water to a rolling boil. Add the pasta and cook until *al dente*: 4–5 minutes for fresh and 8–10 minutes for dried. Drain and reserve 3 tablespoons of the cooking water. Return the pasta to the saucepan together with the cooking water and reserve.

Trim the asparagus and shave the spears to remove any woody bits. Bring a frying pan of water to the boil and add the asparagus. Cook for 4 minutes, then drain. Cut off the tips and reserve. Cut the remainder into short lengths and reserve.

Heat the olive oil in a medium saucepan, add the celery and garlic and fry for 3 minutes, then add the broad/fava beans, the asparagus stalks, the Parma ham/prosciutto, tomatoes and black/ripe olives and cook over a gentle heat for 6 minutes, stirring frequently.

Stir the vegetables into the cooked pasta, then spoon into a warmed serving dish. Scatter with the basil and serve with the grated Parmesan cheese and extra virgin olive oil to drizzle.

Health Rating: 3 points

Tortellini & Summer Vegetable Salad

Serves 6

Ingredients

350 g/12 oz mixed green and plain cheese-filled fresh tortellini
150 ml/¼ pint/⅔ cup extra virgin olive oil
225 g/8 oz/1½ cups fine green beans, trimmed
175 g/6 oz/2½ cups broccoli florets
1 yellow or red pepper, deseeded and thinly sliced
1 red onion, peeled and sliced
175 g/6 oz jar marinated artichoke hearts, drained and halved
2 tbsp capers
75 g/3 oz/½ cup dry-cured pitted black/ripe olives
3 tbsp raspberry or balsamic vinegar
1 tbsp Dijon mustard
1 tsp soft brown sugar
salt and freshly ground black pepper
2 tbsp freshly chopped basil or flat-leaf parsley
2 hard-boiled eggs, quartered, to garnish

Bring a large pan of lightly salted water to a rolling boil. Add the tortellini and cook according to the packet instructions, or until *al dente*. Using a large slotted spoon, transfer the tortellini to a colander/strainer to drain. Rinse under cold running water and drain again. Transfer to a large bowl and toss with 2 tablespoons of the olive oil.

Return the pasta water to the boil and drop in the green beans and broccoli. Blanch for 2 minutes, or until just beginning to soften. Drain, rinse under cold running water and drain again thoroughly. Add the vegetables to the reserved tortellini. Add the pepper, onion, artichoke hearts, capers and olives to the bowl and stir lightly.

Whisk together the vinegar, mustard and brown sugar in a bowl and season to taste with salt and pepper. Slowly whisk in the remaining olive oil to form a thick, creamy dressing. Pour over the tortellini and vegetables, add the chopped basil or parsley and stir until lightly coated. Transfer to a shallow serving dish or salad bowl. Garnish with the hard–boiled egg quarters and serve.

Health Rating: 4 points

Pasta with Courgettes, Rosemary & Lemon

Serves 4

Ingredients

350 g/12 oz/4½ cups dried pasta shapes, such as rigatoni

1½ tbsp good-quality extra virgin olive oil

2 garlic cloves, peeled and finely chopped

4 courgettes/zucchini and thinly sliced

1 tbsp freshly chopped rosemary

1 tbsp freshly chopped parsley

zest and juice of 2 lemons

25 g/1 oz pitted black/ripe olives, roughly chopped

25 g/1 oz pitted green olives, roughly chopped

salt and freshly ground black pepper

To garnish:

lemon slices

fresh rosemary sprigs

Bring a large saucepan of salted water to the boil and add the pasta. Return to the boil and cook until *al dente*, or according to the packet instructions.

When the pasta is almost done, heat the oil in a large frying pan and add the garlic. Cook over a medium heat until the garlic just begins to brown. Take care not to overcook the garlic at this stage, or it will become bitter.

Add the courgettes/zucchini, rosemary, parsley and lemon zest and juice. Cook for 3–4 minutes until the courgettes are just tender. Add the olives to the frying pan and stir well. Season to taste with salt and pepper and remove from the heat.

Drain the pasta well. Add to the frying pan. Stir until thoroughly combined. Garnish with lemon and fresh rosemary. Serve immediately.

Health Rating: 3 points

Vegetarian Spaghetti Bolognese

Serves 4

Ingredients

2 tbsp olive oil

1 onion, peeled and finely chopped

1 carrot, peeled and finely chopped

1 celery stalk, trimmed and finely chopped

225 g/8 oz Quorn mince/soy meat substitute

150 ml/¼ pint/⅔ cup red wine

300 ml/½ pint/1¼ cups vegetable stock

1 tsp ketchup

4 tbsp tomato purée/paste

350 g/12 oz/4 cups dried spaghetti

4 tbsp crème fraîche

salt and freshly ground black pepper

1 tbsp freshly chopped parsley

Heat the oil in a large saucepan and add the onion, carrot and celery. Cook gently for 10 minutes, adding a little water if necessary, until softened and starting to brown.

Add the Quorn mince/soy meat substitute and cook for a further 2–3 minutes before adding the red wine. Increase the heat and simmer gently until nearly all the wine has evaporated.

Mix together the vegetable stock and ketchup and add about half to the Quorn mixture along with the tomato purée/paste. Cover and simmer gently for about 45 minutes, adding the remaining stock if necessary.

Meanwhile, bring a large pan of salted water to the boil and add the spaghetti. Cook until *al dente*, or according to the packet instructions. Drain well. Remove the sauce from the heat, add the crème fraîche and season to taste with salt and pepper. Stir in the parsley and serve immediately with the pasta.

Health Rating: 4 points

Spring Vegetable & Herb Risotto

Serves 2–3

Ingredients

1 litre/1¾ pints/4 cups vegetable stock
125 g/4 oz/½ cup trimmed asparagus tips
125 g/4 oz/1 cup scrubbed baby carrots
50 g/2 oz/½ cup fresh or thawed peas
50 g/2 oz/½ cup trimmed fine French/green beans
1 tbsp olive oil
1 onion, peeled and finely chopped
1 garlic clove, peeled and finely chopped
2 tsp freshly chopped thyme
225 g/8 oz/1 heaping cup Arborio/risotto rice
150 ml/¼ pint/⅔ cup white wine
1 tbsp each freshly chopped basil, chives and parsley
zest of ½ lemon; 3 tbsp crème fraîche
salt and freshly ground black pepper

Bring the vegetable stock to the boil in a large saucepan and add the asparagus, baby carrots, peas and beans. Bring the stock back to the boil and remove the vegetables at once using a slotted spoon. Rinse under cold running water. Drain again and reserve. Keep the stock hot.

Heat the oil in a large, deep frying pan and add the onion. Cook over a medium heat for 4–5 minutes until starting to brown. Add the garlic and thyme and cook for a further few seconds. Add the rice and stir well for 1 minute until the rice is hot and coated in oil.

Add the white wine and stir constantly until the wine is almost completely absorbed by the rice. Begin adding the stock a ladleful at a time, stirring well and waiting until the last ladleful has been absorbed before stirring in the next. Add the vegetables after using about half of the stock. Continue until all the stock is used. This will take 20–25 minutes. The rice and vegetables should both be tender. Remove the pan from the heat. Stir in the herbs, lemon zest and crème fraîche. Season to taste with salt and pepper and serve immediately.

Health Rating: 4 points

Roasted Mixed Vegetables with Garlic & Herb Sauce

Serves 4

Ingredients

1 large garlic bulb, halved horizontally

1 large onion, peeled and cut into wedges

4 small carrots, peeled and quartered

4 small parsnips, peeled

6 small potatoes, scrubbed and halved

1 fennel bulb, thickly sliced

4 fresh rosemary sprigs

4 fresh thyme sprigs

2 tbsp olive oil

salt and freshly ground black pepper

200 g/7 oz/1 cup soft/cream cheese with herbs and garlic

4 tbsp milk

zest of ½ lemon

fresh thyme sprigs, to garnish

Preheat the oven to 220°C/425°F/Gas Mark 7. Put all the vegetables and herbs into a large roasting tin/pan. Add the oil, season well with salt and pepper and toss together to coat lightly in the oil.

Cover with kitchen foil and roast in the preheated oven for 50 minutes. Remove the kitchen foil and cook for a further 30 minutes until all the vegetables are tender and slightly charred. Remove the tin from the oven and allow to cool.

In a small saucepan, melt the soft/cream cheese together with the milk and lemon zest. Remove the garlic from the roasting tin and squeeze the flesh into a bowl. Mash thoroughly, then add to the sauce. Heat through gently. Season the vegetables to taste. Pour some sauce into small ramekins and garnish with 4 thyme sprigs. Serve the roasted vegetables with the sauce for dipping.

Health Rating: 4 points

Baby Onion Risotto

Serves 4

Ingredients

For the baby onions:
1 tbsp olive oil
450 g/1 lb/18 baby onions, peeled and halved if large
pinch sugar
1 tbsp freshly chopped thyme

For the risotto:
1 tbsp olive oil
1 small onion, peeled and finely chopped
2 garlic cloves, peeled and finely chopped
350 g/12 oz/1½ cups Arborio/risotto rice
150 ml/¼ pint/⅔ cup red wine
1 litre/1¾ pints/4 cups vegetable stock, heated
125 g/4 oz/½ cup soft goats' cheese
salt and freshly ground black pepper
rocket/arugula leaves, to serve

For the baby onions, heat the olive oil in a saucepan and add the onions with the sugar. Cover and cook over a low heat, stirring occasionally, for 20–25 minutes until caramelised. Uncover during the last 10 minutes of cooking.

Meanwhile, for the risotto, heat the oil in a large frying pan and add the onion. Cook over a medium heat for 5 minutes until softened. Add the garlic and cook for a further 30 seconds. Add the risotto rice and stir well. Add the red wine and stir constantly until the wine is almost completely absorbed by the rice. Begin adding the stock a ladleful at a time, stirring well and waiting until the last ladleful has been absorbed before stirring in the next. It will take 20–25 minutes to add all the stock, by which time the rice should be just cooked but still firm. Remove from the heat.

Add the thyme to the onions and cook briefly. Increase the heat, allow the onion mixture to bubble for 2–3 minutes until almost evaporated. Add the onion mixture to the risotto along with the goats' cheese. Stir well and season to taste with salt and pepper. Serve with rocket/arugula leaves.

Health Rating: 3 points

Sicilian Baked Aubergine

Serves 4

Ingredients

1 large aubergine/eggplant, trimmed and cubed

2 celery stalks, trimmed

4 large, ripe tomatoes

1 tsp sunflower/corn oil

2 shallots, peeled and finely chopped

1½ tsp tomato purée/paste

5 large, green olives, pitted

5 large, black/ripe olives, pitted

salt and freshly ground black pepper

1 tbsp white wine vinegar

2 tsp caster/superfine sugar

1 tbsp freshly chopped basil, to garnish

mixed salad leaves, to serve

Preheat the oven to 200°C/400°F/Gas Mark 6. Place the aubergine/eggplant on an oiled baking tray/pan. Cover the tray with kitchen foil and bake in the preheated oven for 15–20 minutes until soft. Remove the aubergine from the oven and leave to cool.

Make a small cross in the base of each tomato. Place the celery and tomatoes in a large bowl and cover with boiling water. Remove the tomatoes from the bowl when their skins begin to peel away. Remove the skins, then deseed and chop the flesh into small pieces. Remove the celery from the bowl of water, chop finely and reserve.

Pour the sunflower/corn oil into a nonstick saucepan, add the chopped shallots and fry gently for 2–3 minutes until soft. Add the celery, tomatoes, tomato purée/paste and olives. Season to taste with salt and pepper. Simmer gently for 3–4 minutes.

Add the vinegar, sugar and cooled aubergine to the pan and heat gently for 2–3 minutes until all the ingredients are well blended. Remove from the heat and leave to cool, then garnish with the chopped basil and serve cold with salad leaves.

Health Rating: 5 points

Pasta with Mushrooms & Fontina Cheese

Serves 4

Ingredients

450 g/1 lb pasta, such as orecchiette, fresh or dried

For the sauce:
25 g/1 oz/2 tbsp butter
225 g/8 oz/2¼ cups button/white mushrooms, wiped and chopped
50 g/2 oz/½ cup chestnut/cremini mushrooms, wiped and sliced
200 ml/7 fl oz/¾ cup double/heavy cream
125 g/4 oz fontina cheese, cut into small pieces
salt and freshly ground black pepper
8 spring onions/scallions, trimmed and diagonally sliced

Bring a large saucepan of water to a rolling boil. Add the pasta and cook until al dente: 4–5 minutes for fresh and 10–12 minutes for dried. Drain, reserving 2 tablespoons of the cooking water. Return the pasta and cooking water to the saucepan and reserve.

Melt the butter in a medium saucepan, add both mushrooms and gently fry for 5 minutes. Stir in the cream with the cheese and seasoning and cook gently, stirring frequently, until the cheese melts.

Stir the sauce into the cooked pasta and heat for 2–3 minutes until hot. Serve on warmed plates scattered with the spring onions/scallions.

Health Rating: 2 points

Potato Gnocchi with Pesto Sauce

Serves 6

Ingredients

900 g/2 lb floury potatoes
40 g/1½ oz/3 tbsp butter
1 egg, beaten
225 g/8 oz/2 cups plain/all-purpose flour
1 tsp salt
freshly ground black pepper
50 g/2 oz/2 packed cups fresh basil leaves
1 large garlic clove, peeled
2 tbsp pine nuts
125 ml/4 fl oz/½ cup olive oil
40 g/1½ oz/⅓ cup grated Parmesan cheese, plus an extra
    25 g/1 oz/⅓ cup, to garnish
rocket/arugula salad, to serve

Cook the potatoes in their skins in boiling water for 20 minutes, or until tender. Drain and peel. While still warm, push the potatoes through a fine sieve into a bowl. Stir in the butter, egg, 175 g/6 oz/1½ cups of the flour, the salt and pepper. Sift the remaining flour onto a board or work surface and add the potato mixture. Gently knead in enough flour until a soft, slightly sticky dough is formed. With floured hands, break off portions of the dough and roll into 2.5 cm/1 inch thick ropes. Cut into 2 cm/¾ inch lengths. Lightly press each piece against the inner prongs of a fork. Put on a tray covered with a floured dish towel and chill in the refrigerator for about 30 minutes.

To make the pesto sauce, put the basil, garlic, pine nuts and oil in a food processor and blend until smooth and creamy. Turn into a bowl and stir in the Parmesan. Season to taste. Cooking in several batches, drop the gnocchi into a saucepan of barely simmering salted water. Cook for 3–4 minutes until they float to the surface. Remove with a slotted spoon and keep warm in a covered, oiled baking dish in a low oven. Add the gnocchi to the sauce and toss gently to coat. Serve scattered with the grated Parmesan and accompanied by a rocket/arugula salad.

Health Rating: 2 points

Broad Bean & Artichoke Risotto

Serves 4

Ingredients

275 g/10 oz/1¾ cups frozen broad/fava beans

400 g/14 oz canned artichoke hearts, drained

1 tbsp sunflower oil

150 ml/¼ pint/⅔ cup dry white wine

900 ml/1½ pints/3¾ cups vegetable stock

25 g/1 oz/2 tbsp butter

1 onion, peeled and finely chopped

200 g/7 oz/1 cup Arborio/risotto rice

finely grated zest and juice of 1 lemon

50 g/2 oz/½ cup grated Parmesan cheese

salt and freshly ground black pepper

freshly grated Parmesan cheese, to serve

Cook the beans in a saucepan of lightly salted boiling water for 4–5 minutes until just tender. Drain and plunge into cold water. Peel off the tough outer skins, if liked. Pat the artichokes dry on absorbent paper towels and cut each in half lengthways through the stem end. Cut each half into three wedges.

Heat the oil in a large saucepan and cook the artichokes for 4–5 minutes, turning occasionally, until they are lightly browned. Remove and reserve. Bring the wine and stock to the boil in a separate frying pan. Keep them barely simmering while making the risotto.

Melt the butter in a large frying pan, add the onion and cook for 5 minutes until beginning to soften. Add the rice and cook for 1 minute, stirring. Pour in a ladleful of the hot wine and stock, simmer gently, stirring frequently, until the stock is absorbed. Continue to add the stock in this way for 20–25 minutes until the rice is just tender and the risotto creamy and soft. Add the beans, artichokes and lemon zest and juice. Gently mix in, cover and leave to warm through for 1–2 minutes. Stir in the Parmesan cheese and season to taste with salt and pepper. Serve sprinkled with extra Parmesan cheese.

Health Rating: 4 points

Wild Mushroom Risotto

Serves 4

Ingredients

15 g/½ oz dried porcini mushrooms

1.1 litres/2 pints/4⅔ cups vegetable stock

75 g/3 oz/6 tbsp butter

1 tbsp olive oil

1 onion, peeled and chopped

2–4 garlic cloves, peeled and chopped

1–2 red chillies, deseeded and chopped

225 g/8 oz/2¼ cups wiped and halved wild mushrooms

125 g/4 oz/1¼ cups wiped and sliced button/white mushrooms

350 g/12 oz/1¾ cups Arborio/risotto rice

175 g/6 oz/1 cup peeled cooked prawns/shrimp (optional)

150 ml/¼ pint/⅔ cup white wine

salt and freshly ground black pepper

1 tbsp lemon zest

1 tbsp freshly snipped chives; 2 tbsp freshly chopped parsley

Soak the porcini in 300 ml/½ pint/1¼ cups very hot but not boiling water for 30 minutes. Drain, reserving the mushrooms and the soaking liquid. Pour the stock into a saucepan and bring to the boil, then reduce the heat to keep it simmering.

Melt the butter and oil in a large, deep frying pan, add the onion, garlic and chillies and cook gently for 5 minutes. Add the wild and button/white mushrooms with the drained porcini and continue to cook for 4–5 minutes, stirring frequently.

Stir in the rice and cook for 1 minute. Strain the reserved soaking liquid and stir into the rice with a little of the hot stock. Cook gently, stirring frequently, until the liquid is absorbed. Continue to add most of the stock, a ladleful at a time, stirring after each addition, until the rice is tender and the risotto looks creamy.

Add the prawns/shrimp, if using, and wine along with the last additions of stock. When the prawns are hot and all the liquid is absorbed, season to taste with salt and pepper. Remove from the heat and stir in the lemon zest, chives and parsley, reserving some for the garnish. Garnish and serve.

Health Rating: 3 points

Quattro Formaggi Pizza

Makes one 25 cm/10 inch pizza

Ingredients

1 quantity basic pizza dough (*see right*)
plain/all-purpose flour, for dusting
125 g/4 oz/¹/₂ cup ricotta cheese
2–3 garlic cloves, peeled and crushed (optional)
3 beefsteak tomatoes (optional)
75 g/3 oz blue cheese, such as Gorgonzola
75 g/3 oz small balls mozzarella cheese
40 g/1¹/₂ oz/generous ¹/₄ cup freshly grated Parmesan cheese
1 tbsp freshly shredded basil, to serve

Preheat the oven to 230°C/450°F/Gas Mark 8, 15 minutes before cooking. Place a pizza stone or large baking sheet in the oven to heat up 5 minutes before cooking. Roll the dough out on a lightly floured surface and shape into a 25 cm/10 inch round pizza base. Ensure that the edge is slightly raised so that the cheese does not run off.

Dot the prepared pizza base with small spoonfuls of ricotta cheese and scatter over the crushed garlic, if using. Slice the tomatoes, if using, and arrange on the base. Cut the blue cheese into small pieces, then randomly scatter over the base with the mozzarella balls. Sprinkle with the grated Parmesan cheese.

Bake in the preheated oven for 10–12 minutes until the cheeses have melted and are bubbling and the crust is golden. Sprinkle with the shredded basil and serve immediately.

Health Rating: 2 points

Three-Tomato Pizzas

Serves 4

Ingredients

For the basic pizza dough:
225 g/8 oz/2 cups strong white/bread flour
¹/₂ tsp salt; ¹/₄ tsp quick-acting dried yeast
150 ml/¹/₄ pint/²/₃ cup warm water
1 tbsp extra virgin olive oil

For the topping:
3 plum tomatoes
8 cherry tomatoes
6 sun-dried tomatoes
pinch sea salt
1 tbsp freshly chopped basil
2 tbsp extra virgin olive oil
125 g/4 oz buffalo mozzarella cheese, sliced
freshly ground black pepper
fresh basil leaves, to garnish

Preheat the oven to 220°C/425°F/Gas Mark 7 and place a baking sheet in the oven to heat up. Sift the flour and salt into a bowl and stir in the yeast. Make a well in the centre and gradually add the water and oil to form a soft dough. Knead on a floured surface for about 5 minutes until smooth and elastic. Place in a lightly oiled bowl and cover with plastic wrap. Leave to rise in a warm place for 1 hour. Knock the dough with your fist a few times, then divide into four equal pieces. Roll out one piece on a lightly floured board to form a 20.5 cm/8 inch round. Roll out the other three pieces into rounds, one at a time. While rolling out any piece, keep the others lightly covered with plastic wrap.

Slice the plum tomatoes, halve the cherry tomatoes and chop the sun-dried tomatoes into small pieces. Place a few pieces of each type of tomato on each pizza base, then season to taste with the salt. Sprinkle with the chopped basil and drizzle with the olive oil. Place a few slices of mozzarella on each pizza and season with black pepper. Transfer the pizzas onto the heated baking sheet and cook for 15–20 minutes until the cheese is golden brown and bubbling. Garnish with the basil and serve immediately.

Health Rating: 3 points

Spinach, Pine Nut & Mascarpone Pizza

Serves 2–4

Ingredients

1 quantity pizza dough (*see* page 282)

For the topping:
3 tbsp olive oil
1 large red onion, peeled and chopped
2 garlic cloves, peeled and finely sliced
450 g/1 lb/3 cups frozen spinach, thawed and drained
salt and freshly ground black pepper
3 tbsp passata/tomato puree (or use tomato sauce)
125 g/4 oz/heaping ½ cup mascarpone cheese
1 tbsp toasted pine nuts

Preheat the oven to 220°C/425°F/Gas Mark 7. Shape and thinly roll out the pizza dough on a lightly floured board. Place on a lightly floured baking sheet and lift the edge to make a little rim. Place another baking sheet into the preheated oven to heat up.

Heat half the oil in a frying pan. Gently fry the onion and garlic until soft and starting to change colour.

Squeeze out any excess water from the spinach and finely chop. Add to the onion and garlic with the remaining olive oil. Season to taste with salt and pepper.

Spread the passata/tomato puree on the pizza dough and top with the spinach mixture. Mix the mascarpone with the pine nuts and dot over the pizza. Slide the pizza onto the hot baking sheet and bake for 15–20 minutes. Transfer to a large plate and serve immediately.

Health Rating: 3 points

Chargrilled Vegetable & Goats' Cheese Pizza

Serves 4

Ingredients

1 small (125 g/4 oz) baking potato

1 tbsp olive oil

225 g/8 oz strong white/bread flour

½ tsp salt

1 tsp easy-blend dried/active dry yeast

For the topping:

1 medium aubergine/eggplant, thinly sliced

2 small courgettes/zucchini, trimmed and sliced lengthways

1 yellow pepper, quartered and deseeded

1 red onion, peeled and sliced into very thin wedges

5 tbsp olive oil

175 g/6 oz/1 heaping cup halved cooked new potatoes

400 g/14 oz/2 cups drained canned chopped tomatoes

2 tsp freshly chopped oregano

125 g/4 oz/1 heaping cup cubed mozzarella cheese

125 g/4 oz/½ cup crumbled goats' cheese

Preheat the oven to 220°C/425°F/Gas Mark 7, 15 minutes before baking. Put a baking sheet in the oven to heat up. Cook the potato in lightly salted boiling water until tender. Peel and mash with the olive oil until smooth.

Sift the flour and salt into a bowl. Stir in the yeast. Add the mashed potato and 150 ml/¼ pint/⅔ cup warm water and mix to a soft dough. Knead for 5–6 minutes until smooth. Put the dough in a bowl, cover with plastic wrap and leave to rise in a warm place for 30 minutes.

For the topping, arrange the aubergine/eggplant, courgettes/ zucchini, pepper and onion, skin-side up, on a grill/boiler rack and brush with 4 tablespoons of the oil. Grill for 4–5 minutes.

Turn the vegetables and brush with the remaining oil. Grill for 3–4 minutes. Cool, skin and slice the pepper. Put all of the vegetables in a bowl, add the halved new potatoes and toss gently together. Reserve.

Briefly re-knead the dough, then roll out to a 30.5–35.5 cm/12 -14 inch round, according to preferred thickness. Mix the tomatoes and oregano together and spread over the pizza base. Scatter over the mozzarella cheese. Put the pizza on the preheated baking sheet and bake for 8 minutes. Arrange the vegetables and goats' cheese on top and bake for 8–10 minutes. Serve.

Health Rating: 3 points

Entertaining & Desserts

This section is filled with excellent recipes that will delight your family and friends. The first half is devoted to savoury dishes for dinner parties, such as Pasta Triangles with Pesto & Walnut Dressing and Tagliatelle with Stuffed Pork Escalopes. The second half is filled with recipes for baking and desserts, beginning with Italian bread such as Rosemary & Olive Focaccia before moving on to sweet treats. The Tiramisu will provide an excellent pick-me-up, while other desserts such as the Bomba Siciliana and the Almond Angel Cake with Amaretto Cream are sure to make you a success at any dinner party.

Penne with Vodka & Caviar

Serves 4

Ingredients

400 g/14 oz/3½ cups penne
25 g/1 oz/2 tbsp butter
4–6 spring onions/scallions, trimmed and thinly sliced
1 garlic clove, peeled and finely chopped
125 ml/4 fl oz/½ cup vodka
200 ml/7 fl oz/¾ cup double/heavy cream
1–2 ripe plum tomatoes, skinned, deseeded and chopped
75 g/3 oz caviar
salt and freshly ground black pepper

Bring a large pan of lightly salted water to a rolling boil. Add the penne and cook according to the packet instructions, or until *al dente*. Drain thoroughly and reserve.

Heat the butter in a large frying pan or wok, add the spring onions/scallions and stir–fry for 1 minute. Stir in the garlic and cook for a further 1 minute. Pour the vodka into the pan; it will bubble and steam. Cook until the vodka is reduced by about half, then add the double/heavy cream and return to the boil. Simmer gently for 2–3 minutes until the sauce has thickened slightly.

Stir in the tomatoes, then stir in all but 1 tablespoon of the caviar and season to taste with salt and pepper. Add the penne and toss lightly to coat. Cook for 1 minute, or until heated through. Divide the mixture among four warmed pasta bowls and garnish with the reserved caviar. Serve immediately.

Health Rating: 2 points

Fettuccine with Calves' Liver & Calvados

Serves 4

Ingredients

50 g/2 oz/¹⁄₂ cup plain/all-purpose flour

salt and freshly ground black pepper

1 tsp paprika

450 g/1 lb calves' liver, trimmed and thinly sliced

50 g/2 oz/4 tbsp butter

1¹⁄₂ tbsp olive oil

2 tbsp Calvados

150 ml/¹⁄₄ pint/²⁄₃ cup cider

150 ml/¹⁄₄ pint/²⁄₃ cup whipping cream

350 g/12 oz fresh fettuccine

fresh thyme sprigs, to garnish

Season the flour with the salt, black pepper and paprika, then toss the liver in the flour until well coated. Melt half the butter and 1 tablespoon of the olive oil in a large frying pan and fry the liver in batches for 1 minute, or until just browned but still slightly pink inside. Remove using a slotted spoon and place in a warmed dish.

Add the remaining butter to the pan, stir in 1 tablespoon of the seasoned flour and cook for 1 minute. Pour in the Calvados and cider and cook over a high heat for 30 seconds. Stir the cream into the sauce and simmer for 1 minute to thicken slightly, then season to taste. Return the liver to the pan and heat through.

Bring a large pan of lightly salted water to a rolling boil. Add the fettuccine and cook according to the packet instructions, about 3–4 minutes, or until *al dente*.

Drain the fettuccine thoroughly, return to the pan and toss in the remaining olive oil. Divide among four warmed plates and spoon the liver and sauce over the pasta. Garnish with thyme sprigs and serve immediately.

Health Rating: 2 points

Tagliatelle with Stuffed Pork Escalopes

Serves 4

Ingredients

150 g/5 oz/³/₄ cup finely chopped and blanched broccoli florets

125 g/4 oz/1 cup grated mozzarella cheese

1 garlic clove, peeled and crushed

2 large/extra-large eggs, beaten

salt and freshly ground black pepper

4 thin pork escalopes/cutlets, about 100 g/3¹/₂ oz each

1 tbsp olive oil

25 g/1 oz/2 tbsp butter

2 tbsp flour

150 ml/¹/₄ pint/²/₃ cup milk

150 ml/¹/₄ pint/²/₃ cup chicken stock

1 tbsp Dijon mustard

225 g/8 oz fresh tagliatelle

sage leaves, to garnish

Preheat the oven to 180°C/350°F/Gas Mark 4, 10 minutes before cooking. Mix the broccoli with the mozzarella, garlic and beaten eggs. Season to taste and reserve. With a meat mallet or rolling pin, pound the escalopes/cutlets on a sheet of greaseproof/wax paper until 5 mm/¹/₄ inch thick. Divide the broccoli mixture between the escalopes and roll each one up from the shortest side. Place the pork rolls in a lightly oiled, ovenproof dish, drizzle over the olive oil and bake for 40–50 minutes until cooked.

Meanwhile, melt the butter in a heavy-based pan, stir in the flour and cook for 2 minutes. Remove from the heat and whisk in the milk and stock. Season to taste, stir in the mustard, then cook until smooth and thickened. Keep warm.

Bring a large pan of lightly salted water to a rolling boil. Add the tagliatelle and cook according to the packet instructions, or for about 3–4 minutes until *al dente*. Drain thoroughly and tip into a warmed serving dish. Slice each pork roll into three, place on top of the pasta and pour the sauce over the top. Garnish with sage leaves and serve immediately.

Health Rating: 3 points

Spicy Chicken with Open Ravioli & Tomato Sauce

Serves 2–3

Ingredients

2 tbsp olive oil

1 onion, peeled and finely chopped

1 tsp ground cumin

1 tsp hot paprika

1 tsp ground cinnamon

175 g/6 oz skinless chicken breast fillets/halves, chopped

salt and freshly ground black pepper

1 tbsp smooth peanut butter

50 g/2 oz/4 tbsp butter

1 shallot, peeled and finely chopped

2 garlic cloves, peeled and crushed

400 g/14 oz/2 cups canned chopped tomatoes

125 g/4 oz fresh egg lasagne sheets

2 tbsp freshly chopped coriander/cilantro

Heat the olive oil in a frying pan, add the onion and cook gently for 2–3 minutes, then add the cumin, paprika and cinnamon and cook for a further 1 minute. Add the chicken, season to taste with salt and pepper and cook for 3–4 minutes until tender. Add the peanut butter and stir until well mixed and reserve.

Melt the butter in the frying pan, add the shallot and cook for 2 minutes. Add the tomatoes and garlic. Season to taste. Simmer gently for 20 minutes, or until thickened. Keep the sauce warm.

Cut each lasagne sheet into six squares. Bring a large pan of lightly salted water to a rolling boil. Add the lasagne squares and cook according to the packet instructions, about 3–4 minutes, or until *al dente*. Drain the lasagne pieces thoroughly, reserve and keep warm.

Layer the pasta squares with the spicy filling on individual warmed plates. Pour over a little of the hot tomato sauce and sprinkle with chopped coriander/cilantro. Serve immediately.

Health Rating: 3 points

Farfalle & Chicken in White Wine Sauce

Serves 4

Ingredients

4 skinless and boneless chicken breasts, about 450 g/1 lb in
    total weight
salt and freshly ground black pepper
125 g/4 oz feta cheese
1 small/medium egg, beaten
2 tbsp freshly chopped tarragon
50 g/2 oz/4 tbsp butter
1 tbsp olive oil
1 onion, peeled and sliced into rings
150 ml/¹⁄₄ pint/²⁄₃ cup white wine
150 ml/¹⁄₄ pint/²⁄₃ cup chicken stock
350 g/12 oz fresh farfalle
3–4 tbsp sour cream
2 tbsp freshly chopped parsley

Place the chicken breasts between two sheets of greaseproof/
wax paper and, using a meat mallet or wooden rolling pin, pound
as thinly as possible. Season with salt and pepper and reserve.

Mash the feta cheese with a fork and blend with the egg and half
the tarragon. Divide the mixture between the chicken breasts and
roll up each one. Secure with cocktail sticks/toothpicks.

Heat half the butter and all the olive oil in a frying pan, add the
onion and cook for 2–3 minutes. Remove using a slotted spoon
and reserve. Add the chicken parcels to the pan and cook for
3–4 minutes until browned.

Pour in the wine and the stock and stir in the remaining
tarragon. Cover and simmer gently for 10–15 minutes until the
chicken is cooked.

Meanwhile, bring a large pan of lightly salted water to a rolling
boil. Add the farfalle and cook according to the packet
instructions, about 3–4 minutes, or until *al dente*. Drain, toss in
the remaining butter and tip into a warmed serving dish.

Slice each chicken roll into four pieces and place on the pasta.
Whisk the sauce until smooth, then stir in the sour cream and
the reserved onion. Heat the sauce gently, then pour over the
chicken. Sprinkle with the parsley and serve immediately.

Health Rating: 2 points

Gnocchi Roulade with Mozzarella & Spinach

Serves 8

Ingredients

600 ml/1 pint/2½ cups milk

125 g/4 oz/⅔ cup fine semolina or polenta

25 g/1 oz/2 tbsp butter

75 g/3 oz/¾ cup grated Cheddar cheese

2 medium/large egg yolks

salt and freshly ground black pepper

700 g/1½ lb baby spinach leaves

½ tsp freshly grated nutmeg

150 g/5 oz/1¼ cups grated mozzarella cheese

2 tbsp freshly grated Parmesan cheese

freshly made tomato sauce, to serve

Preheat the oven to 240°C/475°F/Gas Mark 9, 15 minutes before cooking. Oil and line a large Swiss roll tin/jelly-roll pan (23 x 33 cm/9 inches x 13 inches) with nonstick baking parchment.

Pour the milk into a heavy-based pan and whisk in the semolina or polenta. Bring to the boil then simmer, stirring constantly with a wooden spoon, for 3–4 minutes until very thick. Remove from heat and stir in the butter and Cheddar cheese until melted. Whisk in the egg yolks and season to taste with salt and pepper. Pour into the lined tin. Cover and allow to cool for 1 hour.

Cook the baby spinach in batches in a large pan with 1 teaspoon water for 3–4 minutes until wilted. Drain thoroughly, season to taste with salt, pepper and nutmeg, then allow to cool.

Spread the spinach over the cooled semolina mixture and sprinkle over 75 g/3 oz of the mozzarella and half the Parmesan cheese. Bake in the preheated oven for 20 minutes, or until golden.

Allow to cool, then roll up like a Swiss roll. Sprinkle with the remaining mozzarella and Parmesan cheese, then bake for another 15–20 minutes until golden. Serve immediately with freshly made tomato sauce.

Health Rating: 3 points

Penne with Mixed Peppers & Garlic

Serves 4

Ingredients

450 g/1 lb green, red and yellow peppers
2 tbsp olive oil
1 large onion, peeled and sliced
1 celery stalk, trimmed and finely chopped
2 garlic cloves, peeled and crushed
4 rashers/slices smoked streaky/fatty bacon, finely chopped
300 ml/½ pint/1¼ cups chicken stock
salt and freshly ground black pepper
350 g/12 oz/3 cups fresh penne
2 tbsp freshly chopped parsley
2 tbsp finely grated pecorino cheese

To serve:
green salad
warm granary bread

Preheat the grill/broiler and line the rack with kitchen foil. Cut the peppers in half, deseed and place cut-side down on the rack. Cook under the grill until the skins become blistered and black all over. Place the peppers in a plastic bag and allow to cool, then discard the skin and slice thinly.

Heat the oil in a heavy-based pan. Add the onion, celery, garlic and bacon and cook for 4–5 minutes until the onion has softened. Add the peppers and cook for 1 minute. Pour in the stock and season to taste with salt and pepper. Cover and simmer for 20 minutes.

Meanwhile, bring a large pan of lightly salted water to a rolling boil. Add the penne and cook according to the packet instructions, about 3–4 minutes, or until *al dente*. Drain thoroughly and return to the pan. Pour the pepper sauce over the pasta and toss lightly. Tip into a warmed serving dish and sprinkle with the chopped parsley and grated pecorino cheese. Serve immediately with a green salad and warm granary bread.

Health Rating: 3 points

Spaghetti with Smoked Salmon & Prawns

Serves 4

Ingredients

225 g/8 oz baby spinach leaves
salt and freshly ground black pepper
pinch freshly grated nutmeg
225 g/8 oz cooked tiger prawns/jumbo shrimp in their shells
450 g/1 lb fresh angel hair spaghetti
50 g/2 oz/4 tbsp butter
3 small/medium eggs
1 tbsp freshly chopped dill, plus extra to garnish
125 g/4 oz smoked salmon, cut into strips
dill sprigs, to garnish
2 tbsp grated Parmesan cheese, to serve

Cook the baby spinach leaves in a large pan with 1 teaspoon water for 3–4 minutes until wilted. Drain thoroughly, season to taste with salt, pepper and nutmeg. Keep warm. Remove the shells from all but 4 of the tiger prawns/shrimp and reserve.

Bring a large pan of lightly salted water to a rolling boil. Add the pasta and cook according to the packet instructions, about 3–4 minutes, or until *al dente*. Drain thoroughly. Return to the pan. Stir in the butter and the peeled prawns, cover and keep warm.

Beat the eggs with the dill, season well, then stir into the spaghetti and prawns. Return the pan to the heat briefly, just long enough to lightly scramble the eggs, then remove from the heat. Carefully mix in the smoked salmon strips and the cooked spinach. Toss gently to mix. Tip into a warmed serving dish and garnish with the reserved prawns and the dill sprigs. Serve immediately with grated Parmesan.

Health Rating: 3 points

Salmon & Mushroom Linguine

Serves 4

Ingredients

450 g/1 lb salmon fillets, skinned
salt and freshly ground black pepper
75 g/3 oz/6 tbsp butter
3 tbsp flour
300 ml/¹/₂ pint/1¹/₄ cups chicken stock
150 ml/¹/₄ pint/²/₃ cup whipping cream
225 g/8 oz/2¹/₂ cups wiped and sliced mushrooms
350 g/12 oz linguine
50 g/2 oz/¹/₂ cup grated Cheddar cheese
50 g/2 oz/1 cup fresh white breadcrumbs
2 tbsp freshly chopped parsley, to garnish

Preheat the oven to 190°C/375°F/Gas Mark 5, 10 minutes before cooking. Place the salmon in a shallow pan and cover with water. Season well with salt and pepper and bring to the boil, then lower the heat and simmer for 6–8 minutes until cooked. Drain and keep warm.

Melt 50 g/2 oz/4 tbsp of the butter in a heavy-based pan, stir in the flour, cook for 1 minute, then whisk in the chicken stock. Simmer gently until thickened. Stir in the cream and season to taste. Keep the sauce warm. Melt the remaining butter in a pan, add the sliced mushrooms and cook for 2–3 minutes. Stir the mushrooms into the white sauce.

Bring a large pan of lightly salted water to a rolling boil. Add the linguine and cook according to the packet instructions, or until *al dente*.

Drain the pasta thoroughly and return to the pan. Stir in half the sauce, then spoon into a lightly oiled, 1.4 litre/2¹/₂ pint/1¹/₂ quart, shallow, ovenproof dish. Flake the salmon, add to the remaining sauce, then pour over the pasta. Sprinkle with the cheese and breadcrumbs, then bake in the preheated for 15–20 minutes until golden. Garnish with the parsley and serve immediately.

Health Rating: 3 points

Pasta Ring with Chicken & Sun-dried Tomatoes

Serves 6

Ingredients

125 g/4 oz/¹/₂ cup (1 stick) butter, plus extra for brushing

2 tbsp natural white breadcrumbs

40 g/1¹/₂ oz/3 tbsp flour

450 ml/³/₄ pint/1³/₄ cups milk

1 small onion, peeled and very finely chopped

salt and freshly ground black pepper

225 g/8 oz fresh tagliatelle

450 g/1 lb chicken breast fillets, skinned and cut
   into strips

200 ml/7 fl oz/³/₄ cup white wine

1 tsp cornflour/cornstarch

2 tbsp freshly chopped tarragon

2 tbsp chopped sun-dried tomatoes

Preheat the oven to 190°C/375°F/Gas Mark 5, 10 minutes before cooking. Lightly brush a 20.5 cm/8 inch ring mould with a little melted butter and dust with the breadcrumbs.

Melt 50 g/2 oz of the butter in a heavy-based pan. Add the flour and cook for 1 minute. Whisk in the milk and cook, stirring, until thickened. Add the chopped onion, season to taste with salt and pepper and reserve.

Bring a large pan of lightly salted water to a rolling boil. Add the tagliatelle and cook according to the packet instructions, about 3–4 minutes until *al dente*. Drain thoroughly and stir into the white sauce. Pour the pasta mixture into the prepared mould and bake in the preheated oven for 25–30 minutes.

Melt the remaining butter in a frying pan, add the chicken and cook for 4–5 minutes until cooked. Pour in the wine and cook over a high heat for 30 seconds.

Blend the cornflour/cornstarch with 1 teaspoon water and stir into the pan. Add 1 tablespoon of the chopped tarragon and the tomatoes. Season well, then cook for a few minutes until thickened.

Allow the pasta to cool for 5 minutes, then unmould onto a large serving plate. Fill the centre with the chicken sauce. Garnish with the remaining tarragon and serve immediately.

Health Rating: 3 points

Spaghetti with Hot Chilli Mussels

Serves 4

Ingredients

900 g/2 lb fresh live mussels
300 ml/¹/₂ pint/1¹/₄ cups white wine
3–4 garlic cloves, peeled and crushed
2 tbsp olive oil
1–2 bird's-eye chillies/Thai chiles, deseeded and chopped
800 g/28 oz/4 cups canned chopped tomatoes
salt and freshly ground black pepper
350 g/12 oz fresh spaghetti
2 tbsp freshly chopped parsley, to garnish
warm crusty bread, to serve

Health Rating: 3 points

Scrub the mussels and remove any beards. Discard any that do not close when tapped. Place in a large pan with the white wine and half the crushed garlic. Cover and cook over a high heat for 5–6 minutes, shaking the pan from time to time. When the mussels have opened, drain, reserving the juices and straining them through a muslin-lined sieve. Discard any mussels that have not opened and keep the rest warm.

Heat the oil in a heavy-based pan, add the remaining garlic with the chillies and cook for 30 seconds. Stir in the chopped tomatoes and 75 ml/3 fl oz/¹/₃ cup of the reserved cooking liquor and simmer for 15–20 minutes. Season to taste with salt and pepper.

Meanwhile, bring a large pan of lightly salted water to a rolling boil. Add the spaghetti and cook according to the packet instructions, about 3–4 minutes until *al dente*.

Drain the spaghetti thoroughly and return to the pan. Add the mussels and tomato sauce to the pasta, toss lightly to cover, then tip into a warmed serving dish or spoon onto individual plates. Garnish with chopped parsley and serve immediately with warm crusty bread.

Conchiglioni with Crab au Gratin

Serves 4

Ingredients

175 g/6 oz large pasta shells
50 g/2 oz/4 tbsp butter
1 shallot, peeled and finely chopped
1 bird's-eye chilli/Thai chile, deseeded and finely chopped
400 g/14 oz/3 cups drained canned crab meat
3 tbsp plain/all-purpose flour
50 ml/2 fl oz/¼ cup white wine
50 ml/2 fl oz/¼ cup milk
3 tbsp crème fraîche
15 g/½ oz/1½ tbsp grated Cheddar cheese
salt and freshly ground black pepper
50 g/2 oz/1 cup fresh white breadcrumbs
1 tbsp oil or melted butter

To serve:
cheese or tomato sauce
tossed green salad or freshly cooked baby vegetables

Preheat the oven to 200°C/400°F/Gas Mark 6, 15 minutes before cooking. Bring a large pan of lightly salted water to a rolling boil. Add the pasta shells and cook according to the packet instructions, or until *al dente*. Drain thoroughly and allow to dry completely.

Melt half the butter in a heavy-based pan, add the shallot and bird's eye chilli/Thai chile and cook for 2 minutes, then stir in the crab meat. Stuff the cooled shells with the crab mixture and reserve.

Melt the remaining butter in a small pan and stir in the flour. Cook for 1 minute, then whisk in the wine and milk and cook, stirring, until thickened. Stir in the crème fraîche and grated cheese and season the sauce to taste with salt and pepper.

Place the crab-filled shells in a lightly oiled, large, shallow baking dish or tray and spoon a little of the sauce over. Toss the

breadcrumbs in the oil or melted butter, then sprinkle over the pasta shells. Bake in the preheated oven for 10 minutes. Serve immediately with a cheese or tomato sauce and a tossed green salad or cooked baby vegetables.

Health Rating: 3 points

Pappardelle with Spicy Lamb & Peppers

Serves 4

Ingredients

450 g/1 lb fresh minced/ground lamb

2 tbsp olive oil

1 onion, peeled and finely chopped

2 garlic cloves, peeled and crushed

1 green pepper, deseeded and chopped

1 yellow pepper, deseeded and chopped

½ tsp hot chilli powder

1 tsp ground cumin

1 tbsp tomato paste

150 ml/¼ pint/ ⅔ cup red wine

salt and freshly ground black pepper

350 g/12 oz pappardelle

50 g/2 oz fresh white breadcrumbs

25 g/1 oz/2 tbsp butter, melted

25 g/1 oz/¼ cup grated Cheddar cheese

1 tbsp freshly chopped parsley

Preheat the grill/broiler just before cooking. Dry–fry the minced/ground lamb in a frying pan until browned. Heat the olive oil in a heavy–based pan, add the onion, garlic and all the chopped peppers and cook gently for 3–4 minutes until softened. Add the browned lamb to the pan and cook, stirring, until the onion has softened, then drain off any remaining oil.

Stir the chilli powder and cumin into the pan and cook gently for 2 minutes, stirring frequently. Add the tomato paste, pour in the wine and season to taste with salt and pepper. Reduce the heat and simmer for 10–15 minutes until the sauce has reduced.

Meanwhile, bring a large pan of lightly salted water to a rolling boil. Add the pappardelle and cook according to the packet instructions, or until *al dente*. Drain thoroughly, then return to the pan and stir the meat sauce into the pasta. Keep warm.

Meanwhile, place the breadcrumbs on a baking tray, drizzle over the melted butter and place under the preheated grill for 3–4 minutes until golden and crispy. Allow to cool, then mix with the grated Cheddar cheese. Tip the pasta mixture into a warmed serving dish, sprinkle with the breadcrumbs and the parsley. Serve immediately.

Health Rating: 2 points

Farfalle with Courgettes & Mushrooms

Serves 4

Ingredients

25 g/1 oz/2 tbsp butter

2 tsp olive oil

1 small onion, peeled and finely chopped

2 garlic cloves, peeled and crushed

125 g/4 oz/½ cup bacon lardons

450 g/1 lb/2½ cups trimmed and diced courgettes/zucchinis

125 g/4 oz/2 cups wiped and roughly chopped
    button/white mushrooms

350 g/21 oz/3 cups farfalle

salt and freshly ground black pepper

250 ml carton/1 cup crème fraîche

2 tbsp freshly chopped parsley

shaved pecorino cheese, to garnish

mixed salad and crusty bread, to serve

Heat the butter and olive oil in a large pan, add the onion, garlic and bacon lardons and cook for 3–4 minutes until the onion has softened. Add the courgettes/zucchini and cook, stirring, for 3–4 minutes. Add the mushrooms, lower the heat and cook covered, for 4–5 minutes.

Meanwhile, bring a large pan of lightly salted water to a rolling boil. Add the farfalle and cook according to the packet instructions, or until *al dente*. Drain thoroughly, return to the pan and keep warm.

Season the mushroom mixture to taste with salt and pepper, then stir in the crème fraîche and half the chopped parsley. Simmer for 2–3 minutes until the sauce is thick and creamy.

Pour the sauce over the cooked pasta, toss lightly, then reheat for 2 minutes, or until piping hot. Tip into a warmed serving dish and sprinkle over the remaining chopped parsley. Garnish with pecorino cheese shavings and serve immediately with a mixed salad and crusty bread.

Health Rating: 2 points

Cannelloni with Tomato & Red Wine Sauce

Serves 6

Ingredients

2 tbsp olive oil

1 onion, peeled and finely chopped

1 garlic clove, peeled and crushed

250 g/9 oz carton ricotta cheese

50 g/2 oz/scant ⅓ cup pine nuts

salt and freshly ground black pepper

pinch freshly grated nutmeg

250 g/9 oz fresh spinach lasagne sheets

25 g/1 oz/2 tbsp butter

1 shallot, peeled and finely chopped

150 ml/¼ pint/⅔ cup red wine

800 g/28 oz/4 cups canned chopped tomatoes

½ tsp sugar

50 g/2 oz/½ cup grated mozzarella cheese, plus extra to serve

1 tbsp freshly chopped parsley, to garnish

fresh green salad, to serve

Preheat the oven to 200˚C/400˚F/Gas Mark 6, 15 minutes before cooking. Heat the oil in a heavy-based pan, add the onion and garlic and cook for 2–3 minutes.

Cool slightly, then stir in the ricotta cheese and pine nuts. Season the filling to taste with salt, pepper and nutmeg.

Cut each lasagne sheet in half, put a little of the ricotta filling on each piece and roll up like a cigar to resemble cannelloni tubes.

Arrange the cannelloni seam-side down in a single layer in a lightly oiled, 2.3 litre/4 pint/2⅓ quart, shallow, ovenproof dish.

Melt the butter in a pan, add the shallot and cook for 2 minutes. Pour in the red wine, tomatoes and sugar and season well. Bring to the boil, lower the heat and simmer for about 20 minutes until thickened. Add a little more sugar if desired. Transfer to a food processor and blend until a smooth sauce is formed.

Pour the warm tomato sauce over the cannelloni and sprinkle with the grated mozzarella cheese. Bake in the preheated oven for about 30 minutes until golden and bubbling. Garnish and serve immediately with a green salad.

Health Rating: 2 points

Pasta Triangles with Pesto & Walnut Dressing

Serves 6

Ingredients

450 g/1 lb fresh egg lasagne sheets

4 tbsp pesto

4 tbsp ricotta cheese

125 g/4 oz/1 cup walnuts

1 slice white bread, crusts removed

150 ml/¼ pint/⅔ cup sour cream

75 g/3 oz/⅓ cup mascarpone cheese

25 g/1 oz/¼ cup grated pecorino cheese

salt and freshly ground black pepper

1 tbsp olive oil

dill sprig or freshly chopped basil or parsley, to garnish

tomato and cucumber salad, to serve

Preheat the grill/broiler to high. Cut the lasagne sheets in half, then into triangles and reserve.

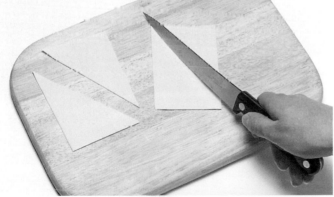

Mix the pesto and ricotta together and warm gently in a pan. Toast the walnuts under the grill until golden. Rub off the papery skins, then place the nuts in a food processor with the bread and grind finely.

Mix the sour cream with the mascarpone in a bowl. Add the ground walnuts and grated pecorino and season to taste. Whisk in the olive oil, then pour into a pan and warm gently.

Bring a large pan of lightly salted water to a rolling boil. Add the pasta triangles and cook according to the packet instructions, or for about 3–4 minutes until al dente

Drain the pasta thoroughly and arrange a few triangles on each serving plate. Top each one with a spoonful of the pesto mixture, then place another triangle on top. Continue to layer the pasta and pesto mixture, then spoon a little of the walnut sauce on top of each stack. Garnish with dill, basil or parsley, and serve immediately with a freshly dressed tomato and cucumber salad.

Health Rating: 2 points

Aubergine & Tomato Layer

Serves 4

Ingredients

2 aubergines/eggplants, about 700 g/1½ lb, trimmed and
   thinly sliced

6 tbsp olive oil

1 onion, peeled and finely sliced

1 garlic clove, peeled and crushed

400 g/14 oz/2 cups canned chopped tomatoes

50 ml/2 fl oz/¼ cup red wine

½ tsp sugar

salt and freshly ground black pepper

50 g/2 oz/4 tbsp butter

3 tbsp plain/all-purpose flour

450 ml/¾ pint/1¾ cups milk

225 g/8 oz fresh egg lasagne sheets

125 g/4 oz/1¼ cups grated mozzarella cheese

2 small/medium eggs, beaten

200 ml/7 fl oz/¾ cup Greek yogurt

fresh basil leaves, to garnish

Preheat the oven to 190°C/375°F/Gas Mark 5, 10 minutes before cooking. Brush the aubergine/eggplant slices with 5 tablespoons of the olive oil and place on a baking sheet. Bake in the preheated oven for 20 minutes, or until tender. Remove from the oven and increase the temperature to 200°C/400°F/Gas Mark 6.

Heat the remaining oil in a heavy-based pan. Add the onion and garlic, cook for 2–3 minutes, then add the tomatoes, wine and sugar. Season to taste with salt and pepper, then simmer for 20 minutes.

Melt the butter in another pan. Stir in the flour, cook for 2 minutes, then whisk in the milk. Cook for 2–3 minutes until thickened. Season to taste.

Pour a little white sauce into a lightly oiled, 1.7 litre/3 pint/1¾ quart baking dish. Cover with a layer of lasagne, spread with tomato sauce, then add some of the aubergines/eggplants.

Cover thinly with white sauce and sprinkle with a little cheese. Continue to layer in this way, finishing with a layer of lasagne.

Beat together the eggs and yogurt. Season, then pour over the lasagne. Sprinkle with the remaining cheese and bake in the preheated oven for 25–30 minutes until golden. Garnish with basil leaves and serve.

Health Rating: 2 points

Cannelloni with Gorgonzola Sauce

Serves 2–3

Ingredients

50 g/2 oz/4 tbsp salted butter

1 shallot, peeled and finely chopped

2 rashers/slices rindless streaky/fatty bacon, chopped

225 g/8 oz/4 cups wiped and finely chopped mushrooms

2 tbsp plain/all-purpose flour

125 ml/4 fl oz/$\frac{1}{2}$ cup double/heavy cream

6 sheets fresh egg lasagne

40 g/1$\frac{1}{2}$ oz/3 tbsp unsalted butter

150 g/5 oz/1$\frac{1}{4}$ cups diced Gorgonzola cheese

150 ml/$\frac{1}{4}$ pint/$\frac{2}{3}$ cup whipping cream

assorted salad leaves, to serve

Health Rating: 1 point

Preheat the oven to 190°C/375°F/Gas Mark 5, 10 minutes before cooking. Melt the salted butter in a heavy-based pan, add the shallot and bacon and cook for about 4–5 minutes. Add the mushrooms to the pan and cook for 5–6 minutes until the mushrooms are very soft. Stir in the flour, cook for 1 minute, then stir in the double/heavy cream and cook gently for 2 minutes. Allow to cool.

Cut each lasagne sheet in half. Spoon some filling on to each piece and roll up from the longest side to resemble cannelloni. Arrange the cannelloni in a lightly oiled, shallow, 1.4 litre/2$\frac{1}{2}$ pint/1$\frac{1}{2}$ quart, ovenproof dish.

Heat the unsalted butter very slowly in a pan and, when melted, add the Gorgonzola cheese. Stir until the cheese has melted, then stir in the whipping cream. Bring to the boil slowly, then simmer gently for about 5 minutes until thickened. Pour the cream sauce over the cannelloni. Place in the preheated oven and bake for 20 minutes, or until golden and thoroughly heated through. Serve immediately with assorted salad leaves.

Lamb & Pasta Pie

Serves 8

Ingredients

400 g/14 oz/2²/₃ cups plain/all-purpose flour

pinch salt

100 g/3¹/₂ oz/¹/₂ cup margarine

100 g/3¹/₂ oz/¹/₂ cup white vegetable fat/shortening

1 small/medium egg, separated

50 g/2 oz/4 tbsp butter

50 g/2 oz/¹/₃ cup flour

450 ml/³/₄ pint/1³/₄ cups milk

salt and freshly ground black pepper

225 g/8 oz/2 cups macaroni

50 g/2 oz/¹/₂ cup grated Cheddar cheese

1 tbsp vegetable oil

1 onion, peeled and chopped

1 garlic clove, peeled and crushed

2 celery stalks, trimmed and chopped

450 g/1 lb minced/ground lamb

1 tbsp tomato paste

400 g/14 oz/2 cups canned chopped tomatoes

Preheat the oven to 190°C/375°F/Gas Mark 5, 10 minutes before cooking. Lightly oil a 20.5 cm/8 inch, spring-form cake tin/pan.

Blend the flour, salt, margarine and white vegetable fat/shortening in a food processor and add sufficient cold water to make a smooth, pliable dough. Knead on a lightly floured surface, then roll out two thirds to line the base and sides of the tin. Brush the pastry with egg white and reserve.

Melt the butter in a heavy-based pan, stir in the 50 g/2 oz/¹/₃ cup flour and cook for 2 minutes. Stir in the milk and cook, stirring, until a smooth, thick sauce is formed. Season to taste with salt and pepper and reserve.

Bring a large pan of lightly salted water to a rolling boil. Add the macaroni and cook according to the packet instructions, or until *al dente*. Drain, then stir into the white sauce with the grated cheese.

Heat the oil in a frying pan, add the onion, garlic, celery and minced/ground lamb and cook, stirring, for 5–6 minutes. Stir in the tomato paste and tomatoes and cook for 10 minutes. Cool slightly.

Place half the pasta mixture, then all the mince in the pastry-lined tin. Top with a layer of pasta.

Roll out the remaining pastry and cut out a lid. Brush the edge with water, place over the filling and pinch the edges together. Use trimmings to decorate the top of the pie.

Brush the pie with beaten egg yolk and bake in the preheated oven for 50–60 minutes, covering the top with foil if browning too quickly. Stand for 15 minutes before turning out. Serve immediately.

Health Rating: 1 point

Baked Macaroni with Mushrooms & Leeks

Serves 4

Ingredients

2 tbsp olive oil

1 onion, peeled and finely chopped

1 garlic clove, peeled and crushed

2 small leeks, trimmed and chopped

450 g/1 lb assorted wild mushrooms, trimmed

75 g/3 oz/6 tbsp butter

50 ml/2 fl oz/¼ cup white wine

150 ml/¼ pint/⅔ cup crème fraîche or whipping cream

salt and freshly ground black pepper

350 g/12 oz/3 cups short-cut macaroni

75 g/3 oz/1½ cups fresh white breadcrumbs

1 tbsp freshly chopped parsley, to garnish

Preheat the oven to 220°C/425°F/Gas Mark 7, 15 minutes before cooking. Heat 1 tablespoon of the olive oil in a large frying pan, add the onion and garlic and cook for 2 minutes. Add the leeks, mushrooms and 25 g/1 oz/2 tbsp of the butter, then cook for 5 minutes. Pour in the white wine, cook for 2 minutes, then stir in the crème fraîche or whipping cream. Season to taste with salt and pepper.

Meanwhile, bring a large pan of lightly salted water to a rolling boil. Add the macaroni and cook according to the packet instructions, or until *al dente*.

Melt 25 g/1 oz/2 tbsp of the butter with the remaining oil in a small frying pan. Add the breadcrumbs, fry until just turning golden brown. Drain on absorbent paper towels.

Drain the pasta thoroughly, toss in the remaining butter, then tip into a lightly oiled, 1.4 litre/2½ pint/1½ quart, shallow baking dish. Cover the pasta with the leek and mushroom mixture, then sprinkle with the fried breadcrumbs. Bake in the preheated oven for 5–10 minutes until golden and crisp. Garnish with chopped parsley and serve.

Health Rating: 3 points

Tomato & Basil Rolls

Makes 10 large rolls

Ingredients

575 g/1¼ lb/4½ cups strong white/bread flour
2 tsp salt
7 g sachet/1¾ tsp fast-action dried yeast
5 tbsp olive oil
2 tbsp tomato purée/paste
100 g/3½ oz/2 cups chopped soft sun-dried tomatoes
25 g/1 oz/1 cup chopped fresh basil
25 g/1 oz/¼ cup finely grated Parmesan cheese
1 tbsp sea salt

Sift the flour and salt into a bowl and stir in the yeast. Add 4 tablespoons of the olive oil, 300 ml/½ pint/1¼ cups lukewarm water and the tomato purée/paste and mix to a soft dough. Knead the dough by hand for 10 minutes, or place in a tabletop mixer fitted with a dough hook and knead for 5 minutes, or until smooth and elastic.

Return to the bowl and cover with oiled plastic wrap. Leave in a warm place for about 1 hour until doubled in size. Turn the dough onto a floured surface and punch it to knock out all the air. Knead in the chopped tomatoes, basil and Parmesan cheese.

Cut the dough into 10 pieces. Roll each piece out into a ball and brush over the tops with the remaining 1 tablespoon olive oil. Make shallow diamond–shaped slashes across the top of each one with a sharp knife.

Cover the rolls with oiled plastic wrap and leave for about 45 minutes until doubled in size. Preheat the oven to 220°C/425°F/Gas Mark 7, 10–15 minutes before baking. Discard the plastic wrap and scatter the sea salt over the rolls. Bake for about 20 minutes until risen and golden and the rolls sound hollow when tapped. Leave to cool on a wire rack.

Health Rating: 3 points

Rosemary & Olive Focaccia

Makes 2 loaves

Ingredients

700 g/1½ lb/5½ cups strong white/bread flour
pinch salt
pinch caster/superfine sugar
7 g/¼ oz sachet easy-blend dried/dry active yeast
2 tsp freshly chopped rosemary
3 tbsp olive oil
75 g/3 oz/½ cup pitted and roughly chopped black/ripe olives
rosemary sprigs, to garnish

To finish:
3 tbsp olive oil
coarse sea salt
freshly ground black pepper

Preheat the oven to 200°C/400°F/Gas Mark 6, 15 minutes before baking. Sift the flour, salt and sugar into a large bowl. Stir in the yeast and rosemary. Make a well in the centre. Pour in 450 ml/¾ pint/1¾ cups warm water and the oil and mix to a soft dough. Turn out onto a lightly floured surface and knead for about 10 minutes until smooth and elastic.

Pat the olives dry on paper towels, then gently knead into the dough. Put in an oiled bowl, cover with plastic wrap and leave to rise in a warm place for 1½ hours, or until it has doubled in size.

Turn out the dough and knead again for a minute or two. Divide in half and roll out each piece to a 25.5 cm/10 inch circle. Transfer to oiled baking sheets, cover with oiled plastic wrap and leave to rise for 30 minutes.

Using the fingertips, make deep dimples all over the dough. Drizzle with the oil and sprinkle with sea salt. Bake in the oven for 20–25 minutes until risen and golden. Cool on a wire rack and garnish with sprigs of rosemary. Grind over a little black pepper before serving.

Health Rating: 2 points

Pesto Muffins

Makes 20–24

Ingredients

50 g/2 oz/4 tbsp butter
225 g/8 oz/2 cups self-raising flour
1 tsp baking powder
pinch salt
75 g/3 oz/³/₄ cup grated mozzarella cheese
2 medium/large eggs
6–7 tbsp milk
1 tbsp green pesto
2 tbsp chopped green olives
3 tbsp sun-dried tomato sauce

Preheat the oven to 180°C/350°F/Gas Mark 4. Lightly oil a mini-muffin tray or line with 20–24 mini cases, depending on the depth of the holes.

Melt the butter over a low heat and leave aside to cool. Sift the flour, baking powder and salt into a bowl and stir in half the mozzarella cheese. In another bowl, beat the eggs with the milk and pesto.

Pour the egg mixture into the flour, then fold in with the cooled butter and chopped olives. Spoon into the muffin cases, then top each one with ¹/₂ tsp sun-dried tomato sauce and the remaining grated cheese.

Bake for 15–25 minutes until well risen and golden. Turn out onto a wire rack to cool slightly. Serve warm with soup or salad. Best eaten fresh on the day of baking.

Health Rating: 3 points

Italian Biscotti

Makes 26–28

Ingredients

150 g/5 oz/²/₃ cup (1¼ sticks) butter

200 g/7 oz/1 cup caster/superfine sugar

¼ tsp vanilla extract

1 small/medium egg, beaten

¼ tsp ground cinnamon

grated zest of 1 lemon

2¹/₃ tbsp ground almonds

150 g/5 oz/1 heaping cup plain/all-purpose flour

150 g/5 oz dark/bittersweet chocolate

Health Rating: 2 points

Preheat the oven to 190°C/375°F/Gas Mark 5, 10 minutes before baking. Lightly oil three or four baking sheets and reserve. Cream the butter and sugar together in a bowl and mix in the vanilla extract. When it is light and fluffy, beat in the egg with the cinnamon, lemon zest and the ground almonds. Stir in the flour to make a firm dough.

Knead lightly until smooth and free from cracks. Shape the dough into rectangular blocks about 4 cm/1½ inches in diameter, wrap in greaseproof/wax paper and chill in the refrigerator for at least 2 hours.

Cut the chilled dough into 5 mm/¼ inch slices, place on the baking sheets and cook in the preheated oven for 12–15 minutes until firm. Remove from the oven, cool slightly, then transfer to wire racks to cool.

When completely cold, melt the chocolate in a heatproof bowl set over a saucepan of simmering water. Alternatively, melt the chocolate in the microwave according to the manufacturer's instructions. Spoon into a decorating bag and pipe over the biscuits. Leave to dry on a sheet of nonstick baking parchment before serving.

Traditional Easter Cake

Serves 10–12

Ingredients

225 g/8 oz prepared shortcrust pastry/pie dough

300 g/10 oz/scant 2¼ cups plain/all-purpose flour, plus extra
 for dusting

1 tbsp caster/superfine sugar

2 tsp almond extract

finely grated zest of 1 lemon

300 ml/½ pint/1¼ cups milk

25 g/1 oz/2 tbsp butter

200 g/7 oz/scant 1 cup ricotta cheese

200 g/7 oz/1 cup caster sugar

4 small/medium eggs, separated

1 tsp vanilla extract or brandy (optional)

1 tbsp finely grated orange zest

For the topping:

finely grated zest of 1 small orange

50 g/2 oz/scant ½ cup icing/confectioners' sugar

Preheat the oven to 180°C/350°F/Gas Mark 4, 10 minutes before
baking. Reserve a quarter of the pastry/pie dough for the topping.
Roll out the remaining pastry on a lightly floured surface and use
to line a lightly oiled, 25 cm/10 inch cake or springform tin/pan.
Lightly prick the pastry with a fork and reserve.

Place the flour into a saucepan with the sugar, almond extract and
lemon zest. Gradually stir in the milk; add the butter. Place over a
low heat and cook, stirring until the mixture is creamy and the milk
has been absorbed. Remove; let cool. Blend the ricotta and sugar
together, then add the egg yolks with the vanilla extract or brandy,
if using, the orange and the cooled flour mixture. Whisk the egg
whites until stiff, then fold into the mixture. Pour into the cake tin.

Roll the reserved pastry out and cut into thin strips. Lightly
brush the edges with water and place the strips on top to form
a lattice effect. Bake in the preheated oven for 50 minutes, or
until the filling is set. Mix the topping ingredients together and
sprinkle over the top. Serve.

Health Rating: 1 point

Chocolate Florentines

Makes 20

Ingredients

125 g/4 oz/½ cup (1 stick) butter or margarine

125 g/4 oz/½ cup packed soft light brown sugar

1 tbsp double/heavy cream

50 g/2 oz/1⅓ cup roughly chopped blanched almonds

50 g/2 oz/½ cup hazelnuts, roughly chopped

75 g/3 oz sultanas/golden raisins

50 g/2 oz/⅓ cup roughly chopped glacé/candied cherries

40 g/1½ oz/⅓ cup plain/all-purpose flour

50 g/2 oz dark/semisweet dark chocolate, roughly chopped

50 g/2 oz milk chocolate, roughly chopped or broken

50 g/2 oz white chocolate, roughly chopped

Preheat the oven to 180°C/350°F/Gas Mark 4, 10 minutes
before baking. Lightly oil a baking sheet.

Melt the butter or margarine with the sugar and double/heavy
cream in a small saucepan over a very low heat. Do not boil.
Remove from the heat and stir in the almonds, hazelnuts,
sultanas/golden raisins and cherries, then stir in the flour.

Drop teaspoonfuls of the mixture onto the baking sheet. Transfer
to the oven and bake for 10 minutes until golden. Leave the
biscuits to cool on the baking sheet for about 5 minutes, then
carefully transfer to a wire rack to cool.

Melt the dark, milk and white chocolates in separate bowls,
either in the microwave following the manufacturer's
instructions, or in a small bowl placed over a saucepan of gently
simmering water.

Spread one third of the biscuits with the dark chocolate, one
third with the milk chocolate and one third with the white
chocolate. When almost set, mark out wavy lines on the
chocolate with the tines of a fork, or dip some of the biscuits in
chocolate to half coat and serve.

Health Rating: 2 points

Amaretti Chocolate Cake

Serves 6–8

Ingredients

175 g/6 oz dark/semisweet dark chocolate
450 ml/³/₄ pint/1³/₄ cups double/heavy cream
4 tbsp brandy or Cointreau, or use fruit juice
500 g/1 lb 1 oz soft amaretti biscuits/cookies
1–2 tsp unsweetened cocoa powder, for dusting

Break the chocolate into pieces and place in a heavy-based saucepan. Add the cream and place over a gentle heat. Heat, stirring frequently with a wooden spoon, until the chocolate has melted and a smooth mixture is formed.

Remove from the heat and stir in the brandy or Cointreau or fruit juice. Leave until cool, stirring occasionally, then pour into a shallow dish.

Place a small circle of baking parchment in the base of a 900 ml/1¹/₂ pint/3³/₄ cup pudding basin/ovenproof bowl and lightly oil the sides of the bowl.

Dip a few biscuits/cookies into the chocolate mixture and place in the base. Top with a thin layer of the chocolate mixture and continue layering, finishing with a layer of biscuits.

Place either a saucer that fits inside the basin on top of the biscuits or fold some foil to make a sturdy lid. Place some weights on top, then leave overnight in the refrigerator.

The next day, run a knife around the side to loosen, then invert onto a serving plate. Shake to remove the basin. Sprinkle with a little unsweetened cocoa powder and serve. Store in the refrigerator.

Health Rating: 2 points

Strawberry Flan

Serves 6

Ingredients

For the sweet pastry/pie dough:
175 g/6 oz/1¹/₃ cups plain/all-purpose flour
50 g/2 oz/4 tbsp butter
50 g/2 oz/¹/₄ cup white vegetable fat/shortening
2 tsp caster/superfine sugar
1 medium/large egg yolk, beaten

For the filling:
1 medium/large egg, plus 1 extra egg yolk
50 g/2 oz/¹/₄ cup caster/superfine sugar
25 g/1 oz/3 heaping tbsp plain/all-purpose flour
300 ml/¹/₂ pint/1¹/₄ cups milk
few drops vanilla extract
450 g/1 lb/3 heaping cups cleaned and hulled strawberries
mint leaves, to decorate

Preheat the oven to 200°C/400°F/Gas Mark 6, 15 minutes before baking. Place the flour, butter and vegetable fat/shortening in a food processor and blend until the mixture resembles fine breadcrumbs. Stir in the sugar, then, with the machine running, add the egg yolk and enough water to make a fairly stiff dough. Knead lightly, cover and chill for 30 minutes. Roll out the pastry/pie dough and use to line a 23 cm/9 inch, loose-bottomed flan tin/tart pan. Place a piece of greaseproof/wax paper in the pastry case/pie crust and cover with baking beans/pie weights or rice. Bake for 15–20 minutes until just firm. Reserve until cool.

Make the filling by whisking the eggs and sugar together until thick and pale. Gradually stir in the flour and then the milk. Pour into a small saucepan and simmer for 3–4 minutes, stirring throughout. Add the vanilla extract to taste, then pour into a bowl and leave to cool. Cover with greaseproof paper to prevent a skin from forming.

When the filling is cold, whisk until smooth, then pour onto the cooked flan case. Slice the strawberries and arrange on top of the filling. Allow to set. Decorate with the mint leaves and serve.

Health Rating: 2 points

Chocolate Fruit Tiramisu

Serves 4

Ingredients

2 ripe passion fruit

2 fresh nectarines or peaches

75 g/3 oz sponge fingers/ladyfingers

125 g/4 oz amaretti biscuits

5 tbsp amaretto liqueur

6 tbsp prepared black coffee

250 g/9 oz/1 heaping cup mascarpone cheese

450 ml/³/₄ pint/1³/₄ cups fresh custard

200 g/7 oz dark/semisweet dark chocolate, finely chopped
   or grated

2 tbsp sifted unsweetened cocoa powder

Cut the passion fruit and scoop out the seeds and reserve. Plunge the nectarines or peaches into boiling water and leave for 2–3 minutes. Carefully remove the nectarines from the water, cut in half and remove the stones. Peel off the skin, chop the flesh finely and reserve.

Break the sponge finger biscuits and amaretti biscuits in half. Place the amaretto liqueur and prepared black coffee into a shallow dish and stir well. Place half the sponge fingers and amaretti biscuits into the amaretto and coffee mixture and soak for 30 seconds.

Lift out both biscuits from the liqueur mixture and arrange in the bases of four deep individual glass dishes.

Cream the mascarpone cheese until soft and creamy, then slowly beat in the fresh custard and mix well together. Spoon half the mascarpone mixture over the biscuits in the dishes and sprinkle with 125 g/4 oz of the finely chopped or grated dark chocolate.

Arrange half the passion fruit seeds and the chopped nectarines or peaches over the chocolate and sprinkle with half the sifted unsweetened cocoa powder.

Place the remaining biscuits in the remaining coffee liqueur mixture and soak for 30 seconds, then arrange on top of the

fruit and cocoa powder. Top with the remaining chocolate, nectarine or peach and the mascarpone cheese mixture, piling the mascarpone high in the dishes.

Chill in the refrigerator for 1¹/₂ hours, then spoon the remaining passion fruit seeds and cocoa powder over the desserts. Chill in the refrigerator for 30 minutes and serve.

Health Rating: 2 points

Almond Angel Cake with Amaretto Cream

Cuts into 10–12 slices

Ingredients

175 g/6 oz/1¾ cups, plus 2–3 tbsp icing/confectioners' sugar

150 g/5 oz/1 heaping cup plain/all-purpose flour

350 ml/12 fl oz egg whites (about 10 large/extra-large egg whites)

1½ tsp cream of tartar

½ tsp vanilla extract

1 tsp almond extract

¼ tsp salt

200 g/7 oz/1 cup caster/superfine sugar

175 ml/6 fl oz/scant ¾ cup double/heavy cream

2 tbsp amaretto liqueur

fresh raspberries, to decorate

Preheat the oven to 180°C/350°F/Gas Mark 4, 10 minutes before baking. Sift together the 175 g/6 oz icing/confectioners' sugar and flour. Stir to blend, then sift again and reserve.

Using an electric whisk, beat the egg whites, cream of tartar, vanilla extract, ½ teaspoon of the almond extract and salt on medium speed until soft peaks form. Gradually add the caster/superfine sugar, 2 tablespoons at a time, beating well after each addition, until stiff peaks form.

Sift about one third of the flour mixture over the egg white mixture and, using a metal spoon or rubber spatula, gently fold into the egg white mixture. Repeat, folding the flour mixture into the egg white mixture in two more batches.

Spoon gently into an ungreased angel-food cake tin/pan or 25.5 cm/10 inch tube tin. Bake in the preheated oven until risen and golden on top and the surface springs back quickly when gently pressed with a clean finger. Immediately invert the cake tin and cool completely in the tin.

When cool, carefully run a sharp knife around the edge of the tin and the centre ring to loosen the cake from the edge. Using the fingertips, ease the cake from the tin and invert onto a cake plate. Thickly dust the cake with the extra icing sugar.

Whip the cream with the remaining almond extract, amaretto liqueur and a little more icing sugar until soft peaks form. Fill a decorating bag fitted with a star nozzle/tip with half the cream and pipe around the bottom edge of the cake. Decorate the edge with the fresh raspberries and serve the remaining cream separately.

Health Rating: 2 points

Polenta Biscuits

Makes 15–20

Ingredients

150 g/5 oz/scant 1 cup polenta/cornmeal
50 g/2 oz/generous 1/3 cup plain/all-purpose flour
125 g/4 oz/1/2 cup (1 stick) unsalted butter, softened
125 g/4 oz/scant 2/3 cup caster/superfine sugar
finely grated zest of 1 small orange
1 large/extra-large egg
1 large/extra-large egg yolk
1 tbsp icing/confectioners' sugar, sifted

Preheat the oven to 190°C/375°F/Gas Mark 5, 10 minutes before baking. Lightly oil two baking sheets. Place the polenta/cornmeal and flour into a mixing bowl and add the butter. Rub the butter into the flour and polenta, then stir in the sugar. Add the orange zest and stir lightly together.

Beat the egg with the egg yolk, then add to the bowl and bring the mixture together either with a spoon or your hands to form a soft but slightly sticky dough.

Spoon into a large decorating bag fitted with a large, fluted nozzle/tip and pipe rosettes onto the prepared baking sheets, allowing room for expansion.

Bake in the preheated oven for 12–15 minutes until firm and golden. Remove from the oven, leave to cool slightly, then place on a wire rack. Leave until cold before sprinkling with a little sifted icing/confectioners' sugar and serving. Store in an airtight container.

Health Rating: 2 points

Ricotta Cheesecake with Strawberry Coulis

Serves 6–8

Ingredients

8 digestive biscuits/Graham crackers
100 g/3½ oz/2/3 cup chopped mixed/candied peel
65 g/2½ oz/5 tbsp butter, melted
150 ml/¼ pint/2/3 cup crème fraîche
375 g/13 oz/1 cup ricotta cheese
100 g/3½ oz/½ cup caster/superfine sugar
1 vanilla pod/bean, seeds only
2 large/extra-large eggs
225 g/8 oz/1½ cups hulled strawberries
2–4 tbsp caster/superfine sugar, to taste
zest and juice of 1 orange

Preheat the oven to 170°C/325°F/Gas Mark 3. Line a 20.5 cm/8 inch springform tin/pan with baking parchment. Put the biscuits/crackers in a food processor together with the peel. Blend until the biscuits are crushed and the peel is chopped. Add 50 g/2 oz/4 tbsp of the melted butter and process until mixed. Tip into the tin and spread firmly and evenly over the bottom.

Blend together the crème fraîche, ricotta cheese, sugar, vanilla seeds and eggs in a food processor. With the motor running, add the remaining melted butter and blend for a few seconds. Pour the mixture onto the base. Transfer to the preheated oven and cook for about 1 hour until set and risen round the edges but slightly wobbly in the centre. Switch off the oven and allow to cool there. Chill in the refrigerator for at least 8 hours, or preferably overnight.

Wash and drain the strawberries. Put into the food processor along with 2 tablespoons of the sugar, the orange zest and juice. Blend until smooth. Add any remaining sugar, to taste. Pass through a sieve to remove the seeds and chill in the refrigerator until needed. Cut the cheesecake into wedges, spoon over some of the strawberry coulis and serve.

Health Rating: 2 points

Classic Panna Cotta

Serves 4

Ingredients

11 g packet gelatine or 3 gelatine leaves
250 ml/8 fl oz/1 cup milk
250 ml/8 fl oz/1 cup double/heavy cream
1 vanilla pod/bean, split in half lengthways,
    or few drops vanilla extract
25 g/1 oz/⅛ cup caster/superfine sugar

For the fruit sauce:
300 g/11 oz frozen red fruits such as raspberries or fruits
    of the forest
1–2 tbsp sugar, or to taste
2–3 tbsp orange juice or water

Pour 75 ml/3 fl oz/5 tbsp almost–boiling water into a heatproof bowl, then sprinkle in the powdered gelatine. Stir until dissolved, then leave to cool. If using gelatine leaves, cover the leaves with the water and leave for 20 minutes, or until softened.

Pour the milk and cream into a heavy–based saucepan and add the vanilla pod/bean or add the vanilla extract together with the sugar. Bring to the boil, reduce the heat and simmer for 5–8 minutes until the sugar has dissolved. Remove from the heat and stir in the gelatine liquid in a thin, steady stream, or add the softened leaves and stir until dissolved. Leave to cool.

Discard the vanilla pod and pour the milk mixture into four 150 ml/¼ pint/⅔ cup ramekins or small dishes. Chill in the refrigerator for at least 1 hour until set.

Meanwhile, make the fruit sauce. Place the fruit into a saucepan with the sugar and orange juice or water. Place over a gentle heat and cook for 5 minutes, or until the sugar has dissolved and the fruit is beginning to collapse. Either serve with whole pieces of fruit or blend to form a smooth sauce. If liked, rub through a fine sieve to remove any pips. Serve with the set panna cottas.

Health Rating: 2 points

Vanilla & Lemon Panna Cotta with Raspberry Sauce

Serves 6

Ingredients

900 ml/1½ pints/3½ cups double/heavy cream
1 vanilla pod/bean, split
100 g/3½ oz/½ cup caster/superfine sugar
zest of 1 lemon
3 sheets gelatine
5 tbsp milk
450 g/1 lb/3 cups raspberries
3–4 tbsp icing/confectioners' sugar, to taste
1 tbsp lemon juice
extra lemon zest, to decorate

Put the cream, vanilla pod/bean and sugar into a saucepan. Bring to the boil, then simmer for 10 minutes until slightly reduced, stirring to prevent scalding. Remove from the heat, stir in the lemon zest and remove the vanilla pod.

Soak the gelatine in the milk for 5 minutes, or until softened. Squeeze out any excess milk and add to the hot cream. Stir well until dissolved.

Pour the cream mixture into six ramekins or mini pudding moulds and leave in the refrigerator for 4 hours, or until set.

Meanwhile, put 175 g/6 oz/1½ cups of the raspberries in a food processor with the icing/confectioners' sugar and lemon juice. Blend to a purée, then pass the mixture through a sieve. Stir in the remaining raspberries with a metal spoon or rubber spatula and chill in the refrigerator until ready to serve.

To serve, dip each of the moulds into hot water for a few seconds, then turn out onto individual serving plates. Spoon some of the raspberry sauce over and around the panna cotta, decorate with extra lemon zest and serve.

Health Rating: 2 points

Italian Polenta Cake with Mascarpone Cream

Cuts into 6–8 slices

Ingredients

1 tsp butter and flour, for the tin/pan

100 g/3½ oz/¾ cup plain/all-purpose flour

40 g/1½ oz/¼ cup polenta/cornmeal

1 tsp baking powder

¼ tsp salt

grated zest of 1 lemon

2 large/extra-large eggs

150 g/5 oz/¾ cup caster/superfine sugar

5 tbsp milk

½ tsp almond extract

2 tbsp raisins or sultanas/golden raisins

75 g/3 oz/6 tbsp unsalted butter, softened

2 medium dessert pears, peeled, cored and thinly sliced

2 tbsp apricot jam/jelly

175 g/6 oz/¾ cup mascarpone cheese

1–2 tsp sugar

50 ml/2 fl oz/¼ cup double/heavy cream

2 tbsp amaretto liqueur or rum

2–3 tbsp toasted flaked almonds

icing/confectioners' sugar, for dusting

Preheat the oven to 190°C/375°F/Gas Mark 5, 10 minutes before baking. Butter a 23 cm/9 inch, springform tin/pan. Dust lightly with flour. Stir the flour, polenta/cornmeal, baking powder, salt and lemon zest together.

Beat the eggs and half the sugar until light and fluffy. Slowly beat in the milk and almond extract. Stir in the raisins or sultanas/golden raisins, then beat in the flour mixture and 50 g/2 oz/4 tbsp of the butter. Spoon into the tin and smooth the top evenly. Arrange the pear slices on top in overlapping concentric circles.

Melt the remaining butter and brush over the pear slices. Sprinkle with the rest of the sugar. Bake in the preheated oven for about 40 minutes until puffed and golden and the edges of the pears are lightly caramelised. Transfer to a wire rack. Cool in the tin for 15 minutes. Remove the cake from the tin.

Heat the apricot jam/jelly with 1 tablespoon water and brush over the top of the cake to glaze.

Beat the mascarpone cheese with the sugar to taste, the cream and amaretto or rum until smooth and forming a soft dropping consistency. When the cake is cool, sprinkle over the almonds and dust generously with the icing/confectioners' sugar. Serve the cake with the liqueur-flavoured mascarpone cream on the side.

Health Rating: 2 points

Cantuccini

Makes 24 biscuits

Ingredients

250 g/9 oz/2 cups plain/all-purpose flour

250 g/9 oz/2¼ cups caster/superfine sugar

½ tsp baking powder

½ tsp vanilla extract

2 medium/large eggs

1 medium/large egg yolk

100 g/3½ oz/¾ cup toasted and roughly chopped mixed
   almonds and hazelnuts

1 tsp whole aniseed

1 medium/large egg yolk mixed with 1 tbsp water, for glazing

Vin Santo dessert wine or coffee, to serve

Health Rating: 2 points

Preheat the oven to 180°C/350°F/Gas Mark 4. Line a large baking sheet with nonstick baking parchment. Place the flour, caster/superfine sugar, baking powder, vanilla extract, the whole eggs and one of the egg yolks into a food processor and blend until the mixture forms a ball, scraping down the sides once or twice. Turn the mixture out onto a lightly floured surface and knead in the chopped nuts and aniseed.

Divide the paste into three pieces and roll into logs about 4 cm/1½ inches wide. Place the logs onto the baking sheet at least 5 cm/2 inches apart. Brush lightly with the other egg yolk beaten with 1 tablespoon water and bake in the preheated oven for 30–35 minutes.

Remove from the oven and reduce the oven temperature to 150°C/300°F/Gas Mark 2. Cut the logs diagonally into 2.5 cm/1 inch slices and lay cut-side down on the baking sheet. Return to the oven for a further 30–40 minutes until dry and firm. Cool on a wire rack and store in an airtight container. Serve with Vin Santo or coffee.

Sweet Pasta with Sesame Seeds

Serves 4

Ingredients

300 g/11 oz/scant 2¹/₄ cups durum wheat flour, plus extra
   for dusting
pinch salt
15 g/¹/₂ oz/generous 1 tbsp caster/superfine sugar
1 tbsp toasted sesame seeds, plus extra to serve
3 medium/large eggs, beaten
1 tbsp olive oil

To serve:
mango slices or orange segments
clear honey, for drizzling

Place the flour, salt, sugar and toasted sesame seeds in a large mixing bowl or on a clean surface and make a well in the centre. Using a fork, gradually work the eggs into the flour until smooth. When about half the eggs have been added, pour the oil into the centre of the flour. Continue adding the eggs and, when all the eggs have been added, knead well to form a stiff dough. Add a little water if the dough is very stiff. It should be moist but not sticky. Knead until smooth, then wrap in plastic wrap and leave for 20 minutes.

When ready to use, lightly flour the pasta dough, then either use a pasta machine fitted with the shape cutter or roll out on a lightly floured board and cut into thin strips with a large, sharp knife. Place on a clean dish towel and leave to dry for 5 minutes.

Either cook the pasta immediately in a large pan of boiling water for 2–3 minutes depending on size or wrap a few strips at a time around your hand to form nests and store in an airtight container.

Once cooked, drain the pasta and arrange on warmed serving plates. Sprinkle with extra toasted sesame seeds, add some mango or orange and drizzle with a little honey. Serve.

Health Rating: 2 points

Almond & Pistachio Biscotti

Makes 12 biscuits

Ingredients

125 g/4 oz/1¹/₃ cups ground almonds
50 g/2 oz/¹/₃ cup shelled pistachios
50 g/2 oz/¹/₃ cup blanched almonds
2 medium/large eggs
1 medium/large egg yolk
125 g/4 oz/1¹/₄ cups icing/confectioners' sugar
225 g/8 oz/1³/₄ cups plain/all-purpose flour
1 tsp baking powder
pinch salt
zest of ¹/₂ lemon

Preheat the oven to 180°C/350°F/Gas Mark 4, 10 minutes before baking. Line a large baking sheet with nonstick baking parchment. Toast the ground almonds and whole nuts lightly and reserve until cool.

Beat together the eggs, egg yolk and icing/confectioners' sugar until thick, then beat in the flour, baking powder and salt. Add the lemon zest, ground almonds and whole nuts and mix to form a slightly sticky dough.

Turn the dough onto a lightly floured surface and, using lightly floured hands, form into a log measuring approximately 30 cm/12 inches long. Place down the centre of the prepared baking sheet and transfer to the preheated oven. Bake for 20 minutes.

Remove from the oven and increase the oven temperature to 200°C/400°F/Gas Mark 6. Cut the log diagonally into 2.5 cm/1 inch slices. Return to the baking sheet, cut-side down, and bake for a further 10–15 minutes until golden, turning once. Leave to cool on a wire rack and store in an airtight container.

Health Rating: 2 points

Hazelnut, Chocolate & Chestnut Meringue Torte

Serves 8–10

Ingredients

For the chocolate meringue:
1 medium/large egg white
50 g/2 oz/¼ cup caster/superfine sugar
2 tbsp unsweetened cocoa powder

For the hazelnut meringue:
75 g/3 oz/½ cup toasted hazelnuts
2 medium/large egg whites
125 g/4 oz/⅔ cup caster/superfine sugar

For the filling:
300 ml/½ pint/1¼ cups double/heavy cream
250 g/9 oz canned sweetened chestnut purée
50 g/2 oz dark/bittersweet dark chocolate, melted
25 g/1 oz dark/bittersweet dark chocolate, grated

Preheat the oven to 130°C/250°F/Gas Mark ½. Line three baking sheets with nonstick baking parchment and draw a 20.5 cm/8 inch circle on each. Beat 1 egg white until stiff peaks form. Add 25 g/1 oz/⅛ cup of the sugar and beat until shiny. Mix the cocoa powder with the remaining 25 g/1 oz/⅛ cup of sugar, adding 1 tablespoon at a time, beating well after each addition, until all the sugar is added and the mixture is stiff and glossy. Spread onto one of the baking sheets within the circle drawn on the underside.

Put the hazelnuts in a food processor and blend until chopped. In a clean bowl, beat the 2 egg whites until stiff. Add 50 g/2 oz/¼ cup of the sugar and beat. Add the remaining sugar about 1 tablespoon at a time, beating after each addition, until all the sugar is added and the mixture is stiff and glossy.

Reserve 2 tablespoons of the nuts, then fold in the remainder and divide between the two remaining baking sheets. Sprinkle one of the hazelnut meringues with the reserved hazelnuts and transfer all the baking sheets to the oven. Bake in the preheated oven for 1½ hours. Turn the oven off and leave in the oven until cold. Whip the cream until thick.

Beat the chestnut purée in another bowl until soft. Add a spoonful of the cream and fold together before adding the remaining cream and melted chocolate and folding together.

Place the plain hazelnut meringue on a serving plate. Top with half the cream and chestnut mixture. Add the chocolate meringue and top with the remaining cream. Add the final meringue. Sprinkle over the grated chocolate and serve.

Health Rating: 1 point

Bomba Siciliana

Serves 6–8

Ingredients

100 g/3½ oz dark/semisweet dark chocolate, in pieces

200 g/7 oz/1 cup fresh chilled custard

150 ml/¼ pint/⅔ cup whipping cream

50 g/2 oz/⅓ cup finely chopped mixed/candied peel

2 tbsp sultanas/golden raisins

1 tbsp chopped glacé/candied cherries

3 tbsp rum

225 g/8 oz/2 cups vanilla ice cream

200 ml/7 fl oz/¾ cup double/heavy cream

3 tbsp caster/superfine sugar

Melt the chocolate in a bowl set over a saucepan of simmering water until smooth, then allow to cool. Whisk together the custard with the whipping cream and slightly cooled chocolate. Spoon the mixture into a shallow, lidded freezer box and freeze.

Every 2 hours, remove from the freezer and whisk thoroughly using an electric or balloon whisk. Repeat three times, then leave until frozen solid.

Soak the mixed/candied peel, sultanas/golden raisins and glacé/candied cherries in the rum and leave until needed.

Chill a bombe or 1 litre/1¾ pint/1 quart dessert mould in the freezer for about 30 minutes. Remove the chocolate ice cream from the freezer to soften, then spoon the ice cream into the mould and press down well, smoothing around the edges and leaving a hollow in the centre. Return the ice cream to the freezer for about 1 hour until frozen hard.

Remove the vanilla ice cream from the freezer to soften. Spoon it into the hollow, making sure to leave another hollow for the cream. Return to the freezer again and freeze until hard.

Whip the cream and sugar until it is just holding its shape, then fold in the soaked fruit. Remove the mould from the freezer and spoon in the cream mixture. Return to the freezer for at least another hour.

When ready to serve, remove the mould from the freezer and dip into hot water for a few seconds, then turn onto a large serving plate. Dip a knife into hot water and cut into wedges to serve.

Health Rating: 1 point

Poached Pears in Marsala Wine

Serves 6

Ingredients

6 firm pears
2–3 lemon slices
50 g/2 oz/¹/₄ cup caster/superfine sugar
300 ml/¹/₂ pint/1¹/₄ cups Marsala wine (or use half wine and half water)
pared zest of ¹/₂ orange
4–6 cloves
1 cinnamon stick, lightly bashed

Choose upright pears with a good stalk. Cut a thin slice off the base of the pears so they stand upright. Peel, making sure you keep the stalk intact and place in a large bowl covered with cold water and 2–3 lemon slices to stop them discolouring.

Put the sugar and 150 ml/¹/₄ pint/²/₃ cup water in a saucepan large enough to hold the pears. Bring to the boil and boil for 2–3 minutes, then remove from the heat. Add the wine, orange zest, cloves and cinnamon stick and return the pan to the heat. Bring back to the boil and reduce to a simmer.

Drain the pears and place in the saucepan, standing upright. Cover with the lid and simmer for 12–15 minutes until the pears are tender. Remove from the heat and occasionally spoon the wine over the pears until they are cool. If space allows, lay the pears down in the wine syrup and turn occasionally. Serve warm or cold.

Health Rating: 5 points

Summer Fruit Semifreddo

Serves 6–8

Ingredients

225 g/8 oz/2 cups raspberries
125 g/4 oz/1 cup blueberries
125 g/4 oz/1 cup redcurrants (buy frozen if you can't find fresh)
50 g/2 oz/¹/₂ cup icing/confectioners' sugar
juice of 1 lemon
1 vanilla pod/bean, split
50 g/2 oz/¹/₄ cup caster/superfine sugar
4 large/extra-large eggs, separated
600 ml/1 pint/2¹/₂ cups double/heavy cream
pinch salt
fresh redcurrants, to decorate

Wash and remove stalks from the fruits if necessary, then put them into a food processor or blender with the icing/confectioners' sugar and lemon juice. Blend to a purée, pour into a jug/pitcher and chill in the refrigerator until needed.

Remove the seeds from the vanilla pod/bean by opening the pod and scraping with the back of a knife. Add the seeds to the caster/superfine sugar and whisk with the egg yolks until pale and thick.

In another bowl, whip the cream until soft peaks form. Do not overwhip. In a third bowl, whip the egg whites with the salt until stiff peaks form. Using a large, metal spoon (to avoid knocking any air from the mixture), fold together the fruit purée, egg yolk mixture, the cream and egg whites.

Transfer the mixture to a round, shallow, lidded freezer box and put into the freezer until almost frozen. If the mixture freezes solid, thaw in the refrigerator until semi-frozen. Turn out the semi-frozen mixture, cut into wedges and serve decorated with a few fresh redcurrants. If the mixture thaws completely, eat immediately and do not refreeze.

Health Rating: 2 points

Cassatta

Serves 6–8

Ingredients

300 g/11 oz dark/semisweet dark chocolate, broken into pieces
200 g/7 oz/1 cup fresh chilled custard
150 ml/¼ pint/⅔ cup whipping cream
275 g/10 oz/2½ cups good-quality pistachio ice cream
25 g/1 oz/¼ cup shelled and toasted pistachios
50 g/2 oz/⅓ cup finely chopped mixed/candied peel
1 tbsp finely chopped glacé/candied cherries
275 g/10 oz/2½ cups good-quality strawberry ice cream

Line a 450 g/1 lb loaf tin/pan with plastic wrap. Place in the freezer. Melt 100 g/3½ oz of the chocolate into a heatproof bowl set over a saucepan of simmering water, stir until smooth, then cool. Place the custard into a bowl. Stir in the cream and the chocolate and stir until mixed. Spoon into a shallow, lidded freezer box and transfer to the freezer. Every 2 hours, remove from the freezer and, using an electric whisk, whisk thoroughly. Repeat 3 times, then leave until frozen solid.

Remove the chocolate ice cream from the freezer and allow to soften. Remove the loaf tin from the freezer and press the chocolate ice cream into the bottom of the tin, press down well and allow it to come up the sides of the tin. Return to the freezer and leave until solid.

Soften the pistachio ice cream, then beat in the pistachios, mixed/candied peel and cherries. Spoon into the tin, pressing down well and smoothing the top. Return to the freezer until hard. Soften the strawberry ice cream and spread onto the pistachio ice cream. Smooth the top. Return to the freezer for at least 1 hour until completely solid.

Meanwhile, melt the remaining chocolate, stir until smooth and cool slightly. Remove the loaf tin from the freezer. Dip into hot water and turn onto a serving dish. Using a teaspoon, drizzle the chocolate over the ice cream in a haphazard pattern. Return the cassatta to the freezer until the chocolate has set. Dip a knife in hot water and use to slice the cassatta. Serve immediately.

Health Rating: 1 point

Marzipan Cake

Serves 12–14

Ingredients

450 g/1 lb/4 cups blanched almonds

300 g/11 oz/2¾ cups icing/confectioners' sugar, plus extra for dusting and rolling

4 egg whites

125 g/4 oz/1 small Madeira or plain sponge cake

2 tbsp Marsala wine

225 g/8 oz/1 cup ricotta cheese

50 g/2 oz/¼ cup caster/superfine sugar

grated zest of 1 lemon

50 g/2 oz/⅓ cup finely chopped mixed/candied peel

25 g/1 oz/1 tbsp chopped glacé/candied cherries

425 g/15 oz/2 cups drained canned peach halves

200 ml/7 fl oz/¾ cup double/heavy cream

Grind the blanched almonds in a food processor until fairly fine. Mix with 200 g/7 oz/⅔ cup of the icing/confectioners' sugar.

Beat the egg whites until stiff, then fold into the almond mixture using a metal spoon or rubber spatula to form a stiffish dough. It will still be quite sticky but will firm up as it rests. Leave for 30 minutes.

Generously dust a work surface/countertop with some of the remaining icing sugar so that the marzipan does not stick. Roll out two thirds of the marzipan into a large sheet to a thickness of about 5 mm/¼ inch. Use to line a sloping-sided baking dish with a base measuring 25 x 20.5 cm/10 x 8 inches. Trim the edges and put any trimmings with the remaining marzipan.

Cut the Madeira cake into thin slices and make a layer of sponge to cover the bottom of the marzipan. Sprinkle with the Marsala wine.

Beat the ricotta cheese with the sugar and add the lemon zest, mixed/candied peel and glacé/candied cherries. Spread this over the sponge. Slice the peaches and put them on top of the ricotta. Whip the cream and spread it over the peaches.

Roll out the remaining marzipan and lay it over the cream to seal the whole cake, pressing down gently to remove any air. Press the edges of the marzipan together. Chill in the refrigerator for 2 hours.

Turn the cake out onto a serving plate. Dust generously with icing sugar. Slice thickly and serve immediately.

Health Rating: 2 points

Neapolitan Tart

Serves 6–8

Ingredients

450 g/1 lb ready-made sweet shortcrust pastry/pie dough
plain/all-purpose flour, for dusting
1 small/medium egg yolk, for glazing

For the filling:
2 medium/large egg yolks
50 g/2 oz/4 tbsp butter, softened
50 g/2 oz/¹⁄₄ cup caster/superfine sugar
finely grated zest of ¹⁄₂ lemon
450 g/1 lb/2 cups ricotta cheese
1 tbsp chopped candied lemon peel
25 g/1 oz/1 tbsp chopped candied orange peel
1 tbsp chopped glacé/candied cherries
50 g/2 oz dark/semisweet dark chocolate, chopped

Preheat the oven to 190°C/375°F/Gas Mark 5, 10 minutes before baking. To make the filling, beat the egg yolks with the butter and sugar until creamy, then beat in the lemon zest.

Beat the ricotta until smooth, then fold into the egg mixture together with the chopped candied peel, cherries and chocolate.

Roll three quarters of the pastry/pie dough out on a lightly floured surface and use to line the base and sides of a 20.5cm/8 inch cake tin/pan or springform tin. Pour in the filling.

Roll out the remaining pastry and cut into 23 cm/9 inch strips and use to form a lattice effect across the pie. Brush the strips with the beaten egg yolk and bake in the preheated oven for 30–40 minutes until the filling is set. Leave to cool before removing from the tin and serving.

Health Rating: 2 points

Chestnut Cake

Serves 8–10

Ingredients

175 g/6 oz/³⁄₄ cup (1¹⁄₂ sticks) butter, softened
175 g/6 oz/³⁄₄ cup caster/superfine sugar
250 g/9 oz canned sweetened chestnut purée
3 medium/large eggs, lightly beaten
175 g/6 oz/1¹⁄₂ cups plain/all-purpose flour
1 tsp baking powder
pinch ground cloves
1 tsp fennel seeds, crushed
75 g/3 oz/¹⁄₂ cup raisins
50 g/2 oz/¹⁄₂ cup pine nuts, toasted
125 g/4 oz/1 cup icing/confectioners' sugar
5 tbsp lemon juice
pared strips lemon zest, to decorate

Preheat the oven to 150°C/300°F/Gas Mark 2. Oil and line a 23 cm/9 inch springform tin/pan. Beat together the butter and sugar until light and fluffy. Add the chestnut purée and beat. Gradually add the eggs, beating after each addition. Sift in the flour with the baking powder and cloves. Add the fennel seeds and beat. The mixture should drop easily from a wooden spoon when tapped against the side of the bowl. If not, add a little milk.

Beat in the raisins and pine nuts. Spoon the mixture into the prepared tin and smooth the top. Put in the centre of the preheated oven and bake for 55–60 minutes until a skewer inserted into the centre of the cake comes out clean. Remove from the oven and leave in the tin.

Meanwhile, mix together the icing/confectioners' sugar and lemon juice in a small saucepan until smooth. Heat gently until hot but not boiling. Using a cocktail stick/toothpick or skewer, poke holes into the cake all over. Pour the hot syrup evenly over the cake and leave to soak into the cake. Decorate with pared strips of lemon zest and serve.

Health Rating: 2 points

Chocolate Pasta

Serves 4

Ingredients

50 g/2 oz dark/semisweet dark chocolate, melted
300 g/11 oz/scant 2¼ cups durum wheat flour, plus extra
    for dusting
pinch salt
3 medium/large eggs, beaten
1 tbsp olive oil

To serve:
fresh raspberries or raspberry sauce
icing/confectioners' sugar, for dusting

Stir the chocolate until smooth and leave to cool.

Place the flour and salt in a large mixing bowl or on a clean
surface and make a well in the centre. Using a fork, gradually
work the eggs into the flour. When about half the eggs have
been added, pour the chocolate and oil into the centre of
the flour. Gradually mix in the rest of the eggs. When all the
eggs have been added, knead well to form a stiff dough. Add
a little water if the dough is too stiff. It should be moist but
not sticky. Knead until smooth, then wrap in plastic wrap and
leave for 20 minutes.

When ready to use, lightly flour the pasta dough, then either
use a pasta machine to form strips or roll out on a lightly
floured board and cut into thin strips. Place on a clean dish
towel and leave to dry for 5 minutes. Make sure you separate all
the strips on the dish towel, otherwise they will stick together.

Either cook the pasta immediately in a large pan of boiling
water for 2–3 minutes depending on size or wrap a few strips
at a time around your hand to form nests and store in an
airtight container.

Once the pasta is cooked, drain, then arrange on warmed serving
plates. Either add fresh raspberries or drizzle over some raspberry
sauce, then dust with icing/confectioners' sugar and serve.

Health Rating: 2 points

Sauternes & Olive Oil Cake

Serves 8–10

Ingredients

125 g/4 oz/1 cup plain/all-purpose flour, plus extra for dusting
4 medium/large eggs
125 g/4½ oz/⅔ cup caster/superfine sugar
grated zest of ½ lemon
grated zest of ½ orange
2 tbsp Sauternes or other sweet dessert wine
3 tbsp very best-quality extra virgin olive oil
4 ripe peaches
1–2 tsp soft brown sugar, or to taste
1 tbsp lemon juice
icing/confectioners' sugar, for dusting

Preheat the oven to 140°C/275°F/Gas Mark 1. Oil and line a 25.5
cm/10 inch, springform tin/pan. Sift the flour onto a large sheet
of greaseproof/wax paper. Reserve.

Using a freestanding electric mixer, if possible, whisk the eggs
and sugar together until pale and stiff. Add the lemon and
orange zest. Turn the speed to low and pour the flour from the
paper in a slow, steady stream onto the eggs and sugar mixture.
Immediately add the wine and olive oil and switch the machine
off as the olive oil should not be incorporated completely.

Using a metal spoon or rubber spatula, fold the mixture very
gently 3 or 4 times so that the ingredients are just
incorporated. Pour the mixture immediately into the prepared
tin and bake in the preheated oven for 20–25 minutes, without
opening the door for at least 15 minutes. Test if cooked by
pressing the top lightly with a clean finger – if it springs back,
remove from the oven. If not, bake for a little longer. Leave the
cake to cool in the tin on a wire rack. Remove the cake from
the tin when cool enough to handle.

Meanwhile, skin the peaches and cut into segments. Toss with
the brown sugar and lemon juice and reserve. When the cake is
cold, dust generously with icing/confectioners' sugar, cut into
wedges and serve with the peaches.

Health Rating: 3 points

Frozen Amaretti Soufflé with Strawberries

Serves 6–8

Ingredients

125 g/4 oz/1 cup amaretti biscuits/cookies

135 ml/4½ fl oz/½ cup plus 1 tbsp amaretto liqueur

grated zest and juice of 1 lemon

1 tbsp powdered gelatine

6 medium/large eggs, separated

175 g/6 oz/¾ cup soft brown sugar

600 ml/1 pint/2½ cups double/heavy cream

450 g/1 lb/4 cups halved fresh strawberries

1 vanilla pod/bean, split and seeds scraped out

2 tbsp caster/superfine sugar

few finely crushed amaretti biscuits/cookies, to decorate

Wrap a collar of greaseproof/wax paper around a 900 ml/1½ pint/scant 1 quart soufflé dish or 6–8 individual ramekins to extend at least 5 cm/2 inches above the rim and secure with string. Break the amaretti biscuits/cookies into a bowl. Sprinkle over 6 tablespoons of the amaretto liqueur and leave to soak.

Put the lemon zest and juice into a small, heatproof bowl and sprinkle over the gelatine. Leave for 5 minutes to sponge, then put the bowl over a saucepan of simmering water, ensuring that the bottom of the bowl does not touch the water. Stir occasionally until the gelatine has dissolved completely.

In a clean bowl, whisk the egg yolks and sugar until pale and thick, then stir in the gelatine and the soaked biscuits. In another bowl, lightly whip 450 ml/¾ pint/1¾ cups of the cream and, using a large, metal spoon or rubber spatula, fold into the mixture. In a third clean bowl, whisk the egg whites until stiff, then fold into the soufflé mixture. Transfer to the prepared dish or individual ramekins and level the top. Freeze for at least 8 hours, or preferably overnight.

Put the strawberries, vanilla pod/bean and seeds, sugar and remaining amaretto liqueur into a bowl. Leave overnight in the refrigerator, then allow to come to room temperature to serve.

Place the soufflé in the refrigerator for about 1 hour. Whip the remaining cream to decorate the soufflé. Sprinkle a few finely crushed amaretti biscuits on top and serve with the strawberries and sauce.

Health Rating: 2 points

Baked Stuffed Amaretti Peaches

Serves 4

Ingredients

4 ripe peaches
grated zest and juice of 1 lemon
8 amaretti biscuits/cookies
50 g/2 oz/²⁄₃ cup chopped blanched almonds, toasted
50 g/2 oz/¹⁄₂ cup toasted pine nuts
3 tbsp light muscovado/golden brown sugar
50 g/2 oz/4 tbsp butter
1 medium egg yolk
2 tsp clear honey
crème fraîche or Greek/plain yogurt, to serve

Preheat the oven to 180°C/350°F/Gas Mark 4. Halve the peaches and remove the stones. Take a very thin slice from the bottom of each peach half so that it will sit flat on the baking tray/pan. Dip the peach halves in lemon juice and arrange on a baking tray.

Crush the amaretti biscuits/cookies lightly and put into a large bowl. Add the almonds, pine nuts, sugar, lemon zest and butter. Work with the fingertips until the mixture resembles coarse breadcrumbs. Add the egg yolk and mix well until the mixture is just binding.

Divide the amaretti and nut mixture between the peach halves, pressing down lightly. Bake in the preheated oven for 15 minutes, or until the peaches are tender and the filling is golden. Remove from the oven and drizzle with the honey.

Place two peach halves on each serving plate and spoon over a little crème fraîche or Greek/plain yogurt, then serve.

Health Rating: 3 **points**

Apricot Granita

Serves 4–6

Ingredients

75 g/3 oz/generous ⅓ cup caster/superfine or granulated sugar
450 g/1 lb fresh, ripe apricots or 300 g/11 oz/1¾ cups dried, ready-to-eat apricots
300 ml/½ pint/1¼ cups orange juice or apricot nectar or use water and juice mixed together
few drops almond extract
1 large/extra-large egg white
2 fresh apricots or redcurrant sprays (buy frozen if you can't find fresh)

Set the freezer to rapid freeze if necessary. Place the sugar with 200 ml/7 fl oz/¾ cup water in a saucepan over a gentle heat and simmer gently until the sugar has dissolved, then bring to the boil and boil for 5 minutes. Reserve.

If using fresh apricots, rinse, cut in half and discard the stones/pits. If using dried apricots, chop roughly. Place the apricots in the sugar syrup and add the juice and water, if using. Bring to the boil, then reduce the heat and simmer for 10–15 minutes until really soft. Add the almond extract.

Remove from the heat, cool slightly, then pass through a blender or food processor to form a purée. Leave until cold, then stiffly whisk the egg white and stir into the apricot purée. Pour into a freezerproof container.

Place in the freezer and freeze for 2 hours, or until just frozen. Stir about every 20–30 minutes to break up the ice crystals until the mixture is almost frozen. (If too hard, then leave in the refrigerator for a few minutes to soften.) Spoon into chilled glasses or dishes, decorate with fresh apricots or sprays of red currants and serve immediately.

Health Rating: 4 points

Almond & Pine Nut Tart

Serves 6

Ingredients

250 g/9 oz/1¼ cups ready-made sweet shortcrust pastry/pie dough
75 g/3 oz/¾ cup blanched almonds
75 g/3 oz/⅓ cup caster/superfine sugar
pinch salt
2 medium/large eggs
1 tsp vanilla extract
2–3 drops almond extract
125 g/4 oz/½ cup (1 stick) unsalted butter, softened
2 tbsp plain/all-purpose flour
½ tsp baking powder
3–4 tbsp raspberry jam/jelly
50 g/2 oz/½ cup pine nuts
icing/confectioners' sugar, to decorate
whipped/whipping cream, to serve

Preheat the oven to 200°C/400°F/Gas Mark 6. Roll out the pastry/dough and use to line a 23 cm/9 inch, fluted flan tin/pan. Chill in the refrigerator for 10 minutes, then line with greaseproof/wax paper and baking beans/pie weights. Bake blind in the preheated oven for 10 minutes. Remove the paper and beans. Bake for a further 10–12 minutes until cooked. Leave to cool. Reduce the oven temperature to 190°C/375°F/Gas Mark 5.

Grind the almonds in a food processor until fine. Add the sugar, salt, eggs and vanilla and almond extracts and blend. Add the butter, flour and baking powder and blend until smooth.

Spread a thick layer of the raspberry jam/jelly over the cooled pastry case/pie crust, then pour in the almond filling. Sprinkle the pine nuts evenly over the top and bake for 30 minutes until firm and browned. Remove the tart from the oven and leave to cool. Dust generously with icing/confectioners' sugar and serve cut into wedges with whipped cream.

Health Rating: 2 points

Raspberry & Almond Tart

Serves 6–8

Ingredients

For the pastry:
225 g/8 oz/2 cups plain/all-purpose flour
pinch salt
125 g/4 oz/¹/₂ cup (1 stick) butter, cut into pieces
50 g/2 oz/¹/₄ cup caster/superfine sugar
grated zest of ¹/₂ lemon
1 medium/large egg yolk

For the filling:
75 g/3 oz/²/₃ stick butter
75 g/3 oz/6 tbsp caster/superfine sugar
75 g/3 oz/³/₄ cup ground almonds
2 medium/large eggs
225 g/8 oz/2 cups fresh or thawed raspberries
2 tbsp flaked/slivered almonds
icing/confectioners' sugar, for dusting

Preheat the oven to 200°C/400°F/Gas Mark 6, 15 minutes before cooking. Blend the flour, salt and butter in a food processor until the mixture resembles breadcrumbs. Add the sugar and lemon zest and blend again for 1 minute.

Mix the egg yolk with 2 tablespoons cold water and add to the mixture. Blend until the mixture starts to come together, adding a little more water if necessary, then tip out onto a lightly floured surface. Knead until smooth, wrap in plastic wrap and chill in the refrigerator for 30 minutes. Roll the dough out thinly on a lightly floured surface and use to line a 23 cm/9 inch, fluted tin/tart pan. Chill in the refrigerator for 10 minutes.

Line the pastry case/shell with greaseproof/wax paper and baking beans/pie weights. Bake for 10 minutes, then remove the paper and baking beans and return to the oven for a further 10–12 minutes until cooked. Allow to cool slightly, then reduce the oven temperature to 190°C/375°F/Gas Mark 5.

Blend together the butter, sugar, ground almonds and eggs until smooth. Spread the raspberries over the base of the pastry, then cover with the almond mixture. Bake for 15 minutes.

Remove from the oven. Sprinkle with the flaked or slivered almonds and dust generously with icing/confectioners' sugar. Bake for a further 15–20 minutes until firm and golden brown. Leave to cool, then serve.

Health Rating: 2 points

Zabaglione with Rum-soaked Raisin Compote

Serves 6

Ingredients

2 tbsp raisins

1 strip thinly pared lemon zest

½ tsp ground cinnamon

3 tbsp Marsala or Italian fortified wine

3 medium/large egg yolks

3 tbsp caster/superfine sugar

125 ml/4 fl oz/½ cup dry white wine

150 ml/¼ pint/⅔ cup lightly whipped double/heavy cream

crisp biscuits/cookies, to serve

Health Rating: 2 points

Put the raisins in a small bowl with the lemon zest and ground cinnamon. Pour over the Marsala or fortified wine to cover and leave to macerate for at least 1 hour.

When the raisins are plump, lift out of the Marsala wine and reserve the raisins and wine, discarding the lemon zest.

In a large heatproof bowl, mix together the egg yolks and sugar. Add the white wine and Marsala wine and stir well to combine.

Put the bowl over a saucepan of simmering water, ensuring that the bottom of the bowl does not touch the water. Whisk constantly until the mixture doubles in bulk.

Remove from the heat and continue whisking for about 5 minutes until the mixture has cooled slightly. Fold in the raisins and then immediately fold in the whipped cream. Spoon into dessert glasses or goblets and serve with crisp biscuits/cookies.

Cappuccino Granita

Serves 4–6

Ingredients

about 25 g/1 oz/¹/₈ cup caster/superfine or granulated sugar,
   to taste
4–6 tbsp amaretto liqueur (optional)
900 ml/1¹/₂ pints/3³/₄ cups freshly brewed coffee
1 large/extra-large egg white
150 ml/¹/₄ pint/²/₃ cup double/heavy cream
grated dark/semisweet dark chocolate, to serve

Set the freezer to rapid freeze if necessary. Add the sugar
and the liqueur to taste to the coffee and stir until the sugar
has dissolved.

Whisk the egg white until stiff, then carefully stir into the
coffee. Take care not to destroy all the air bubbles.

Pour the coffee into a shallow, freezerproof container and
freeze for 2 hours, or until almost frozen. Stir about every 20
minutes to break up the ice crystals. (If too hard, then leave in
the refrigerator for a few minutes to soften.)

Whip the cream until soft peaks are formed. Spoon the granita
into cups or small dishes and top with swirls of cream. Sprinkle
with grated chocolate and serve.

Health Rating: 1 point

Coffee Ricotta

Serves 6

Ingredients

700 g/1¹/₂ lb/3 cups fresh ricotta cheese
125 ml/4 fl oz/¹/₂ cup double/heavy cream
25 g/1 oz/2 tbsp espresso beans, freshly ground
50 g/2 oz/¹/₄ cup caster/superfine sugar
3 tbsp brandy
50 g/2 oz/4 tbsp butter, softened
75 g/3 oz/¹/₂ cup caster/superfine sugar
1 medium/large egg, beaten
50 g/2 oz/¹/₂ cup plain/all-purpose flour

Preheat the oven to 220°C/425°F/Gas Mark 7, 15 minutes
before baking. Beat the ricotta and cream together until
smooth. Stir in the ground coffee beans, sugar and brandy.
Cover and refrigerate for at least 2 hours (the flavour improves
the longer it stands).

Meanwhile, oil two baking sheets and line with nonstick
baking parchment.

Cream together the butter and sugar until fluffy. Gradually beat
in the egg, a little at a time. Sift the flour into a bowl, then fold
into the butter mixture to form a soft dough. Spoon the
mixture into a decorating bag fitted with a 1 cm/¹/₂ inch plain
nozzle/tip. Pipe 7.5 cm/3 inch lengths of the mixture onto the
baking sheets, spaced well apart. Use a sharp knife to cut the
dough off cleanly at the nozzle.

Bake in the preheated oven for 6–8 minutes until just golden at
the edges. Cool on the baking sheets for 5 minutes before
transferring to a wire rack to cool completely.

To serve, spoon the coffee and ricotta mixture into small coffee
cups. Serve with the biscuits/cookies.

Health Rating: 1 point

Goats' Cheese & Lemon Tart

Serves 4

Ingredients

For the pastry:
125 g/4 oz/¹/₂ cup (1 stick) butter, cut into small pieces
225 g/8 oz/2 cups plain/all-purpose flour
pinch salt
50 g/2 oz/¹/₄ cup caster/superfine sugar
1 medium/large egg yolk

For the filling:
350 g/12 oz/1¹/₂ cups mild fresh goats' cheese
3 medium/large eggs, beaten
150 g/5 oz/³/₄ cup caster/superfine sugar
grated zest and juice of 3 lemons
450 ml/³/₄ pint/1³/₄ cups double/heavy cream
fresh raspberries, to decorate

Preheat the oven to 200°C/400°F/Gas Mark 6, 15 minutes before baking. Rub the butter into the plain/all-purpose flour and salt until the mixture resembles breadcrumbs, then stir in the sugar. Beat the egg yolk with 2 tablespoons cold water and add to the mixture. Mix together until a dough is formed, then turn the dough out onto a lightly floured surface and knead until smooth. Chill in the refrigerator for 30 minutes.

Roll the dough out thinly on a lightly floured surface and use to line a 4 cm/1¹/₂ inch deep, 23 cm/9 inch, fluted flan tin/tart pan. Chill in the refrigerator for 10 minutes. Line the pastry case/pie crust with greaseproof/wax paper and baking beans/pie weights or kitchen foil and bake blind in the preheated oven for 10 minutes. Remove the paper and beans or foil. Return to the oven for a further 12–15 minutes until cooked. Leave to cool slightly, then reduce the oven temperature to 150°C/300°F/Gas Mark 2.

Beat the goats' cheese until smooth. Whisk in the eggs, sugar, lemon zest and juice. Add the cream and mix well. Carefully pour the cheese mixture into the pastry case and return to the oven. Bake in the oven for 35–40 minutes until just set.

If it begins to brown or swell, open the oven door for 2 minutes. Reduce the temperature to 120°C/250°F/Gas Mark ¹/₂ and leave the tart to cool in the oven. Chill in the refrigerator until cold. Decorate and serve with fresh raspberries.

Health Rating: 1 point

Cannoli with Ricotta Cheese

Makes 24

Ingredients

For the pastry:
25 g/1 oz/2 tbsp butter
25 g/1 oz/2 tbsp caster/superfine sugar
3 tbsp dry white wine
pinch salt
150 g/5 oz/1¼ cups plain/all-purpose flour
1 medium/large egg, lightly beaten
vegetable oil, for deep-frying

For the filling:
450 g/1 lb/2 cups ricotta cheese
125 g/4 oz/½ cup caster/superfine sugar
2 tbsp orange water
1 tsp vanilla extract
50 g/2 oz/⅓ cup chopped glacé/candied cherries
2 tbsp chopped angelica
125 g/4 oz/⅔ cup chopped mixed/candied peel
75 g/3 oz dark/semisweet dark chocolate, finely chopped
icing/confectioners' sugar, for dusting

Beat together the butter and the 25 g/1 oz sugar until light and fluffy. Add the white wine and salt and mix together well. Fold in the flour and knead to form a soft dough. Reserve for 2 hours.

Lightly flour a work surface/countertop and roll the dough out to a thickness of about 5 mm/¼ inch. Cut into 12.5 cm/5 inch squares, then wrap the pastry around the cannoli or cream horn moulds using the beaten egg to seal. Make 3–4 at a time.

Heat the vegetable oil to 180°C/350°F in a deep fryer and fry the cannoli for 1–2 minutes until puffed and golden. Drain well on paper towels and leave to cool.

Remove the moulds when the cannoli are cool enough to handle. Repeat until all the cannoli are cooked.

Beat the ricotta with the 125 g/4 oz/½ cup sugar, orange water and vanilla extract until creamy. Add the cherries, angelica, mixed/candied peel and chopped chocolate.

Fill each cannoli using a decorating bag with a large, plain nozzle/tip or a small spoon. Dust with icing/confectioners' sugar and serve cool but not cold.

Health Rating: 1 point

Roasted Figs with Dolcelatte

Serves 4

Ingredients

8–12 fresh figs
4 tbsp Marsala wine or orange juice
125 g/4 oz Dolcelatte cheese, cut into 8–12 small squares
orange segments, to decorate

Preheat the oven to 180°C/350°F/Gas Mark 4,10 minutes before roasting the figs.

Lightly rinse the figs and make a cross at the top of each fig. Push gently to open the fruit slightly, then place in an ovenproof dish and pour over the Marsala wine or orange juice.

Roast in the oven for 3 minutes, or until the figs are hot. Place the small pieces of cheese in the top of each fig, then return to the oven and cook for a further 2–3 minutes until the cheese is beginning to melt.

Arrange on four small serving plates, pouring the melted cheese and wine mixture over the figs. Decorate with the orange segments and serve. (These figs can be served with a little salad as a starter or in place of the cheese course.)

Health Rating: 4 points

Tiramisu

Serves 4

Ingredients

225 g/8 oz/1 cup mascarpone cheese
25 g/1 oz/$^{1}/_{4}$ cup icing/confectioners' sugar, sifted
150 ml/$^{1}/_{4}$ pint/$^{2}/_{3}$ cup strong brewed coffee, chilled
300 ml/$^{1}/_{2}$ pint/1$^{1}/_{4}$ cups double/heavy cream
3 tbsp coffee liqueur
125 g/4 oz Savoiardi or sponge fingers/ladyfingers
50 g/2 oz dark/bittersweet dark chocolate, grated or made into small curls
unsweetened cocoa powder, for dusting
assorted summer berries, to serve

Lightly oil and line a 900 g/2 lb loaf tin/pan with a piece of plastic wrap.

Put the mascarpone and icing/confectioners' sugar into a large bowl and, using a metal spoon or rubber spatula, beat until smooth. Stir in 2 tablespoons chilled coffee and mix thoroughly.

Whip the cream with 1 tablespoon of the coffee liqueur until just thickened. Stir a spoonful of the whipped cream into the mascarpone mixture, then fold in the rest. Spoon half of the mascarpone mixture into the prepared loaf tin and smooth the top.

Put the remaining coffee and coffee liqueur into a shallow dish just bigger than the sponge fingers/ladyfingers. Using half of them, dip one side of each sponge finger into the coffee mixture, then arrange on top of the mascarpone mixture in a single layer. Spoon the rest of the mascarpone mixture over the sponge fingers and smooth the top. Dip the remaining sponge fingers in the coffee mixture and arrange on top of the mascarpone mixture. Drizzle with any remaining coffee mixture. Cover with plastic wrap and chill in the refrigerator for 4 hours.

Carefully turn the tiramisu out onto a large serving plate. Sprinkle with the grated chocolate or chocolate curls. Dust with cocoa powder, cut into slices and serve with a few summer berries.

Health Rating: 2 points

Pine Nut & Hazelnut Cake

Serves 8

Ingredients

125 g/4 oz/¹/₂ cup (1 stick) unsalted butter, softened, plus extra
    for greasing
125 g/4 oz/generous ³/₄ cup skinned hazelnuts
15 g/¹/₂ oz/scant 2 tbsp pine nuts
125 g/4 oz/scant ²/₃ cup caster/superfine sugar
4 large/extra-large eggs, separated
25 g/1 oz/generous ¹/₈ cup sifted plain/all-purpose flour
125 g/4 oz/¹/₂ cup ricotta cheese
grated zest of 1 small orange
4 tbsp apricot jam/jelly
1 tbsp orange juice
40 g/1¹/₂ oz dark/semisweet dark chocolate, grated

Preheat the oven to 200°C/400°F/Gas Mark 6, 15 minutes
before baking. Lightly grease and baseline a 25 cm/10 inch,
shallow cake tin/pan. Place all the nuts on a baking tray and
roast in the oven for 6–8 minutes until golden. Remove from
the oven, leave to cool, then chop finely.

Place the butter in a mixing bowl and beat in 75 g/3 oz/
generous ¹/₃ cup of the sugar. Add the egg yolks one at a time,
beating well after each addition. Stir in the flour. Place the
ricotta in a separate bowl and stir until light and creamy. Add
the chopped nuts together with the orange zest, then stir into
the flour mixture.

Whisk the egg whites until stiff, then carefully stir into the mixture.
Stir lightly until the egg whites are thoroughly incorporated.
Spoon the mixture into the tin and tap lightly on the surface to
remove any air bubbles. Bake for 30–40 minutes until the top is
firm to the touch. Remove and leave to cool before turning out,
discarding the lining paper. Place on a wire rack.

Heat the jam/jelly and orange juice, then rub through a sieve
and use to brush over the cake. Place the grated chocolate on a
piece of baking parchment and use to coat the cake completely
in the chocolate. Serve.

Health Rating: 2 points

Florentine-topped Cupcakes

Makes 18

Ingredients

150 g/5 oz/²/₃ cup (1¹/₄ sticks) butter, softened
150 g/5 oz/³/₄ cup caster/superfine sugar
175 g/6 oz/1¹/₂ cups self-raising flour
3 medium/large eggs
1 tsp vanilla extract
75 g/3 oz/¹/₂ cup glacé/candied cherries
50 g/2 oz angelica, chopped
50 g/2 oz ¹/₃ cup chopped mixed/candied peel
50 g/2 oz/scant ¹/₂ cup dried cranberries

To decorate:
75 g/3 oz dark/semisweet dark or milk chocolate, melted
50 g/2 oz/¹/₂ cup flaked almonds

Preheat the oven to 180°C/350°F/Gas Mark 4. Line two 12-hole
muffin trays with 18 paper cases.

Place the butter and sugar in a bowl, then sift in the flour. In
another bowl, beat the eggs with the vanilla extract, then add
to the first mixture and beat until smooth. Fold in half the
cherries, angelica, peel and cranberries. Spoon into the cases,
filling them three quarters full.

Bake for about 18 minutes until firm to the touch in the centre.
Turn out to cool on a wire rack.

Spoon a little melted chocolate on top of each cupcake, then
scatter the remaining cherries, angelica, peel and cranberries
and the almonds into the wet chocolate. Drizzle the remaining
chocolate over the fruit topping with a teaspoon and leave to
set for 30 minutes. Keep for 2 days in an airtight container.

Health Rating: 2 points

Index